The Simply Happy COOKBOOK

ALSO BY STEVE AND KATHY DOOCY
The Mr. & Mrs. Happy Handbook
The Happy Cookbook
The Happy in a Hurry Cookbook

ALSO BY STEVE DOOCY
Tales from the Dad Side

The *Simply Happy* COOKBOOK

NOTHING COMPLICATED—EVERYTHING DELICIOUS!
100-Plus Recipes to Take the Stress Out of Cooking

STEVE AND KATHY DOOCY

WILLIAM MORROW
An Imprint of HarperCollins*Publishers*

CONT

ENTS

TO OUR FAMILY—
WHO MAKE US SIMPLY HAPPY

INTRODUCTION

Welcome to *The Simply Happy Cookbook,* the newest installment in our Happy Cookbook series. Three books on one theme—happiness? We've written a trilogy! One of our kids joked that we have become the Tolkiens of taste. Actually *happy* taste—based on the proven fact that we all have foods that can trigger deep memories of emotions and feelings that often transport us to a cheery place somewhere in our past.

Why do we call this *The Simply Happy Cookbook*? In the last couple of years, nothing has been simple. For stretches of time the only thing we had to look forward to was dinner before bed. So if that was the day's highlight, it had to be great— but it couldn't be too complicated.

For this book we've *curated* (SAT word popularized during the lockdown) one hundred more comforting recipes—with stories about why they trigger a pang of personal happiness to someone—and we engineered them to be as simple as possible to get on the table. With supply chain issues, we know some ingredients can be hard to get, so we use as few ingredients as possible, and we use some premade sauces and store-bought ingredients to save you time. And we have slow cooker recipes that taste like they've been stewing away all day—and they have—but they only take a few minutes to prep before you put the lid on and forget about them for eight hours.

These delectable dishes are made with pantry staples that are easy to get in every part of America. After our first cookbook, somebody wrote and said they could not find burrata cheese in their town, so Kathy and I made a note, and that's now a requirement for inclusion in our cookbooks—every ingredient has to be widely available either in your grocery store or at your local Walmart. We checked at ours!

Because sometimes it feels like America has run out of things to cook, we dreamed up some new recipes that you probably won't see anyplace else. We got sick of people never returning casserole pans when we'd take them a dinner, so we figured a way to have them *eat the dish* with our A to Ziti Loaf. Our Lasagna Grilled Cheese Sandwiches will change the way you think of grilled cheese forever. We think you'll fall in love with Billionaire Bacon and Cranberry Brie, Bourbon Brisket in a Biscuit, Cast-Iron Cabernet Cheeseburgers, Jolt in a Jar, and German Chocolate Ice Cream Pie. And I don't know any other cookbook that has recipes for Iowa Caucus Casserole, Mona Lisa's Chicken, I Can't Believe It's Not Potato Salad, or Heifer in a Haystack Casserole. Don't worry—no haystacks were used in the making of that hot dish.

The recipes and stories and ideas come from our family and friends, some of whom you may recognize: Dana Perino, Greg Gutfeld, Jesse Watters, Ainsley Earhardt, John Rich, Rachel Campos-Duffy, Paula Bongino (Dan's wife), Susan Richie (Kid Rock's mom), Melanie Luttrell (Marcus's wife), Amy Baier (Bret's wife), and Pete Hegseth.

Special thanks to Guy Fieri, who hired me to work a day in his chicken kitchen, and Paula Deen, the queen of Southern cooking—who humbled us when she whipped up one of our recipes on her show! Also, I can't tell you how many people told us they'd bought our first two cookbooks—but they don't cook! They'd heard friends and family members rave about the heartwarming and sometimes hilarious stories about our family, and they said, *You've got to get it,* and they did.

So this book has plenty of new stories you've never heard. You'll discover how we almost named future White House correspondent Peter Doocy after a town in Tennessee. Find out which prominent Doocy family member arrived in our lives after a one-way trip on the fabled Orphan Train—and we still have no idea where they came from. Learn how Kathy's eye cancer story helped save the eye and probably the life of a total stranger. Which Super Bowl quarterback helped one of our kids make a home run in a local rec-league game? We will reveal that shocker . . . and we all worried about our *permanent records* back in high school, so I called for mine—and you'll be horrified what was in it!

With one story for every one of the hundred recipes, you'll say, "Wait, there's a cookbook in there too?" Yes, indeed . . . it's two books in one!

Thank you to all of those who reached out to us with suggestions for this cookbook. We got an email from a viewer named Sue who reminded us that a lot of our readers are empty nesters—as Kathy and I are—and we should have more recipes for just two people. Sue's right—so we're presenting more recipes that make just a few portions, or are super

easy to divide and make smaller quantities. Just know that leftovers are a gift from the cooking gods, so if you're going to go to the *trouble* . . . you might as well make it *double.*

So thank you for picking up our latest cookbook! We hope you enjoy all these easily accessible recipes and memories from our family and friends. We know everybody's life is still complicated—but we can all do something to untangle it a little. Just turn on the stove and turn back the clock.

Ultimately what we're trying to do is help America come up with fun, interesting, delicious things to make for dinner—and maybe some great leftovers for the middle of the night. I know you're thinking we're not supposed to get up at 1 a.m. and have a snack—but if that was the case . . . why is there a light in the fridge?

#AskingForAFriend.

By the way—we love hashtags, because they remind us of waffles! And our new Red Velvet Waffles recipe is on page 36.

Because I'm the longtime reporter and writer in the family, the recipes are written in my voice, but make no mistake—Kathy is the brains behind the operation. As a couple married over thirty-six years, we're proof that behind every husband who thinks he wears the pants in the family is . . . the wife who told him which pants match his shirt. Sound familiar?

Enjoy, and remember, if you're going to have three meals today, you might as well make sure one of them makes you *simply happy.*

—*Steve & Kathy Doocy*

SIMPLY HAPPY HACKS

In almost everything we do at the Doocy house, Kathy reminds me to use the KISS approach, *Keep It Simple, Steve*. And she's right—why make it complicated when it's so much easier to do it simply?

Because all three of the Doocy kids got married within the span of one year, Kathy and I have invested a good deal of effort into explaining some simple kitchen and cooking hacks to the newlyweds. Many are fundamental things seasoned home cooks already know—but when kids start cooking on their own they have questions. Of course we'd like to think they were paying attention to their elders in the kitchen growing up—but the reality is while we were cooking they were watching *90 Day Fiancé* on their phones, trying to figure out why that woman from Topeka moved to Peru for that loser with the pushy mother.

These simple suggestions come from everywhere. Some are hand-me-downs from our families, others are things we've seen people on TV say or do, and a couple are from quick and clever social media how-to videos. Unfortunately sometimes when a TikTok clip shows how to make a seven-course meal in nineteen seconds, it leaves out some important details. Luckily the world still has actual cookbooks you can refer to for clear instruction.

Here are some of our favorite simple kitchen principles and cooking shortcuts so you can pull together a meal as painlessly as possible.

SIMPLE FOOD PREP PRINCIPLES

Here's a refresher in basic kitchen rules of the road.

RAW EGG DISHES: Some old family recipes use raw or barely heated eggs; at our house that included Caesar salad and eggnog. We now know that's not always healthy, so today we use liquid pasteurized eggs from the dairy case at the grocery. If you use eggs in recipes, make sure the eggs are cooked or completely heated to kill any bacteria.

FLOUR POWER: Right out of the bag it's such a beautiful bright white color, but it's actually a raw food, often ground fresh from the wheat fields of my native Kansas, and could have some unfriendly germs according to the FDA. Even if you grew up eating uncooked cookie dough or batter, it's a no-go. That includes cake mixes and milkshakes, and never use regular homemade cookie dough to make cookie dough ice cream.

WASH PREWASHED? Kathy and I have this conversation every time we open a "triple-washed" or "prewashed" bag of salad. She says wash it, and I do, but the FDA warns that you must make sure that when you wash it, it doesn't touch anything that's unclean, such as cutting boards, counters, tongs, or utensils.

DON'T WASH CHICKEN: Why did we all wash chicken before cooking years ago? To get rid of the bacteria! But now we know rinsing doesn't wash the germs off; the only way to kill them off is cooking to the correct temperature of 165°F. And when you wash a chicken, the bacteria splash into the sink and on the counter and you have more disinfecting to do. This goes for turkey and other poultry, too!

MARINATING: Never marinate food at room temperature—always in the fridge—to avoid breeding bacteria.

OVENPROOF PANS: Some of these recipes call for an ovenproof pan, meaning a pan without handles or other elements that can't take exposure to heat. Also, a pan with a nonstick coating is generally not to be heated above about 500°F, so don't use nonstick pans on your outdoor grill. I made that mistake once, and will never do it again. In general, take note of the manufacturer's instructions on your pans for best and safest use!

COOKING OIL SPRAY: This is an easy and wonderful way to coat something with oil, but never spray it near an open flame on your stove or the grill, or onto already heated surfaces like pots or pans, as it can be flammable. We also store the spray away from the stove, for safety's sake.

350°F ISN'T ALWAYS 350°F: When our oven was on the fritz, the oven repair man spent over an hour measuring how hot it really was. He set it to 350°F—and according to his thermometer it fluctuated between 325°F when the element would turn on and 380°F when it would shut off. Up down, up down. So the temperature you set it at is more of an average. Since then we use the dial as a guide but ultimately we use our eyes to see when something is browned and appears done, then a thermometer to make sure it's actually completely cooked.

IS IT DONE YET? In 2020 the USDA updated its list of cooking temperatures that foods need to hit for them to be completely and safely cooked. This is fundamental—the food is not safe to eat until the interior temperature hits the numbers below. Check them with an accurate food thermometer.

> Beef, pork, lamb, veal—145°F (with 3 minutes of resting time before cutting or eating)
>
> Ground beef—160°F
>
> Ground poultry—165°F
>
> Chicken, turkey, duck, goose—165°F
>
> Fish and shellfish—145°F
>
> Eggs—160°F
>
> Leftovers—165°F

TWO-HOUR RULE: According to the FDA, foods on a buffet table should not stay out longer than 2 hours unless they are being kept hot or cold. Never add extra food to a previously filled dish of food, because then one dish would have two expiration times.

REHEATING LEFTOVERS: Reheat food only once. So if you have a big batch of leftovers, reheat only the amount of food you're going to eat at that meal.

HOW LONG DO LEFTOVERS LAST? According to the Mayo Clinic, leftovers can be eaten for 3 or 4 days with proper refrigeration. We generally toss food after the second day; it's not worth the downside.

MICROWAVING: Never use metal pans or aluminum foil in a microwave! Kathy and I saw somebody warm up take-out food in a microwave—apparently they didn't realize there was foil inside—and *poof,* the whole thing burst into flames. When a plastic container is labeled microwave safe, that simply means it won't melt. Today the worry is about chemicals from plastics leaching into food—so we only use glass or microwave-safe porcelain cookware made for microwaves.

DISHWASHER FILTER: We clean our dishwasher filter once a week—for sparkling dishes every load. Your dishwasher operating manual will show how to remove the filter, rinse it to remove the big particles, and use a brush to clean out gunk stuck to the fine-mesh filter. Another rinsing and it's time to put it back in place. Remember, your dishes are only as clean as your filter.

SIMPLE COOKING

Here are some tips and tricks we've picked up along the way that make recipes easier:

SHRED CHICKEN IN A MIXER: We often need shredded chicken for barbecue or chicken salad and shredding it with two forks is kind of a drag. We saw somebody do the mixer method on TV and now it's our go-to. Put boneless cooked chicken in the bowl of a stand mixer and snap on the paddle attachment. Run the machine for 20 to 30 seconds, until the chicken is completely and professionally shredded. This works on baked chicken, a rotisserie bird from the store, or our Perfect Poached Chicken on page 218. The fastest meal we make is with a still-warm store-bought rotisserie chicken, shredded in the mixer, tossed with barbecue or Buffalo sauce, and placed on buns to make sandwiches. If it takes more than 5 minutes, you're doing it wrong!

ADD CHICKEN BROTH TO PASTA WATER: To give pasta a little more flavor, add a couple cups of chicken broth to the water, bring to a boil, and add the noodles.

MAKE PASTA HEALTHIER: When cooking pasta, in the last 2 minutes throw in a cup of frozen peas or vegetables. It adds color and some delicious nutrients.

BEST BACON: After a lifetime of pan-frying, we only bake our bacon now; it makes less of a mess than pan-frying and it's easier and tastier. Lay bacon slices in a single layer on a nonstick sheet pan and bake in a 425°F oven for 12 minutes, then flip and bake until deeply browned and bacony, another 5 to 7 minutes.

PERFECT STEAK FRIES: Instead of using a knife, use an apple slicer and corer to create perfect potato wedges out of a whole unpeeled russet potato. That long cylinder from the center can be sliced in half or quarters to make more big fries.

HOT HANDS: When cutting hot peppers— especially jalapeños—we wear disposable gloves. If you have a little cut or abrasion on your hand, the capsaicin in the pepper will burn bad!

SLOW COOKER: We love the convenience of the slow cooker, but cleanup is so much easier when you coat the inside with cooking spray before you start a project. Trust me—it makes a big difference.

LEFTOVER PESTO: Jarred pesto has a limited shelf life after opening and we don't want it to go to waste, so we'll use it in place of mayo on a chicken or turkey sandwich, and we'll drizzle some pesto on top of a green salad, followed by a zigzag of ranch dressing. The combination is crazy tasty!

AVOCADOS: When you're in the produce aisle, it's hard to gauge how bruised an avocado is by the number of people who squeezed it before *you* squeezed it. So we buy avocados in bags of 5 or 6 when they are very green and let them ripen on the kitchen counter for a couple of days. The key is finding them before everybody has manhandled them. Best way to do that is to feel one of the avocados through the netting to see if the avocados are firm and still cold. The cold usually means they were just put out for sale. The earlier you shop in the day, the more likely you'll find them cold, otherwise grab a bag of very firm avocados that has not been squeezed by a dozen shoppers. When the avocados do ripen after a couple of days on the counter, we'll return them to our fridge and the cold stops the ripening clock on them, keeping them from getting too ripe too fast.

COLD PIZZA: Don't warm up in the microwave; it never gets crispy. Here's the best way to heat up cold pizza: Warm a nonstick skillet over medium heat, lay in a slice of pizza, and warm it until there are new golden highlights on the bottom of the crust. You'll get a pizzeria-style crispiness that the microwave can't match—and the cheese on top won't get too melty.

PERFECT HARD-BOILED EGGS: Place eggs in a saucepan and cover with cold water. Bring to a rapid boil over high heat, put a tight-fitting lid on, and boil another 30 seconds. Remove from the heat and let sit for 15 minutes. Run cold tap water into the pan to cool down the eggs, then remove the shells promptly—the longer you leave them on, the harder they are to remove.

STORE-BOUGHT STAPLES

Erma Bombeck once said, "I come from a family where gravy is considered a beverage." Today Americans' gravy consumption may be down, but we're really getting sauced. As our daughter Sally says, "Life is all about the sauces," and she's right. After we've made a salad, piece of meat, or side dish, to jazz it up, we'll guiltlessly add a store-bought sauce that makes the meal 25 percent tastier. These are our current favorite go-to store bought sauces.

THAI SWEET CHILI SAUCE: An easy zesty dip or topping for salmon, vegetables, French fries, or egg rolls.

CHICK-FIL-A SAUCE: We use this on any variety of chicken—including rotisserie! Use instead of mustard or mayo on sandwiches or salmon, and it's fantastic on fries. I've used it as a salad dressing and even put it on eggs one morning. It goes great with everything!

HERDEZ AVOCADO HOT SAUCE: Everybody loves avocado, but the fruit itself is only perfectly ripe for about 3 minutes. This terrific avocado sauce has a little kick, and we use it on chili and Tex-Mex.

YUM YUM SAUCE: This is the sauce they serve at hibachi restaurants, and now it's available in most groceries. We use it on grilled shrimp and as a salad dressing. Terry Ho's yum yum sauce is Kathy's favorite; mine is the tangy and fantastic Bibibop Asian Grill yum yum sauce. We report—you decide!

BALSAMIC REDUCTION GLAZE: We use it on tomato and mozzarella (naturally), over chicken and fish, drizzled on salad pizza, and even over watermelon and blueberries.

HIDDEN VALLEY RANCH GOLDEN SECRET SAUCE: This sauce has a terrific honey mustard BBQ flavor and it's great on chicken, burgers, fries . . . it's even tasty on salmon!

BEST SINGLE DRIED HERB BLEND: herbes de Provence. This has been Kathy's go-to seasoning for thirty-plus years. A combination of thyme, rosemary, oregano, marjoram, and more—instead of all those little herb jars that can grow stale, and are sometimes hard to find with supply chain issues . . . we just use this one.

ALL-STAR STEAK SEASONING: Every kitchen needs a shaker of Montreal steak seasoning—a mix of salt and pepper plus hints of garlic, onion, and paprika. Pete Hegseth won the *Fox & Friends* BBQ Contest simply by shaking it on a batch of cheeseburgers. It's great, for Pete's sake!

BEST PASTA NOODLE: Bucatini is a long-strand pasta like a thick spaghetti, with a hole down the center that absorbs the sauce's flavor. We think it's by far the best noodle. There was a bucatini shortage in 2020, which we're sure was caused by the BLT Pasta recipe in our *Happy in a Hurry Cookbook*. Apologies, America. Stock up when you see it!

SIMPLY HELPFUL EQUIPMENT

You already have the essential equipment; here are some of the extra items we have in our kitchen. Nothing will break the bank; they'll just make things a little easier, and that means they'll make you a little happier.

KITCHEN TIMER: It's the easiest cooking mistake: You've lost track of time and you overcook something. It doesn't have to happen. Kathy uses a $3 grocery store timer that looks like a ladybug and it works great. Or use your phone's timer—just don't forget to set it! You might think you know when 6 minutes are up, but trust me—you're better off with a timer.

INSTANT-READ THERMOMETER: Is the chicken done? You can't tell from the outside, but poke one of these into the thickest part of the chicken and it tells you instantly if it's in the right temperature zone. We use a Taylor brand instant-read digital thermometer every day, and as of this writing it was $10 on Amazon. Great in the kitchen and outside on the grill.

SMART THERMOMETER: Kathy gave me a Yummly brand Bluetooth thermometer for Christmas and it's made cooking a big piece of meat in the oven or smoker a snap. Ken, our family doctor, sent us a wireless Meater Plus model, and it's terrific, too. You simply pair either of these with your smartphone and stick it into the meat when you start cooking, and it tells you when it's done. This eliminates the guesswork and allows more time for adult beverage drinking, which is key during recipes that involve long meat roasting or smoking.

KEVLAR KITCHEN GLOVE: When using kitchen choppers and slicers and knife sharpeners your bare hands get so close to the blade, Kevlar gloves are a great layer of added protection to make sure that you're cooking and not bleeding. They don't turn you into Superman, but they make a sometimes perilous task (like removing chopper blades) less hazardous.

POT AND PAN PROTECTORS: We hate to get scratches on the coating of our nonstick pots and pans, and a set of pan protectors keeps them separated when you stack them in your cupboard. About $10, available online.

AIR FRYER: It's almost as speedy as a microwave and gives food a crispy edge. Paula Deen gave us our first one, and now it's the most used gizmo in our kitchen—we swear by it. It cooks faster than your oven, so keep an eye on it.

KITCHEN SHEARS: Sometimes it's easier to snip than chop, especially with herbs . . . and bacon! Plus with shears, you don't dirty a cutting board. One pair will work for the entire meal prep—but if you're going to use it on both vegetables and uncooked meat, snip the vegetables first to avoid cross-contamination.

PIZZA DOCKER: If you make an occasional pizza from fresh dough at home, you've got to have a pizza docker. It pokes holes all over the crust so that no giant bubbles blow up during baking. Our friend Sonny got us using one and now we don't make a pizza pie without it.

OVERFLOW BOX: Over thirty-six years of marriage, we've accumulated a couple hundred small kitchen gizmos. Some we only use once a year, if that, but we'd hate to throw them away—because then we'd definitely need it. So we've weeded out the seldom-used devices and placed them in a clear plastic overflow box that sits in our pantry, keeping them separate from the more frequently used utensils in the drawer.

SPRITZ COOKIE PRESS: This gizmo was ever present in our Scandinavian household growing up. It's the easiest way to make a buttery sugar cookie that looks like it came from a high-end bakery, and it's essential to making the cookies on page 305. It's a blast for your holiday baking—give it a shot!

RICE COOKER: I don't know how our rice cooker always knows exactly when the rice is done, but it does, and we love ours. And it's so simple—just use the ratio of rice to water found in the package directions, turn on the cooker, and wait for the beep—and it will keep the rice warm until you're ready to serve. One added tip: Always triple-rinse the rice to get rid of the starch that can make rice gummy.

APPETIZERS AND SMALLER BITES

*T*HE NERVOUS YOUNG MAN TRIED TO LOOK INCON-spicuous as he stood outside the high-end jewelry store he'd cased a week earlier. Just as the security guard at the door left his post momentarily—the outsider put on a mask that covered most of his face. Quickly he went inside and directly to the most expensive gems, where a concerned clerk zipped behind the counter and asked, "Can I help you?" That's when the masked man whipped a note out of his pocket and slid it in front of the salesman.

The store clerk was looking a little puzzled when the masked man blurted out, "Do you have engagement rings like that?"

The guy squinted and said, "Not really . . . but I can make one. How much you want to spend?"

And that's pretty much exactly what happened when Peter Doocy bought his now-wife Hillary Vaughn her diamond wedding ring in Washington, DC. He was freaked out about shopping for the ring because I'd told Peter as a child never to be the joker who wears a mask into a jewelry store. But who could have predicted a pandemic?

Since our last cookbook came out two years ago, so much has happened with the Doocy family. Peter is of course now a famous White House correspondent whom President Biden has called, *among other things*, "the most interesting man I know in the press." POTUS also called Peter "a one-horse pony," which we're still trying to figure out.

Because our cookbooks are also storybooks about life around our kitchen table, we thought with this first chapter we'd bring you up to date on what the Doocy family has been up to since our *Happy in a Hurry Cookbook*.

Soon a bride, hitching a ride.

That book ended with the breaking news that our younger daughter, Sally, was engaged to Ali Sadri, whom she'd been dating for seven years.

So let's pick it up from there . . .

Sally and Ali were planning a May 2020 wedding of their dreams. Invitations for 180 people were mailed, a champagne wall was being planned, the four-course sit-down dinner was taste-tested and approved, an eleven-piece orchestra was hired, a greenhouse of blue and white hydrangeas was arranged to be harvested and air-expressed to arrive the day of the wedding. And of course, as is customary, we paid for everything in advance.

Then, Covid—you know what happened, you were there.

In the terrifying early days of the pandemic, Kathy was told by her doctor if she got Covid, her preexisting conditions meant that she'd probably die. At that time New York and New Jersey were the world's hot spots, so we outfitted Kathy in two medical-grade masks and a plastic face shield and put her on a plane to Florida to ride out the wave. Sally—whose wedding was postponed at that point—moved in with her mom to help with whatever was needed and work remotely. Meanwhile, her fiancé, Ali, was trapped in his Manhattan apartment. He rarely ventured out into the halls, but when he did he'd see men and women outfitted as if they were on a hazmat squad, in N-95 masks and moon suits. They worked a couple of blocks away at one of New York's most prominent hospitals—which was raging with Covid. When Ali told me about his neighbors, I told him to pack a bag—"I'll be there in forty-five minutes"—and I evacuated him to the Doocy bunker across the river in New Jersey.

Ali had dated Sally for years, so of course I knew him—but I didn't really *know* him, until

My Covid commute was fifteen seconds to the living room.

our pandemically forced staycation. We were locked down together in the house, in which I was hosting *Fox & Friends* from our living room and Ali was working remotely from the kitchen table. Poor kid, held hostage in a house with his future father-in-law for nineteen weeks.

On the bright side—if you have to be holed up with somebody for 133 days, make sure they're working on a cookbook. Ali became my official food taster. Mister Lucky wound up with three hots—and a cot. I calculate that I made Ali 261 from-scratch meals—plus dessert.

As I tweaked the hundred-plus recipes Kathy and I had come up with, what I wanted to hear from Ali after the meal was "That was the best thing I've ever had—thank you, Mr. Doocy, you're the world's greatest future father-in-law!"

But Ali, new to the Doocy family, thought I wanted the truth—*ha!*

Ali was an analyst with an MBA who'd list the pros and cons of every recipe as if he were analyzing the valuation of an apartment building in Portland. I didn't want the downside—I could figure that out—I just wanted him to say "mmm-mmm good!"

Why couldn't I be quarantining with a yes-man?

But as I'd wash the dirty dishes, I'd think about his suggestions and sometimes reconfigure a recipe in my head. His honest opinions and suggestions improved the recipes and there's not one page in that second cookbook that didn't have the Kathy and Steve Doocy

Inspector Ali.

Still gorgeous.

and Ali Sadri Seal of Approval. Ali obviously has good taste—he picked our daughter!

As the months dragged on, we got closer to the new date of their twice-postponed wedding.

Sally briefly returned to our home as their wedding date approached to attempt a final fitting for her wedding dress; it had taken months to make and was sequestered in the back room of a shuttered Madison Avenue designer. Sally was panicked because the dress shop would not answer by phone or email. With less than ten days before their rescheduled wedding, somebody called her back and we immediately jumped in the car and rushed to the city for final adjustments as the seamstress smiled (we think) behind a plastic face shield and stylish mask.

Sally and Ali then flew to Florida for the wedding, and with the house quiet, I wrote my father of the bride speech. Their wedding hashtag was When Ali Met Sally, and for my speech I found a great quote from *When Harry Met Sally*. I asked Ali what his favorite movie was, and he said *Saving Private Ryan*. I looked for an inspirational and appropriate quote from that movie, but all I could find were lines about stopping the bleeding.

You'll read more about the postponed, then slimmed down to *ten people* wedding later in the book—but it was slightly socially distanced and absolutely splendid. And I don't say that just because I saved a boatload of dough by not having to pay for swanky dinner, drinks, an orchestra—plus tip—for an extra 170 people. It was perfect because we were together and safe.

Two months after their wedding, our *Happy in a Hurry Cookbook* rolled out. We were still in the grip of the pandemic, and the planned book tour was completely canceled. Our *Fox & Friends* crew was back in the studio, but it was long before the vaccines and we still had to stand ten feet apart. That book featured our family recipes and delicious dishes from Ainsley and Brian's loved ones and we wanted to show them on TV, but company Covid restrictions meant non-Fox people could not come into the building for any reason—including food prep. Because the building management would not

Big day, big banner.

Trunk show.

allow our food stylist, Maureen Luchejko, into the building, she instead prepared half a dozen recipes in the back of her Toyota RAV4, parked outside our studios on 48th Street. Our show runners would bring the prepped food from the curb into the studio—and warm up the hot dishes like Brian's artichoke pie in a toaster oven backstage. Then, via FaceTime, Maureen told our producers how to arrange the table for the TV cameras. Everything she made outside tasted exactly as if it were out of our kitchen, and nobody at home watching would have ever known those recipes were prepped in the back of a vehicle parked in a tow-away zone. It was like the ultimate Uber Eats—from an actual Uber.

It must have worked out okay, because the book would debut at number one on the *New York Times* bestseller list. It was the most popular book in the world on Amazon—for a whole week, knocking Bob Woodward off the top of the list. Bob has not spoken to me since. Okay, he's never spoken to me, but that's beside the point.

We think one reason the book worked was that it came out six months before the vaccines were approved, and people were still locked down and quite simply had gotten bored with their cooking repertoires, and we had some great ideas. The most popular dessert in America the rest of that year was our Ritz cracker crust peanut butter pie, a family recipe from our friend Christie de Nicola. My grandma Berndt's Hash Brown Crust Quiche was the

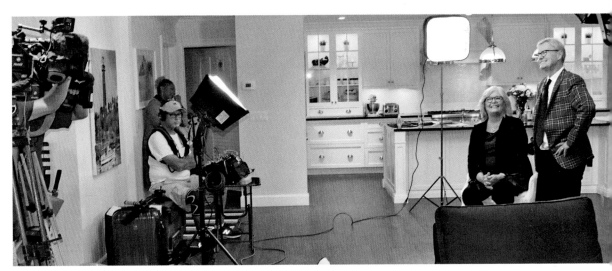

Live *from our kitchen!*

most searched breakfast recipe on Google after I demo'd it on TV. And we believe our BLT Pasta made with bucatini was responsible for the very real nationwide bucatini shortage in 2020.

On that first day of publication we ran a videotape that explained how and why Kathy and I became cookbook writers after she'd been diagnosed with eye cancer, and during radiation therapy Kathy started a project writing down our kids' favorite recipes of hers—just in case.

Halfway across the country, Pastor Terry Keeney was watching. Kathy's cancer sounded exactly like what his friend Vickie Sonnenberg in Tennessee had just been diagnosed with the week before—so he called her and told her to find Kathy's story online and see if it might help her. I heard about Vickie's story when Pastor Terry posted a thank-you to Kathy for sharing her story on Facebook.

When I heard about Vickie, I tracked her down, and as I dialed the last four digits of her phone number, I realized they were the same last four digits of Kathy's cell phone. Coincidence, I've always said, is God's way of working anonymously. Telling Vickie that she and Kathy had the same number was the first thing I said when I got her on the phone.

"Steve, your wife and I have more in common than people realize."

Just like Kathy, Vickie had no idea she had eye cancer before she and her husband had gone to the mall to get a new prescription for glasses. The results were normal, but as they were about to leave the nurse told them that they had a new 3D machine that could look at the back of their eyes to see if there were any problems, but it cost an extra $15. Vickie told me she was from a family with ten children and spent her life in hand-me-downs—"I am as tight as bark on a tree"—and said to the nurse they weren't going to spend the money on the test.

Then her husband, who had just been successfully treated for prostate cancer, told the nurse, "We're going to do it"—and they did.

Her husband's eyes were fine, but something was not right at the back of Vickie's eye—they thought the retina was detaching, and she was immediately sent to a specialist, who spotted a melanoma tumor and got them in quickly to see a surgeon. He gave Vickie two treatment options, radiation therapy or enucleation—taking out the whole eye. She said she would have to think and pray on it. They told her not to take too long; it really couldn't wait. Vickie thought carefully and decided to get rid of all the cancer at once—she would have her entire eye removed.

But two days later, Vickie's friend saw Kathy talk on TV about how she battled and overcame cancer, and he immediately called Vickie and said she had to listen to Kathy Doocy's story. So she did, and it changed her mind—instead of having her eye removed, she would have the same surgery Kathy did by a highly recommended surgeon who happened to have been trained by Kathy's doctors. The good news: Vickie's radiation treatment was successful—and she kept both eyes and her vision.

Vickie told me she had just been to her doctor and the tumor continued to shrink. The doctor also said, "Next time you see that optometrist, thank him for saving your life." She has thanked him plenty of times since. "I truly believe in guardian angels," Vickie told me, and that optometrist was her guardian angel.

"If I hadn't seen that show and heard your wife's story, Steve, Vickie would not have gone down that road," Pastor Terry told me. "And I don't think she would have made it. Thank God I

Mary Doocy, public servant.

saw it." Then he paused a moment. "Honestly," Terry said with his voice cracking on the phone, "your wife probably saved her life."

Over that summer Kathy and I made our annual trip back to Philadelphia for her checkup at Wills Hospital in the heart of the city. The good news was that the surgery and radiation worked—she has some vision challenges, but Kathy has been cancer-free for more than five years.

Just know that Kathy donates a lot of money from these cookbooks toward eye cancer research—which we pray will someday eradicate this awful killer. So thank you for supporting these books, which is helping to fund this important cause. By telling her story and educating people, Kathy has become an accidental national voice about the importance of having your eyes checked for ocular melanoma and about the treatment option that saved her life.

I'm sure she has been a guardian angel to more people than we will ever know.

After we'd promoted the cookbook, making videos and live TV demonstrations for a couple of months, I started noticing that Kathy was apparently washing my jeans in super-hot water because they were suddenly tight. But it wasn't the washer or the dryer; it was an occupational hazard of cookbookery. I had gained a little weight. Luckily, every January I go on a diet, and that year I decided on keto, and simultaneously observed dry January, a month to give my liver a break as I swore off all forms of alcohol—except Purell.

I lost my target poundage in two weeks. But I had half a month left, so I added the ambitious goal of losing the love handles I'd had since I turned thirty. By the end of the month the love handles were gone and I was at a weight that I'd not seen on a bathroom scale since I was twenty-three. That's when our daughter Sally, who runs our social media accounts, told me that the number one topic on our pages was *Is Steve okay? He's gotten really thin.*

Surprised that people noticed I had gone on a diet, I Googled my own name and saw: *"Does Steve Doocy have cancer?"*

I clicked on that link and it took me to Kathy's cancer story. But people weren't asking about Kathy—they were asking about me.

So many of you watch me almost every day and consider me an actual friend. And when there's anything amiss, you worry about me. For that, *I sincerely thank you.*

Just know I am fine—knock on wood—and I'm really good at dieting!

Fast-forward to today, I'm off keto, dry January is over, and I'm back to my normal diet—which is everything in this cookbook. I'm also back to my previous weight, but I've replaced some flab with muscle—thanks to Pilates and

Hillary said, "I Doocy!"

record and ponders whether to let me in, I'll be pointing down to our angel on earth, Mary, who'll look up and nod to St. Peter and mouth the words *"Let him in—he's with me."*

And as for Peter and his new wife, Fox Business correspondent Hillary—who is no doubt at this moment wearing that ring he sketched out for the jeweler in DC—they've made their home just outside Washington. For their wedding, I was honored to be Peter's best man. Here's a small portion of my rhyming toast to the seventeen just-vaccinated people who gathered in South Carolina that beautiful night:

> Peter and Hillary are married—and we're
>   all kind of dizzy.
> I'm so honored to be your best man—
>   apparently Bret Baier is busy.
> Now, Peter, you're at the White House
>   wearing your best khaki,
> Conversing on TV with the press
>   secretary, Jen Psaki,
> And we are delighted today that you have
>   finally married Hillary,
> Rather than your earlier path—that could
>   have been a distillery.
> You've both covered riots and shutdowns
>   and pandemics and strife,
> And if you can survive that—it's easy to be
>   husband and wife.
> Hillary, we know Peter simply adores
>   you—that's no baloney,
> And, Hillary, welcome to the family—of
>   America's favorite one-horse pony.

It was a beautiful ceremony, and one of the highlights of an otherwise challenging year. For more than two years we were all so careful with the pandemic. All of us had gotten double vaccinated, boosted, and tested before we gathered our family together this

working out—and still no love handles! If *Men's Health* would like me to be on the cover of their swimsuit issue, please contact our family lawyer and middle child, Mary Doocy.

Mary continues her vigilant work in federal law enforcement in our nation's capital. A tireless advocate for justice, since law school Mary has always been a public servant, and she's always loved helping people. Kathy and I couldn't be more proud of her achievements and mettle. She approaches her job the way inspirational congresswoman Shirley Chisholm once described that kind of work: "Service is the rent you pay for room on this earth." And she was right.

I know the day I'm standing at the Pearly Gates and St. Peter scrutinizes my permanent past Christmas. It was a blessed and wonderful holiday season . . . until I woke up with a sore throat. After I stood in line for five hours, the ER doctor told me, "Happy New Year, Steve—you have Covid."

I isolated at the other end of the house and wore a surgical-grade mask for days, but it was too late; Peter got it, and then after going to extraordinary lengths for more than two years to protect Kathy, she woke up with Omicron. It was the number one thing we'd worked so hard to prevent, because we'd been told it could have the worst possible outcome. After quick intervention by our doctor, Kathy hit a few speed bumps, but she recovered no worse for wear. We'd done what Michael J. Fox advised against: "Don't spend a lot of time imagining the worst-case scenario. It rarely goes down as you imagine it will, and by some fluke if it does, you'll have lived it twice."

He's right, but given the life-or-death challenge involved, if given the chance for a do-over, we probably wouldn't do a single thing differently. It was the smart thing to do to keep each other safe. But we were also very lucky, and you know exactly what I'm talking about, because wherever you are reading this, we've all been going through the last couple of years together and we're all ready to move on. Right? So let's . . .

And with that, you are officially up to date on the Doocy family since our last cookbook. We hope you'll enjoy our new recipes and stories!

THE FIVE O'CLOCK CHARCUTERIE BOARD

THE FIVE ON THE FOX NEWS CHANNEL SHOULD BE CALLED *THE HAPPY HOUR*, BECAUSE during the 5 p.m. ET hour when it airs, much of America is having a relaxing drink to unwind. Maybe that's why the show is so popular . . . the country is half in the bag.

I'm kidding—it's popular because the hosts are hilarious and very smart and some of the best broadcasters working today. But speaking of drinks, having invited Dana Perino and her husband, Peter, over for dinner, we know that as we're watching the program, if she was at our house during happy hour she'd be drinking sauvignon blanc—with ice. The ice keeps it chilled and slows down your alcohol consumption, which keeps your mind from going blanc.

Greg Gutfeld's go-to drink is a good Dark 'n' Stormy, made with Gosling's dark rum, angostura bitters, and ginger beer. "It reminds me of Jamaica," Greg told me. "Or maybe the Bahamas . . . but it's definitely a memory of being shirtless."

Live with The Five.

"I'm into bourbon," Jesse Watters revealed. "Harold Ford Jr. gave me a fancy bourbon bottle with the little guy on the horse on the top."

"Do you mean Blanton's?"

"That's it! And it was *very* expensive!"

I already knew that, because I had received that exact same bottle as a gift from a young man who was buttering me up to ask for my daughter's hand in marriage. What was Harold Ford asking for—other than fifteen more seconds for his *One More Thing?*

So that's what they're drinking. What would be on their charcuterie board if they had one splayed out on that big table they work around? Here are their world-exclusive answers.

GREG'S INGREDIENTS: SWEET AND SAVORY

Pez candy

Pop Rocks candy

Pigs in a blanket, with spicy mustard and ketchup

Deviled eggs (check out our Dinner Party Dill-Deviled Eggs on page 27)

DANA'S DELICIOUS TREATS: FLORAL AND FABULOUS

Dana's Dazzling Salami Roses (page 12)

Wheel of soft Brie or our Billionaire Bacon and Cranberry Brie (page 22)

Marcona almonds

Carrot and cucumber sticks

WATTERS'S WORLD OF SNACKS

Chicken liver pâté

Sliced meat: pepperoni or soppressata

Manchego cheese, cut into thin wedges, fanned out

Seedless grapes

Honey mustard

Red and green pepper slices with dill sauce

Crackers: Wheat Thins, Triscuits, or Carr's (his mom's favorite)

BOARDING SCHOOL

The best instruction on building your board is to know there is no wrong way to lay this out. You want it to look like a tapestry of wonderful tastes; people will eyeball everything on the board and grab whatever looks good. When in doubt, park things where they look cool—it's all about the pageantry of the presentation!

Quantities for each ingredient depend upon how many people you're serving and the size of the board you're using. Find the right size board for your purposes, and make sure it's clean—you'd hate to ptomaine poison the cast of America's favorite ensemble news program.

First things on the board are the big items, such as bowls of dip or wheels of Brie. Put runny condiments and candies in small bowls. Greg says he likes the idea of putting Pez or Pop Rocks candy on the deviled eggs—*for texture*. He's probably kidding, he is the Comedy King of Late Night—so he could be sleep deprived. We recommend putting any candies into a small dish, but Mr. Gutfeld might suggest a jar to create a *jar*-cuterie.

Refrigerated foods can be out of the fridge for only 2 hours, so chill small plates for elements such as Jesse's pâté or Greg's deviled eggs (best to put out only a few deviled eggs at a time and freshen the plate with new cold eggs as needed).

Dana's Dazzling Salami Roses are pretty big, so they also go on in the early round of assemblage, followed by her wheel of soft Brie, which is best served at room temperature. For a new Brie recipe, try our super-savory and -melty Billionaire Bacon and Cranberry Brie (page 22). It's one of our tastiest new appetizers!

Now that your board is set on the larger items, fill the bare spaces with thinly sliced or cured meats and fanned-out cheeses, both snuggled up to the plates, bowls, or Brie.

Cue the crackers and/or bread slices, then fill any remaining empty spaces with nuts, olives, and sliced vegetables and fruits. Sprigs of herbs look great as an accent as long as their scent doesn't overwhelm the food. Given the program is called *The Five*, the perfect herb would be thyme. Am I right?

Have a few cheese knives nearby and you're ready for *The Five* . . . I mean happy hour!

DANA'S DAZZLING SALAMI ROSES

There are tons of videos online if you want a 1-minute lesson in how to make salami roses. Start with thinly sliced salami on the larger side (not pepperoni size) and a wineglass.

Set a wineglass on your counter. Fold a slice of salami in half over the edge of the glass, so that the slice is half in the glass and half hanging over the edge. Add another folded slice, overlapping it slightly with the first. Continue adding slices around the glass, using up to about 12 slices. Set a small measuring cup (say ¼ cup) into the wineglass about 1 inch deep to hold the salami slices in place. Refrigerate the glass in the fridge to chill and firm up the salami rose. When you're ready to serve, remove the measuring cup, invert the wineglass over the board and gently ease out the salami rose. Repeat to make as many salami roses as you like!

TOMATO AND PESTO PIE

IN A BOX SOMEWHERE I HAVE A BLUE RIBBON FROM OUR 1971 COUNTY FAIR FOR THE best, most perfect tomatoes in Clay County, Kansas. A few weeks later another batch of my tomato crop was sent to the state fair, but the person from our 4-H club who took them there forgot and left them in their car trunk for three hours on the hottest day of the year. They were blistered and split open, but inexplicably they still won a second-place red ribbon, which I'm pretty sure I probably used as a coaster.

Our family tomato patch was amazing, thanks to my dad, who never used any chemicals or fertilizers. At the end of the season, he would select a single beautiful tomato and carefully remove the seeds and dry them in the garage to plant the next year. You know what you call those? Heirloom tomatoes. Jim Doocy was growing heirloom tomatoes fifty years before your grocery store knew they were *a thing* and started selling them for $5 a pound.

Kid pricing.

I grew up growing tomatoes, as did our kids, a couple of pint-size capitalists who started hawking them out on the street. Two basil leaves—three cents. Large tomatoes—a nickel. If they sold out their entire inventory, they'd have 45 cents in their college fund. Of course to honor their entrepreneurship, Kathy would take them to Dairy Queen and spend $12 on treats, meaning the Doocy produce business was operating at an $11.55 deficit. Today Peter and Mary both have jobs in DC—and that is *exactly* how Washington works!

We make this simple recipe when we have a bumper crop of garden tomatoes and basil or simply a jar of store-bought pesto sitting in the fridge screaming *I'm not going to last forever!* This is a blue-ribbon recipe—hope you enjoy!

Makes 8 appetizer-size slices

3 medium heirloom tomatoes (grab the prettiest ones) or 3 medium red tomatoes on the vine

1 refrigerated pie crust, at room temperature

¾ cup shredded mozzarella cheese

1 tablespoon olive oil

Sea salt and freshly ground black pepper

1 large egg

Basil pesto, for drizzling

1. Preheat the oven to 375°F.

2. Use a serrated knife to core the tomatoes and cut them into ¼-inch-thick slices. Use a toothpick to remove the seeds and watery liquids; this may seem a bit fussy but it keeps the pie bottom from getting soggy.

3. Roll out the pie dough on parchment paper into a round that's an inch wider. Lift that parchment paper and pie crust into your sheet pan. If it runs up the sides, that's okay, we're going to bend back the edges later. Scatter the mozzarella across the dough, up to 1 inch from the edge, as you would if this were a pizza.

4. Arrange the tomatoes on top of the cheese, allowing them to slightly overlap and leaving about 1½ inches free around the edge of the pastry. Brush the olive oil over the tomatoes, then sprinkle with salt and pepper. Fold up the edges galette-style: Starting on one side, bend a 1½-inch portion of the dough up and over the tomatoes and gently press it flat into the tomatoes. Move over a couple inches and do the same, pleating the point where they overlap. Go around the dough, folding it all around. It doesn't have to be perfect—rustic is the look we're going for. Whisk an egg and brush it thoroughly over all the exposed pie dough for a golden outer crust.

5. Bake until the crust is deep golden brown and the cheese is bubbling up between the tomatoes, 23 to 26 minutes. Let the pie rest 5 to 10 minutes, then drizzle on as much pesto as you like.

6. Slice with a pizza cutter into 8 wedges and enjoy! This tart is best served the day it's made.

IT'S NACHO CHICKEN!

ONE DAY WHEN WILL CAIN WAS REPORTING FROM A DINER IN TEXAS, HE SHOWED THE audience what he'd ordered for breakfast, a beautiful plate of migas, a simple Mexican egg dish of eggs, cheese, and tortilla chips. "Steve, I don't know if migas is in your cookbook, but if not, it should be . . ."

"Actually, Will, it is . . ." I responded. "But instead of plain tortilla chips, we suggest you use something that changes the whole dish into a flavor explosion—Doritos!" And they do, and they're delicious. We ended that segment with everybody on the set suddenly starving.

Don Presutti, our technical manager, said, "When you mentioned those chips, it reminded me that I've got a great recipe for you: Doritos Chicken."

Wow—he had me at Doritos.

Brilliant idea! It tastes like a zesty chicken taco—without a shell. It's baked *in its shell!*

Originally we were going to call it Don's Easy Cheesy Chip Chicken, but Mrs. Doocy stated the obvious: "If we use Nacho Cheese Doritos . . . *It's Nacho Chicken!*"

Why is she always right?

Now when I hear Don brag to his friends that his recipe is in this cookbook, I have to remind him, "Don . . . *It's Nacho Chicken!*"

I hope Don doesn't take it the wrong way. It may be cheesy to say, but Don—you're a gouda guy.

Makes 4 or 5 servings

One 9.25-ounce bag Nacho Cheese Doritos

½ cup all-purpose flour

½ teaspoon freshly ground black pepper

3 large eggs

3 large boneless, skinless chicken breasts

Cooking oil spray

Chick-fil-A sauce or Old El Paso Creamy Queso Sauce, for drizzling

1. Adjust an oven rack to the center position and preheat the oven to 375°F convection. (You can also make these in an air fryer; they'll cook a couple minutes faster.)

2. In a food processor, pulse half the bag of Doritos to the consistency of store-bought bread crumbs. Transfer them to a large zip-top bag, process the rest, and add them to the bag.

3. Now let's set up a chicken batter assembly line. In a shallow flat-bottomed bowl, combine the flour and pepper and mix. In a second shallow flat-bottomed bowl, whisk the eggs.

4. Place a chicken breast on a cutting board and trim any excess fat. Cut 5 or 6 long, straight chicken strips from the breast, each ½- to ¾-inch wide. Save any extra little odd-size strips as well. Repeat to cut the other breasts into strips.

5. Grease a sheet pan well. Working with one strip at a time, coat the chicken strips completely in the flour, then completely in the egg. Finally, add the strip to the bag with the Doritos crumbs and give it a good shake until completely coated in crumbs. Place the strip on the prepared sheet pan. Repeat to coat all the strips, then mist them with cooking spray.

6. Bake the strips for 12 minutes, then carefully flip them with tongs and bake until the outside is crispy and the interior reads 165°F on an instant-read thermometer, 6 or 7 minutes longer.

7. Remove the strips to plates or a serving platter. We serve these with a zigzag of Chick-fil-A sauce or queso sauce, which makes them simply amazing.

PAULA'S PERFECT EMPANADA EGG ROLLS

DAN BONGINO REMEMBERS ONE OF HIS SECRET SERVICE ASSIGNMENTS IN 2006, WHEN he was providing personal security for Jenna Bush during a trip to Argentina. Her twin sister, Barbara, was also traveling, and they were staying in the fashionable Palermo neighborhood and apparently having a crazy good time, out and about for lunch, dinner, and dancing late into the night. Dan's job was to protect the Bush daughters, and that included never revealing to their father, President George W. Bush, what time his girls returned to their hotel.

So why did Dan spill those juicy details about Jenna and Barbara to me? He didn't. I found them in news reports from the time. But he did confess to me that during his brief leisure time in South America, he developed an unhealthy addiction to something that he has never publicly admitted before—empanadas!

Working around the clock, the only place he could grab something to eat was at a bakery next to the Bush twins' hotel. Their specialty was their fresh daily empanadas—adorable little fried meat and potato pies. They were so delicious Dan would sometimes eat fifteen a day, with the Secret Service picking up his per diem. If you're a taxpayer horrified at this largesse, stop complaining—it was still cheaper than a porterhouse.

During breaks in the action, Dan would call home to check on his family. He told his wonderful wife, Paula, that he'd fallen for the empanadas next door but felt a little guilty because they were fried and greasy. "I can make them healthier," Paula told him, and when he came back home, she'd created her own version. She added more vegetables, used leaner meat, and rather than wrapping them in a thick pastry dough, she used ultrathin egg roll wrappers. And they aren't fried—they're baked!

"Paula's the best," Dan told me once. "I married up." And he's right.

You'll love this recipe! The Doocys serve these as appetizers, and the Bonginos make them an entree, although Dan no longer eats fifteen at a time—he's down to ten. It was either that or buy a new wardrobe of stretch pants with expanding waistbands.

Makes about 20 empanada-style egg rolls

---

2 pounds lean ground beef (they use ground sirloin)

2 medium white potatoes, peeled and cut into ½-inch dice

2 packets Goya Sazón Azafran seasoning (or 2 teaspoons adobo seasoning)

½ teaspoon table salt

¼ cup finely chopped red onion

1. Adjust an oven rack so that it is no closer than 6 inches from the top and preheat the oven to 400°F. Line a sheet pan with parchment paper.

2. In a large skillet, combine the ground beef and potatoes. Sprinkle on the Goya seasoning and salt and cook over medium-high heat, stirring often to break up the meat, until all the pink is gone from the meat, about 10 minutes. Add the onion, bell peppers, tomato, garlic, and cilantro (if using), mix, and cook until the vegetables are soft, 10 to 15 minutes. Occasionally

1 red bell pepper, cut into
½-inch squares

1 green bell pepper, cut into
½-inch squares

1 large tomato, cut into
medium dice

1 garlic clove, chopped

1 tablespoon chopped fresh
cilantro (optional)

20 large egg roll wrappers

Cooking oil spray

OPTIONAL ACCOMPANIMENTS

Guacamole

Ranch dressing

Thai sweet chili sauce

Taco sauce

mash the vegetables (especially the potatoes) with a spatula
and stir and cook some more, until the mixture is pretty mushy.
Remove from the heat.

3. Now to make the egg rolls! Lay out an egg roll wrapper and
scoop about ¼ cup of the filling onto the center. In a small bowl
of water, wet your finger and run it around the outer edges of the
wrapper. Fold the bottom corner up and over the meat mixture,
then fold in the sides and roll it closed. Press lightly along the
edges to seal it up, then lay it on the prepared sheet pan. Repeat
to make the rest of the egg rolls. Lightly mist all the egg rolls with
cooking spray.

4. Bake the egg rolls until the wrappers are crispy with deep
golden highlights on the edges, 10 to 12 minutes. Rotate the
pan front to back once during the baking time.

5. Let the egg rolls cool at least 5 minutes before serving. For
groups Paula will slice them on the diagonal for sharing, but her
family likes them served whole. Guacamole goes great on the
side, as does a little dipping sauce like ranch dressing, Thai sweet
chili sauce, or taco sauce. And because these are a nonfried
version of the empanada, you'd better park a healthy side salad
next to them!

BILLIONAIRE BACON AND CRANBERRY BRIE

KATHY AND I WERE HAVING A FESTIVE LUNCH AT A SCENIC SPOT WHERE THE VERY RICH and famous often tie on the feedbag. The menu seemed pretty standard until I spotted something I'd never heard of: *billionaire bacon*. I immediately felt a pang of envy—not only do the super rich have their own jets and polo ponies, they have their own bacon!

When the waiter came around, Kathy ordered a very blue-collar pasta salad, but I had to have a cheeseburger with this bourgeoisie bacon. Fifteen minutes and two tiny Diet Cokes later, lunch arrived—and the verdict was immediate. That bacon was phenomenal! When our server came back, I asked him why they call it billionaire bacon. *"Don't know."* Is this a favorite of billionaires? *"Not sure . . . I'm new."* Finally, the most important query: Any idea how they make it? *"In the kitchen?"*

As I left I spotted a longtime acquaintance who'd also ordered the bacon. I pointed and said, "That is so good!" And he replied, "My eighty-five-year-old momma made this!"

"How?" I asked.

"Simple," he said. "She'd bake it in brown sugar . . ."

Wait . . . his mother is a billionaire? She drives a Malibu. Who knew? Secondly, the secret ingredient is brown sugar—for its big-money moniker, I expected it to be baked in *Benjamins*!

Our friend Bret told us he's been making his own version of Billionaire's Bacon for years in his smoker, and he gave us some ideas to make it simply. So the next time we cooked bacon, we encrusted it with brown sugar and baked it brown, and it was beautiful! Now we brown-sugar a lot of our bacon, and it's perfect for this baked Brie recipe—one that Kathy's been making since we first met. Along with the bacon and Brie it has nuts and fruit, so it's like an entire charcuterie board on a single plate. Kathy's updated her process to make it simpler—rather than bake it for half an hour in the oven, she lops off the top rind of the Brie and watchfully microwaves it. It's reminiscent of a fabulous fondue—which we're fond of.

You will *love* this!

Makes 20 appetizer-size servings

---

3 slices bacon

¼ cup packed light brown sugar

One 6-inch wheel Brie (we use Président brand)

One 14-ounce can whole-berry cranberry sauce

⅓ cup caramelized pecans or walnuts (find them in the fancy cheese department)

Sliced baguette or crackers, for serving

1. Adjust an oven rack to the center position and preheat the oven to 425°F.

2. Scatter the brown sugar on a plate and press each piece of bacon into the sugar on both sides, then set it on a nonstick sheet pan.

3. Bake for 12 minutes, then carefully flip the bacon using tongs and bake until deep brown and crispy, about 5 minutes longer. Remove to a plate to cool—*don't* use paper towels; the bacon will stick!

4. Place the cranberry sauce in a small microwave-safe bowl, cover the bowl, and microwave for about 3 minutes, stirring once halfway, until the berries separate from the sauce. Remove and keep warm.

5. Stand the Brie on one edge and use a long knife to carefully slice off just the top ⅛ inch of the rind, rotating the wheel as you cut to make it easier. If some rind is left, just skim-cut it off.

6. Place the Brie cut side up in the center of a nice microwave-safe serving plate. Microwave the Brie on high for 30 seconds, then pull it out and examine it. You will notice that it first starts to melt just inside the outer rind. Microwave in 15-second increments until the center is a little melty when you poke it with a fork. (Note that the firmer your Brie is, the longer it will take to microwave, and if you overcook it you'll melt the edges and have a runny mess.) Remove it immediately when it's done.

7. Next, add the flavors—use as much of each as you like! Cut or chop the bacon and sprinkle it on top of the Brie. Using a slotted spoon, strain out the whole cranberries from the sauce and place them on the top of the bacon and Brie. Finally, arrange the nuts on top of the cranberries.

8. To serve, spoon the Brie onto a sliced baguette or dip into it with your favorite sturdy cracker. If it firms up too much while serving, pop it back into the microwave for another 15 seconds to refresh. Refrigerate any leftovers; it heats up great (once) the next day!

JALAPEÑO POPPER PUFFS

OUR DAUGHTER SALLY AND HER HUSBAND, ALI, LIVE IN DALLAS, WHERE THEY MET AS students at Southern Methodist University. The team's mascot is a Shetland pony named Peruna, so for Sally's send-off party before she went off to college, we lassoed a real-live pony for rides around the backyard. Just FYI, it's not easy or cheap to rent an animal in the New York City area. It was the only time we'd ever booked an animal that had an agent at William Morris. It was a nice party.

Sally and Ali go to every SMU football game they can because they love the team and SMU has one of the most elaborate tailgates in America. Ali and his friends Andrew and Michael are such avid tailgaters that they lease their own party spot along the Boulevard. To simplify logistics, Michael bought a tricked-out trailer with the school's logo that they keep all their chairs, tables, and cooking contraptions in. Then come game day they simply drive it to their spot and get the party started. All they need is food, beverages, and ice to enjoy while celebrating the good plays or complaining about the bad.

Sally loves jalapeños and Ali loves cheese, and these are a snap to make because we use a flavored spreadable cheese. Plus they look amazing!

If you see Sally and Ali at their tailgate on the Boulevard, there's a good chance they'll have an empty tray where this appetizer once sat. It's a crowd-pleaser, and cheaper than renting a horse— just saying!

Makes 18 popper puffs

---

9 jalapeños (about 3 inches long work best)

One 8-ounce package spreadable cheese (we use Président Pub Cheese, cheddar and bacon flavor)

2 tablespoons all-purpose flour, for rolling out the puff pastry

2 sheets frozen puff pastry (we use Pepperidge Farm), thawed according to package directions

1 large egg

Mild wings sauce and/or ranch dressing, for serving (optional)

1. Preheat the oven to 425°F.

2. To prep the peppers, we start by putting on kitchen gloves— your choice. Cut off the stems and slice the peppers in half lengthwise. Remove the seeds and white membranes (the hottest parts of the pepper). This is easy to do by scraping the inside of each pepper half with a spoon. Make sure you get every seed!

3. In a medium saucepan, bring a couple inches of salted water to a rolling boil over high heat. Drop in the peppers and cook for about 3 minutes to soften them. Remove from the heat, drain, and run under cold water. Set aside.

4. When the peppers are cool enough to handle, spoon about 1 tablespoon of the spreadable cheese into each of the jalapeño halves. Set aside.

5. On a floured work area, roll out one sheet of puff pastry, making it several inches wider in every direction. Cut the dough into 9 equal squares, like a tic-tac-toe grid. Repeat with the second sheet of puff pastry so you have 18 pastry squares.

6. Fill a small bowl with water. Set out one puff pastry square. Lay a stuffed jalapeño half on it, diagonally and cheese side down. Wet your finger and run it around the edge of the puff pastry square, then fold it closed as you would an egg roll. If you'd like to trim the dough smaller to make it neater, that's fine, or simply fold it over and use a fork to crimp the bottom so the cheese doesn't melt and run out. Repeat to wrap the rest of the stuffed jalapeño halves in pastry. Place the wrapped jalapeños cheese side up on an ungreased nonstick sheet pan. Drain the water bowl, crack an egg in there, and whisk it until smooth to create an egg wash. Brush the egg wash over all the exposed pastry.

7. Bake the pastries until the tops are golden and gorgeous, 20 to 24 minutes.

8. Set aside to rest for least 10 minutes; the cheese will be molten when first out of the oven. If you'd like a dipping sauce you can serve with a mild wings sauce or ranch dressing, both tasty.

The tailgate trailer.

As they say at SMU, "Pony up!"

HOT HONEY ON A HOT DATE (WITH BACON)

ONE DAY I SAW A DIET DOCTOR ON TV EXTOLLING THE VIRTUES OF MEDJOOL DATES. HE said they had great phytonutrients and might reduce inflammation or something impressive like that—and it must be true; he said it on television. I mentioned in passing to Kathy to pick up some Medjool dates if she saw any at the store. So she picked up a package—at Costco, the warehouse club famous for massive quantities. The package was large enough for the Red Cross to distribute after a natural disaster. I didn't question Kathy for buying them—I'd asked her to do it. I only questioned how she got them into the car without a forklift.

Needing phytonutrients that might reduce inflammation or something, we sampled a couple of them, and they were tasty, but after a couple of weeks they started migrating farther and farther toward the back of the cupboard. So I asked Kathy for ideas how to dispose of the dozens of dates.

"Stuff some of them with goat cheese and wrap them in bacon!"

During the 5 p.m. appetizer hour I seared a batch of them, and the verdict was immediate: "Fantastic!"

This is now part of our regular snack rotation. And as a bonus, when acquaintances ask Kathy or me about our upcoming plans, we'll say, "It's hot date night!" And they will look at us with envy—especially if they haven't had a hot date in years. Too bad—they have plenty at Costco.

Makes 20 hot dates

---

20 large Medjool dates, pitted

½ cup goat cheese crumbles, or more as desired

10 slices bacon (not thick-sliced), halved crosswise

½ cup honey

2½ tablespoons hot sauce (we use Frank's RedHot original sauce), or more to taste

1. Make a single lengthwise cut in each date without cutting through to the other side. Hinge it open and use your fingers to stuff in a healthy 1 teaspoon of goat cheese crumbles. (The dates can hold a surprising amount of cheese—use as much as you have on hand and that fits!) Gently squeeze them closed.

2. Using a half bacon strip and one stuffed date, wrap the bacon around the date, starting at one end and spiraling around the date like a barber pole. This will give you maximally crispy bacon. Repeat to wrap the rest of the dates.

3. In a large nonstick skillet, place the bacon-wrapped dates so that the end of the bacon is tucked under the date. Sear a couple minutes over medium-high heat, until the bacon is crispy enough to stay in place. Roll each date over a quarter-turn to sear a couple minutes, then continue searing and rotating until all sides are crispy and delicious. Let rest 5 to 10 minutes on paper towels.

4. To make the hot honey sauce, in a small bowl combine the honey and hot sauce. Add more hot sauce if you want it spicier!

5. Serve these delicious little dates with the hot honey on the side. Now that's a date night!

DINNER PARTY
DILL-DEVILED EGGS

MY GRANDMA DOOCY'S BASEMENT HAD SHELVES LINED WITH DOZENS OF JARS OF CU-cumbers from her garden that were busy turning into pickles. Her "refrigerator pickles," brined with onions and green peppers, weren't actually in the refrigerator. Her "Texas" pickles were boiled in jars; no idea why they called them "Texas." Fourteen-day pickles took many complicated steps over two weeks and involved more work than I did my entire sophomore year of college. Then there was my father's favorite, the dill, which he would compliment by saying to his mother *every time*, "Mom—it's *dill-icious*."

Only a dad could pull off that pun.

Grandma proudly presented a bowl of pickles on the table at every meal I can remember. Brining and canning pickles was her thing, and she was great at it.

A few years ago we were at a fancy party, where waiters circulated through the room with gorgeous hors d'oeuvres. The third tray that came out was a platter of dill-pickled deviled eggs. This immediately reminded me of *both* my grandmas—Grandma Doocy's pickles and Grandma Sharp's favorite appetizer, deviled eggs, which she made every Sunday. Two of my favorite tastes in one delightful little bite.

The tuxedoed caterers served the deviled eggs not sliced in half, the traditional way. Instead they were standing upright, fully loaded—like a boss. We loved the look of them, and we've been making ours like the pros ever since.

Speaking of fully loaded—the happy hour at that party lasted more than two hours, and by the time dinner finally rolled out—I was a little pickled.

Makes 12 deviled eggs

Grandma's priceless pickles.

12 large eggs

⅓ cup mayo (we use Duke's)

½ teaspoon mustard powder

2 tablespoons juice from the dill pickle jar

¼ cup finely diced dill pickles

2 tablespoons finely minced fresh dill fronds (stalks removed), plus more for garnish

1. First, hard boil the eggs (see page xiii); don't overcook because the yolk will be harder to remove. Shell the eggs promptly. These deviled eggs are not served the traditional way, with the eggs sliced in half the long way; here they are served as a whole egg sitting majestically on one end, so we'll need to do a little surgery to give the eggs a flat base. Lay an egg on its side and find the pointier end. Take a sharp knife and slice off about ¼ inch of the little point. The egg will sit on that cut. Now, at the other end of the egg, slice off *a little less* than ½ inch, which should reveal the yolk. Remove the little bit of yolk from the part you just sliced off and put it in a medium bowl, then take a butter knife and carefully remove all the yolk from inside the egg and add it to the bowl as well. Process all the eggs this way, setting them on their ends on a platter as you work.

2. Add the mayo and mustard powder to the bowl with the yolks and mash with a rubber spatula until smooth—it will be a little dry. Add the pickle juice, diced dill pickle, and fresh dill and mix until smooth.

3. Now to fill up the eggs! The easiest way is to make a low-tech pastry bag out of a zip-top plastic bag. Spoon all the egg yolk mixture into a bag, smoosh it into one corner, and use kitchen scissors to cut ½ inch off the corner. Squeeze out the yolk mixture into the eggs, adding an artistic flourish on the tops by squeezing out a little extra. When all the eggs are filled, plant a tiny fresh dill frond to garnish the tops—like a flag.

4. These deviled eggs are delicious to eat right now, but if you refrigerate them for 1 hour to chill, they're even better.

2

BREAKFAST AND BRUNCH

WE'VE TRIED TO KEEP THE NAMES OF OUR RECIpes simple, so as soon as you read them you'll have a pretty good idea what ingredients are involved. Creamy Crusted Horseradish Salmon leaves little to the imagination. However, our Dental Hygienist Pot Roast from our first cookbook might have confused some home cooks.

That pot roast is a fantastic recipe, and so many of you have written saying you love it. Meanwhile, since it was published a few years ago, three of our current and past dental hygienists have claimed credit for it.

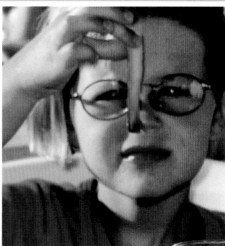

So names are important to us, but of course the toughest decisions were what to call our kids. Before Kathy and I got married, she was friends with a very famous movie star who shall remain nameless (unless you ask me after I've had a few drinks), and they named their kids after important figures from literary history.

When we found out Kathy was pregnant with our first child—the one who's now a very famous White House correspondent—we started searching for the perfect name. As first-time parents, we wanted to make sure his name said something about him and something about us. Given her movie star pal who had dramatic, poetic, thought-provoking names, the bar was high and high-minded. The pressure was on Kathy to come up with a doozy for young Doocy, so we started with literary figures.

The name game.

When I suggested *F. Scott Doocy,* she gave me that look—*Why didn't I marry that guy from St. Elsewhere?*

She wanted dramatic, but I (not so) secretly wanted our children to have funny names. I had the track record that proved it; up until that point the only thing I'd ever named was a cat, which I dubbed G. Gordon Kitty.

Kathy wasn't sold on funny, so rather than considering actual names used by people, we started contemplating *things* that could be a name. Watching a fashion show on TV, we briefly pondered Taffeta, Velvet, and Flannel. "Nobody would ever label a kid anything close to a textile," I pronounced—until Michael Jackson dubbed his child Blanket.

Our trip down Fashion Avenue was replaced by a drive down *actual* street names. Madison was a contender for a couple blocks, inspired by a friend from Kansas who had named his child Montana. Suddenly we were searching for a location-based name, when we stumbled on a magnificent moniker we 100 percent agreed would be our child's name:

Memphis!

I know you're thinking we must have had a radon leak at our house, so let me explain. In addition to being the name of a great city on the banks of the Mississippi that's known for music and Graceland, Memphis is also a name from Greek mythology. But what sold us on the name was that this was the 1980s, and "Memphis" was the name of a popular design movement from Italy. The Memphis style was characterized by colors and shapes that were bold, unconventional, playful. *Bold, unconventional, playful* . . . just what we wanted our baby to be! They would be the only Memphis in their homeroom, and we loved it. Memphis was just perfect, until reality—also known as my mother—weighed in.

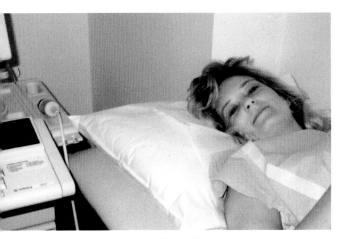

Picking the paint color.

"Stephen, you've never even been to Memphis!" Her urgent, pleading voice suggested that I might be day-drinking.

"Memphis is in Tennessee and you're from Kansas. How does *Topeka Doocy* sound?"

"Well . . ." I tried to buy a little time, but my mother was done. "It's a dumb name, Stephen. Or should I call you *Wichita*?"

Kathy could tell from my side of the conversation that it was time for a backup plan—and we did have a runner-up. Early in Kathy's pregnancy a once-in-a-lifetime event occurred—Halley's Comet returned to the vicinity of Earth. It was literally a cosmic sign from on high—we agreed after about thirty seconds of consideration that our firstborn's name would be Halley Doocy. Period, done, print the announcements.

A few months later Kathy and I leaned in to look at a small black and white monitor in a darkened room, examining very grainy blobs that the doctor assured us were parts of somebody we were related to. "There's the heartbeat," the doctor said, pointing at something fluttering, and then, "That's one foot, and there's the other." And then he announced, "Kathy, call

Sherwin-Williams for blue paint—your baby is a boy!"

Suddenly Halley—which is a perfectly good name for a girl and a comet—flamed out. We bought the paint, and because time was getting short, we wound up doing what so many parents do—we went with a name that was simple and safe and saintly. After sixteen hours of labor, our first child was born—and promptly named after Saint Peter.

A few years later, our first daughter was christened after Saint Mary. Finally, shortly after Kathy learned she was pregnant with our third, I suggested that we should name the baby after Saint Paul. Kathy liked the idea and talked it through: "Peter, Mary, and Paul." She paused and reordered them. "Wait . . . you want to name your kids Peter, *Paul,* and Mary?"

I explained why it was a brilliant and hilarious choice: "And if the baby is a girl, the kids would be Peter, *Paula,* and Mary." A joke—inside a joke—I loved it!

"We are not naming three children after the 'Puff the Magic Dragon' people!"

A few weeks later, only four months into the pregnancy, Kathy called me at work. She was heading to the hospital, having gone into premature labor—at sixteen weeks. I rushed and met her there.

"Those are some giant contractions," the emergency room doctor announced. He then terrified us by saying, "Kathy, you're dilated . . . at a four."

I wasn't a doctor but I knew that was very bad; she was only four months into a nine-month pregnancy. Kathy's ob-gyn arrived and took over her care. The immediate worry was that the baby would be born *that day*—with few organs fully developed, and weighing less than a pound, the chances for survival were tiny. It was one of those days in your life when your whole prayer was simply *God—help the baby*.

The doctor ordered a series of IV medicines, and I sat there for hours holding Kathy's hand until hours of that *drip drip drip* finally stabilized her. The doctor's diagnosis was bleak; for the next five months Kathy was on 100 percent bed rest. They outfitted her with a contraction monitor that we would hook up to our home phone line at the end of every day, so I could transmit the day's contractions and they could adjust her medicine. She went home that night, but before we left, the doctor asked to speak to Peter and Mary, who were in the waiting room with a babysitter.

The doctor, who was excellent, explained to three-year-old Mary and five-year-old Peter that their mom was going to have to be in her bedroom for a long time, and they could not ask for anything. The doctor explained that if they needed anything, first ask their dad, if he was home. Otherwise they would have to do everything by themselves—something our kids were not accustomed to.

To their credit, Peter and Mary pitched in and did what was asked of them. I raced home from work in Washington, DC, very early every day to keep things afloat, cooking, cleaning, nursing Kathy, and playing with the kids. One afternoon Mary asked me if I'd carry her Little Tykes car down the outside deck stairs, which I'd done a million times—and as I was halfway down the staircase a hornet buried its stinger in the back of my calf. It felt like I was being stabbed by a red-hot needle. Reflexively I twisted to swat it away—but in that move I lost the grip on the car and then my balance and promptly fell down ten stairs—breaking the fall with my outstretched foot . . . that I watched in slow motion bend backward.

For a few seconds I was in shock—and then a wave of pain hit me like I'd never felt before.

Peter was first on the scene, "Dad, do you want the boo-boo bear?" The boo-boo bear was a cold pack we kept in the freezer for the kid's minor injuries. This was way past the boo-boo bear's pay grade. Gritting my teeth and writhing in terrible pain, I contemplated my next move. It was the only option. I calmly instructed him, "Go get Mommy."

Kathy had not been outside in a month. She tried to get me up on my feet but I couldn't stand, so she and Peter got a wagon, and like a big broken toy, they dragged me to the driveway, where I pulled myself into the car and drove to the emergency room. Kathy went back to bed and the kids took care of her. At the ER a series of X-rays revealed that half a dozen tiny little bones in my foot were broken into tiny little pieces, and nearly all the soft tissue and ligaments in that part of me were pulled clean off the bone. They gave me a shot, some pills, a cast, and some crutches and I went home and made dinner.

The next day we had to go to the grocery store. Peter pushed the cart and Mary grabbed the groceries; they were like tiny Instacart shoppers with a cranky and slow-moving supervisor shadowing them on crutches. At the checkout, with my leg throbbing, I discovered that Mary and Peter had put pretty much every food they'd ever desired in the cart—and I could not have cared less. I had bigger fish to fry—literally. Peter had selected Mrs. Paul's fish sticks for dinner, and at that moment they were in a bag, slowly thawing.

Over the next five months, I recovered from my injury and Kathy's pregnancy continued. We all held our breath, praying that Kathy's

Cast party.

later, the week before Mother's Day, I was at the Tysons Corner mall outside Washington, DC, at the very fancy Tiffany & Co., to have a silver heart bracelet engraved commemorating our three kids. The sales associate said the bracelet was too small to engrave whole names and suggested using the kids' initials, which I thought would be just fine.

With a pad and pencil she asked for their names—in order. Slowly I announced "Peter" and she put down a *P*, I said "Mary" and she wrote an *M*. Then I said "Sally" and she scrawled an *S*. The clerk paused, reviewed her work, and immediately glared at me. "That spells PMS."

This was news to me!

"Are you sure you want your wife wearing a bracelet that says PMS?" I nodded.

She clearly thought this was a terrible idea. "Sir, do you even know what PMS means?"

"I do," I said with a wry smile. "It means I gave my kids funny names after all."

body and the baby inside would figure a way to make it across the finish line.

At the end of July, after the longest eight and a half months of our lives, our baby was born at a very healthy seven pounds. She was absolutely perfect. She cried when she emerged, and so did we.

We didn't discuss a name in those final months of the pregnancy, just in case. Although one night after we watched the movie *Dennis the Menace*, Peter suggested we name her Mr. Wilson. He was kidding, we think.

Our last born has the notoriety of being our only child not named after a saint—but she is an absolute gift from God. We named her Sally because we liked the name and she looked like a Sally.

After we got home with Sally, Kathy resumed all her mom jobs—chauffeur, chef, family COO—and I went back to work. Ten months

Peter reporting on Sally's birth.

RED VELVET WAFFLES

THE HISTORY OF THE RED CAKE IS HARD TO PIN DOWN. I MEAN, WHO CAN CLAIM CREDIT for the unique color of a cake? Betty Crocker, put your hand down . . .

The bright red color made the red velvet cupcakes from the Magnolia Bakery across the street from the Fox News Channel our kids' go-to favorite when they'd visit me at work. We'd go immediately after the show at 9:01 a.m. Cupcakes for breakfast, #BestDadEver!

We had a blowout party in our backyard to mark daughter Sally's high school graduation and she chose the red velvet cake, because it's tasty and because red is one of the school colors at SMU in Dallas. One of our kids picked red velvet as their wedding cake! Clearly it's one of our favorite flavors of cake.

Years later, Sally, Ali, and Mary were in Dallas at a fancy restaurant and Ali spotted on the menu red velvet waffles. *Waffles?* So at the kids' suggestion Kathy and I figured out this simple recipe that will turn your breakfast into something bright red, white, and blueberry!

Makes about 5 waffles

---

1 large egg

2½ tablespoons vegetable oil

Half of a 15.25-ounce box Duncan Hines Perfectly Moist Red Velvet cake mix (1⅔ cups)

4 ounces cream cheese, at room temperature

4 tablespoons (½ stick) unsalted butter, at room temperature

3 tablespoons whole milk

½ teaspoon pure vanilla extract

2 cups powdered sugar

Canned whipped cream

1 cup blueberries

10 strawberries, hulled, each cut into 4 or 5 slices

1. In a medium bowl, whisk the egg, oil, and ½ cup lukewarm water until combined. Add the cake mix and stir the mixture as smooth as you can get it, using a rubber spatula to scrape the sides of the bowl; it will be very thick. Let the mixture rest for 10 minutes.

2. Preheat a waffle iron to medium-high heat (if yours can be adjusted). Measure ⅓ cup of the batter into the center of the waffle iron and close the top. When the light indicates it's done, open the lid and let the bottom cook for another minute—the top will be a deep red color (the longer it cooks the browner it gets, so don't let it linger). Use a fork to carefully remove the waffle from the iron to a plate. Repeat to make the rest of the waffles. Set the waffles aside to firm up while you make the cream cheese drizzle.

3. In a medium bowl, combine the cream cheese, butter, milk, and vanilla. Use a mixer (or a spoon) to blend well, then add the powdered sugar and mix until silky smooth. To drizzle on the waffles, put that cream cheese mixture into a zip-top plastic bag, squeeze it down to one corner at the bottom of the bag, and snip off ½ inch of the bag's corner. Squeeze out the cream cheese, making a zigzag on the top of each waffle.

4. A healthy squirt of whipped cream goes in the middle. Sprinkle on the blueberries and sliced strawberries and serve.

BARCELONA BREAKFAST
HUEVOS ROTOS (BROKEN EGGS)

MY MOM USED TO MAKE GREAT SUNNY-SIDE UP EGGS, BUT I HAD ONE COMPLAINT; SHE'D fry them until they formed a crispy little edge around the outside that I'd refer to as stringy leather, which I'd always cut off. She'd take note, but she wasn't going to change her method just for me, because everybody else in the family loved the crispy part. What she got perfect every time was the runny yolk for excellent toast dipping.

Barcelona Brunch Bunch.

We went to Barcelona, Spain, for one family vacation, and at breakfast I spied *huevos rotos* on the menu. I knew *huevos* meant eggs, but I had no idea what *rotos* meant. I ordered it, and when the waiter brought the dish to the table it looked like eggs and potatoes. Then he placed the plate in front of me, picked up my spoon, and poked open an egg, releasing the yolk to run all over the meat and potatoes below. I asked what *huevos rotos* meant, and he said, "Broken eggs."

I never would have ordered *broken* eggs, I want perfect eggs! But these were perfect, because they had my mom's kind of runny yolk. Next time I'm in Spain I'll respectfully suggest they rename this treasured dish *huevos rotos sin cuero fibroso*, or "broken eggs with no stringy leather."

We love this hearty breakfast! It comes together in less than half an hour, and with just one bite we're back at brunch in Barcelona, without the jet lag or language barriers. And all without "breaking" the budget!

Makes 3 hearty servings

One 24-ounce bag steam-in-bag, microwave-ready red potatoes

2 tablespoons olive oil

½ medium red onion, roughly chopped

½ pound bulk chorizo, or links with casings removed, crumbled

Table salt and freshly ground black pepper

3 large eggs

1. Microwave the potatoes according to the package directions. Open the bag carefully to vent and to cool.

2. Meanwhile, in a large nonstick skillet with a lid, heat the olive oil over medium-high heat. Add the onion and chorizo and sauté until the meat is thoroughly cooked and the onions are lightly browned, about 10 minutes.

3. Cut the cooled potatoes into ½-inch slices. Move the cooked chorizo to the sides of the pan and place the potatoes cut side down into the flavorful chorizo grease. Lightly salt and pepper the potato tops. Cook, undisturbed, until you get a nice fried edge on one side, 3 to 5 minutes. Mix the potatoes in with the chorizo and cook a few more minutes to get some color on the other side of the spuds.

4. Reduce the heat to medium-low and create three open spaces in the potato mixture all the way to the bottom of the pan. Crack an egg into each of these wells so they cook directly on the pan. Lightly salt and pepper the eggs. Take care not to break the yolks—you want them runny later! Cover the pan and cook until the eggs are done to your liking, 4 to 7 minutes. Remember, if you cook them too long the yolks won't be runny—so the yolk's on you!

5. To serve, scoop the meat and potatoes onto serving plates and top with an egg. Serve immediately. The first order of business is to break the yolk so it runs down over everything. Perfect!

Not broken yet!

MAPLE BACON AND CREAM CHEESE CINNAMON ROLLS

ONE OF OUR KIDS AT A VERY YOUNG AGE HAD A PROBLEM PRONOUNCING THE LETTER *T*—it always came out as an *F*. It meant that whenever Colonel Sanders popped up in a commercial for Kentucky Fried Chicken, our kid would shout out the name of the franchise with an *F* in place of the *T* in Kentucky—which made them sound like a pint-size Howard Stern.

Our kid had never heard the F-word, so we'd wince but laugh at how hilariously innocent it was. So imagine Kathy's surprise when she was pushing the stroller near the mall food court and our kid recognized the sign for that chicken joint and out of nowhere mispronounced Kentucky in the worst possible way. People half a mall away at Nordstrom were thinking, *Did that toddler just say?... No way...*

As I was baking this recipe this morning, Kathy told me a story I'd never heard. "Guess what my first words were?"

"Concierge?"

She didn't think that was funny. Then she pointed at our breakfast, "Sweet roll." Then she explained. When she was growing up, every morning her mom would ask Kathy and her brothers what they wanted to eat. Her older brothers were both athletes and started their day with a beef steak topped with a pat of butter. Then her mom would ask, "Who wants a sweet roll?" Kathy had heard that over and over as a baby, and one morning she broke her lifetime of silence. Kathy's mom brought her a sweet roll, and I'm sure the one-year-old immediately realized it was a heck of a lot tastier than that runny oatmeal.

"Everybody thought it was so funny, so I kept saying it."

When do babies start talking? The answer is . . . when they have something to say. And she was hungry!

Married thirty-six years, I'd never heard that story until this morning as I was baking these off-the-charts cinnamon rolls. Easy to make, easier to eat. We make only two at a time when it's just Kathy and me at home. They're reminiscent of Kathy's sweet rolls and sweeter memories.

Kathy's story also reminded me how relieved we were when that chicken franchise changed its corporate name to KFC.

Sweet roll!

Makes 5 rolls

A KFC in the UK.

10 slices bacon

2½ tablespoons pure maple syrup

One 17.5-ounce can Grands! cinnamon rolls with cream cheese icing

4 ounces cream cheese, at room temperature

½ tablespoon whole milk or half-and-half

1. Preheat the oven to 425°F. Grease an 8 × 8-inch baking pan.

2. Lay the bacon slices on a nonstick sheet pan. Bake for 12 minutes, then remove from the oven and use tongs to flip the slices. Brush 2 tablespoons of the maple syrup over the slices, return to the oven, and bake until browned and cooked but still flexible, not crispy, 3 to 4 minutes. Remove to a plate—not a paper towel or the syrup will stick. Set aside to cool.

3. Reduce the oven temperature to 350°F. Open the cinnamon roll package and set aside the icing container—we will doctor that up in a minute. On a clean work surface, carefully separate and unwind each cinnamon roll to make a long piece of dough. Place 2 pieces of bacon on one length of dough, so they stretch from end to end. Roll up the dough with the bacon inside, leaving about 1 inch of open dough at the end. Pinch the roll shut at the end. Place it in the prepared baking pan and repeat to roll up the rest of the bacon and dough. It's okay to have the rolls slightly touching because they'll blow up a bit as they bake. If the bacon is sticking up above the dough, gently push it straight down (if you can) so it hits the bottom of the pan.

4. Bake until the tops are deeply browned, 30 to 35 minutes. The bacon makes the dough take a bit longer to bake, so don't take out the rolls until they are deeply browned.

5. Meanwhile, let's make the frosting. In a medium bowl, combine the icing included in the cinnamon roll can, the cream cheese, milk, and the remaining ½ tablespoon maple syrup. Use a rubber spatula to blend until perfectly smooth.

6. When the rolls are done baking, remove them from the oven, let them rest a couple minutes, and slather on the frosting as generously as you like.

7. These are too messy to eat by hand, so serve them warm with a knife and fork. Enjoy—that is one sweet and savory *sweet roll*!

BRUNCH PIGS IN BLANKETS

WHEN PETER WAS GROWING UP, HE WORSHIPPED THE NEW YORK YANKEES. I PERSONALLY put up baseball wallpaper in his room, he'd save clippings from the *Post* and put them on his wall, and when a real-life Yankee would come on *Fox & Friends* to promote something, Kathy would drive Peter into New York before school so he could get an autographed ball and a photo with a guy in pinstripes. The other kids in his class thought that was the coolest.

Through the years we've been lucky enough to attend many Yankees games as invited guests of people or organizations with luxury suites. Peter's favorite part? They always had in vast quantities his single favorite baseball food: pigs in a blanket.

"With a hot dog you only eat one, realistically," Peter tells me, "but with pigs in a blanket you can eat fifteen before you realize you've had too many"—a situation he's found himself in more than once. He loves them so much that when he was walking home from school during baseball season, Kathy would warm up a dozen pigs in a blanket for his after-school snack. When Peter graduated from high school, we had a big party in the backyard and served pigs in a blanket. At the rehearsal dinner for his wedding, there were pigs in a blanket.

Peter estimates that his single-day record for pig consumption is nineteen. But that's only at one sitting. Now with this tasty breakfast version we make, you can start your pigs intake first thing in the morning.

So next time you see Peter at a White House briefing, if you see a little smudge of syrup on his tie, you'll know what he warmed up that morning in his toaster oven.

Makes 12 pigs

---

1 sheet frozen puff pastry (we use Pepperidge Farm), thawed according to package directions

One 9.6-ounce package Johnsonville fully cooked breakfast sausages (the Vermont maple syrup flavor is amazing)

1 large egg

OPTIONAL FOR TOPPING/ SERVING

Grated Parmesan cheese

Everything bagel seasoning

Cinnamon-sugar spice

Pancake syrup

1. Adjust an oven rack to the center position and preheat the oven to 400°F. Line a sheet pan with parchment paper.

2. Remove any papers that are poking out of the ends of the puff pastry and unfold it on a cutting board. You will see where it was folded into thirds; set the pastry on the board with those folds running from top to bottom. Use a rolling pin to roll out the dough, making it about 1½ inches longer from top to bottom. Take a sharp knife or pizza cutter and slice along each of those original fold marks. Cut each of those long pieces crosswise into 4 equal rectangles. You'll have 12 total rectangles.

3. Time to pig it up! Sausages vary slightly in length, so lay one lengthwise on top of a single dough rectangle to make sure that the sausage ends will poke out a bit; if not, trim the dough back so it's a little narrower. Dip a finger in water and run it along the edge of dough on the side of the sausage, then roll up the sausage in the dough from the other side. Close up the pig, pinch the sides together, and crimp lightly with a fork to hold everything in place. Repeat to roll up all the pigs.

4. Whisk the egg with 1 tablespoon of tap water to make an egg wash, then use a brush to paint all sides of all the pastry. Place the pigs seam side down on the prepared sheet pan.

5. Now the creative part; we love to top them with a variety of flavors. My favorite is grated Parmesan; others like a light salting of everything bagel seasoning. And we'll shake cinnamon-sugar on a few. Some go with nothing. Choose one or several flavors and top as many as you like.

6. Bake until the pastry is perfectly puffed and deep golden brown, 9 to 11 minutes.

7. Serve the pigs with a side squirt of syrup, which makes the *perfect* dipping sauce for these gems. The syrup was the brilliant suggestion of our cameraman, Ed, who is a very sharp guy . . . just like his focus!

No pigs in blankets are safe around this kid.

JOHN RICH'S CHEESY GRIT CAKES AND EGGS

SO AT 8:07 ONE DECEMBER MORNING DURING *FOX & FRIENDS,* **I GOT A TEXT FROM FOLDS** of Honor founder Major Dan Rooney. It said simply, "JR wants to be in your next cookbook!" For a moment I had no idea who JR was, then a photo appeared, featuring country recording star John Rich wearing a Folds of Honor sweatshirt, serving up scrambled eggs at a charity breakfast. I said to myself, I bet the guy holding the plate had no idea that his server, John Rich, had at that moment the number one song in the country, "Santa's Got a Dirty Job."

John invented this recipe when he was on tour. He'd ordered eggs Benedict for breakfast and they were served not on an English muffin, but something cornmeal-y, which reminded him of something he'd eaten his whole life. "Granny Rich made grits all the time," John told me. "My dad fed me grits from an early age." So he started thinking of replacing the muffin with something grit-based, which he calls "working-class budget food."

From bourbon to breakfast.

"Basically, what you get is all that flavor in the grit cakes as your base instead of stacking meat and a poached egg on top of an English muffin," he said, and then added, "Mine is way better—I call them grit cakes."

Kathy who grew up in California, was not a big grits gal, but she adores these. John says he told Guy Fieri about these breakfast cakes, and if he were ever a contestant on *Guy's Grocery Games,* he'd cook this recipe. John says Guy marveled, "Dude, how did you think of doing *that* with grits?"

Exactly, dude!

I noticed on his initial ingredient list John had not listed the number of eggs needed, so I tried some true-grit humor and simply asked, "Hominy eggs?"

"Four," he responded, and yes, that's corny.

Makes 4 servings

½ pound bulk pork sausage (we use Jimmy Dean's original)

½ cup finely diced red onion

1 large jalapeño, seeded and finely diced

Three 1-ounce packages Quaker Instant Grits

¾ cup whole milk

¾ cup shredded Cheddar cheese

2 tablespoons unsalted butter

4 large eggs

Table salt and freshly ground black pepper

Salsa or picante sauce, for topping

1. Crumble the sausage into a large nonstick skillet and set over medium-high heat. Add the onion and jalapeño and sauté until the sausage is completely cooked and lightly browned and the onions have softened, 8 to 10 minutes.

2. In a medium microwave-safe bowl, combine the grits and milk. Stir, cover, and microwave for 2 minutes on high. Let sit for 30 seconds, then immediately blend in the Cheddar, which will melt right away.

3. Drop the cooked sausage mixture into the grits bowl and mix well. Divide the mixture into 4 equal portions. When cool enough, use your hands to form 4 flat patties about ¾ inch thick.

4. Wipe out the skillet and return it to medium heat. Melt the butter and carefully place the patties in the pan. Cook until they have a nice thick crisp crust on the bottom, about 5 minutes. Carefully flip with a spatula and cook until there is a good crust on the other side and the patties are completely cooked through, about another 5 minutes.

5. Place each patty on a plate. In the skillet, cook the eggs to over easy (or to your liking). Place an egg on each patty set at a jaunty angle—slightly off-center—so you can see some of the grit cake. So pretty! Lightly salt and pepper the eggs the way you like them, then drizzle on your favorite salsa or picante sauce. Final instruction from Mr. Rich: "Eat it!"

6. If you have leftovers, heat them up the next day in a skillet to maintain maximum crispiness!

SKILLET CRUSTLESS QUICHE

WHEN I WAS A KID IN THE BOY SCOUTS, I REMEMBER THE EXCITEMENT OF OUR SEMI-annual campouts, where we'd throw hatchets, tie knots, and communicate over a short distance by waving flags, also known as semaphore. I got pretty good at it, but my mischievous Scout partner thought it was hilarious to use semaphore to spell out every filthy word he knew. Ironically he always got the letter *F* wrong, which limited the precision of his gutter vocabulary. Meanwhile, our Scout leaders were oblivious to what was going on. They were just happy that we weren't smoking Luckies out by the latrine.

A downside to camping out was that none of our male Scout leaders had any idea how to cook. But they knew they were bad; I guess they thought it was cool. I remember one guy proudly proclaimed, "Sorry, boys, I'm such a lousy cook that I can't even boil toast!" He was being funny . . . I think.

But that changed one summer when a Scout leader father who worked as a short-order cook showed us how to use a cast-iron skillet over a campfire. He was amazing, and each morning he'd make us his specialty of ham and cheese and eggs. Years later I realized he'd been making a quiche—which I'd avoided making because quiche was a fancy dish cooked up by the Parisians, and at that time in my life the only French cuisine I'd mastered was their fries.

We updated this with spinach after watching Wolfgang Puck add it to a TV quiche. I wonder how my flag-waving Scout partner would spell out Mr. Puck. Actually, I know exactly how he'd spell it—but he can't because his flags were confiscated by camp security in 1967.

Makes 4 servings

---

6 large eggs, at room temperature

½ cup heavy cream, at room temperature

¼ teaspoon table salt

¼ teaspoon freshly ground black pepper

2 tablespoons unsalted butter

1 medium shallot, thinly sliced

½ cup small-diced cooked ham

3 cups baby spinach

½ cup crumbled feta cheese

Hot sauce, for serving (optional)

1. Adjust an oven rack to the center position and preheat the oven to 375°F.

2. In a medium bowl, combine the eggs, cream, salt, and pepper and whisk until completely incorporated.

3. In a small ovenproof skillet (we use an 8-inch Lodge cast-iron skillet), melt the butter over medium-high heat. Add the shallot and sauté until fragrant, about 1 minute. Add the ham and warm that up for another minute, then quickly stir in the spinach. It will reduce substantially in about a minute. Add the feta and give a stir to warm it through.

4. Quickly but carefully pour the egg mixture over the mixture in the pan and let it cook undisturbed for 90 seconds as it forms an egg crust on the bottom. Stick your spatula in the center of the pan and slightly mix all the ingredients in the middle without disturbing the bottom egg layer. Leave the pan on the stove a couple minutes, until you see steady bubbles coming up from the middle of the pan. Transfer the skillet to the oven and bake until the top is a beautiful golden brown, has risen slightly in the middle, and no longer jiggles in the center, about 20 minutes. Test for doneness by inserting a butter knife near the center; if it comes out clean, it's done. Bake a couple more minutes if not.

5. Let the quiche rest a minute or two before slicing into 4 wedges. Shake some hot sauce on top if you like. We also serve this with fresh berries for a balanced brunch. Refrigerate any leftovers and heat them up the next day—45 seconds in the microwave will do it.

FULLY LOADED FRUITY FRENCH TOAST

WE HAVE PHOTOS FROM PETER'S FIRST BIRTHDAY WHERE HE'S LOOKING AT HIS BIRTHDAY cake as if it were some mystery item dropped via drone onto his high chair, because before that day Peter had never tasted sugar. Kathy had read a bunch of parenting books, and back then they all said sugar was on the no-fly list. We can admit it now because the statute of limitations on helicopter parenting expired in 1992.

That all changed on his first birthday, when we finally decided to spoil him a bit. Kathy spent $52 in 1988 dollars on a hazelnut cake from a fancy French bakery. If you're keeping score, that's three rookie mistakes. (1) We'd never fed him sugar; (2) we spent too much on a cake; (3) hazelnut? For a little kid? *Seriously?*

Tiny sugar-free Peter took that first taste, and a few seconds later the glucose made contact with his bloodstream. He got the biggest grin and his eyes rolled back in his head as he giggled in glee. He ate an adult-size piece and proceeded to smear the rest all over his clothes. Peter, welcome to the Sugar High Club.

Three decades later, Peter still loves sweets, and this recipe is our brunchy homage to his first birthday cake. To update the hazelnut, this has a wonderful Nutella filling. However, to make up for our food sins of the past, it also includes an epic portion of delicious fresh fruit—so please don't try to make a citizen's arrest next time you see us at the mall.

We eventually figured out that kids can eat almost anything if it's done in moderation. It was on our way home from the hospital after Kathy gave birth to our third child, Sally, when we pulled up to a McDonald's window and bought Sally her first Happy Meal. That's a joke—Sally didn't get her first fry until she was *six months old*. She'd been crying uncontrollably in the backseat of our Explorer when five-year-old Peter shut her up with a single Mickey D's fry. We wondered from the front seat why she'd suddenly stopped crying—and caught him red-handed. It was the perfect pacifier—no wonder they call them Happy Meals.

At least he wasn't spoon-feeding her Nutella—for that she'd have to wait until her first birthday.

Enjoy this breakfast!

Peter turns one.

Makes 3 servings

2 large eggs

⅓ cup half-and-half (we use fat-free)

½ teaspoon ground cinnamon

6 slices cinnamon swirl bread with raisins (we use Pepperidge Farm)

1½ tablespoons chocolate-hazelnut spread (we use Nutella)

2 tablespoons unsalted butter

1 banana, diced

Whipped cream, for topping

12 strawberries, hulled and cut into 4 or 5 slices

¾ cup blueberries

Pure maple syrup (optional)

1 tablespoon strawberry jelly (optional)

1. In a wide shallow bowl, combine the eggs, half-and-half, and cinnamon and whisk until perfectly smooth. Set aside.

2. Spread one piece of bread with ½ tablespoon of hazelnut spread, leaving about a ½-inch gap between the spread and the crust. Place another piece of bread on top and lightly press the pieces together; the hazelnut spread glues it shut. Repeat to make the other two sandwiches.

3. In a large skillet, melt the butter over medium heat. Dip the sandwiches in the egg mixture on both sides, letting the egg drip back into the bowl, then set them in the heated skillet. Cook until the bottom is lightly browned, 3 or 4 minutes. Flip and cook the other side for 3 to 4 minutes to brown it.

4. Remove the sandwiches to plates with the hot side up. Add the diced banana first, then the whipped cream on and around the French toast (the banana layer will keep it from melting too fast). Dividing evenly, scatter the strawberries and blueberries on each piece. To add a little sweetness, either drizzle some maple syrup on the plate around the French toast or whisk 1 tablespoon strawberry jelly with 2 teaspoons of water in a small bowl until smooth and drizzle it over the whipped cream and fruit. Serve up immediately and enjoy the hidden hazelnut flavor!

MADELEINE'S BACON MONKEY BUNDT

MY JUNIOR AND SENIOR YEARS OF HIGH SCHOOL WERE GREAT FOR MY SISTER CATHY, who got to ride shotgun in my 1965 Fleetwood Cadillac—with 175,000 miles on it. A deep green color, it looked like a million bucks, and nobody could tell it got nine miles per gallon and was burning motor oil to the tune of a can every other day.

As Cathy said, "You know what I remember about riding with you? Whatever the weather—it could have been minus fifteen degrees or it could have been a hundred—you always drove all the way to school with the window down!" My sister was absolutely correct, but I had a very good motivation. The window was down so I could dry my hair after my morning shower. Twenty miles of open window at seventy miles an hour equaled one Kansas barber blowout.

There was also one stop we loved to make—we'd pull up to the Tasty Pastry Bakery and order a couple of their very famous nut rolls or sticky buns. We did this almost every day. Who cared? It was the 1970s and my cholesterol level was three.

Those sticky buns remind me of pull-apart monkey bread. I have my grandma Doocy's monkey bread recipe—it's got to be at least fifty years old. She used fresh bread dough, which takes more time—so here we use our friend Madeleine Van Duren's recipe. She makes it with quick refrigerated biscuits every Christmas morning. And because her husband, Todd, insisted that she serve this with a side of bacon, here the bacon is baked into the Bundt!

Madeleine will double or even triple the recipe depending on how many people are overnighting at their house and are expecting to be fed. Guests will wake up and wander into the kitchen and pick at the monkey bread and pull it apart as gifts are unwrapped around the tree. Now it's a fixture at the Doocy house for special-occasion brunches and breakfasts.

By the way, the reason I could afford to stop for snacks every morning was that every day my mom would pay me one dollar to be my sister's chauffeur. I should have spent it on a can of motor oil, but a kid's gotta eat.

Makes 10 servings

---

8 slices bacon

Cooking oil spray

½ cup sugar

1 tablespoon ground cinnamon

Two 16-ounce cans refrigerated biscuits (Grands! work great)

¾ cup (1½ sticks) unsalted butter

1 cup packed light brown sugar

1. Preheat the oven to 425°F.

2. Spread the bacon on a nonstick sheet pan. Bake for 12 minutes, then remove from the oven and use tongs to flip the slices. Return to the oven and bake until browned and cooked but not crispy (the bacon will bake more later), 3 to 5 minutes. Set the bacon on a plate to cool.

3. Reduce the oven temperature to 350°F.

4. Mist a 10-inch Bundt pan with cooking spray. Use kitchen shears to snip 2 of the bacon slices into 1-inch pieces and sprinkle them evenly on the bottom of the pan.

A big batch of Madeleine's monkey bread.

Monkey Bread
cup white sugar
cinn. too suit } Roll Dough Balls in this

2 sticks oleo
1 cup Br. sugar
1 cup white sugar
melt pour over bread dough.
pinch dough into small balls.
Bake 25-30 min.
350 degrees

If you use bread dough, you might have to let it rise before pinching into balls, and then after you pour mixture on,

Grandma's original recipe.

5. In a medium bowl, mix the sugar and cinnamon. Open the cans of biscuits and lay the tubes of biscuit dough unseparated on a cutting board. Cut the dough in half lengthwise, then cut each length in half again. Each "biscuit" is now cut into quarters; take a moment to separate all the pieces.

6. Working with the dough chunks, take a piece, roll it into a rough ball, and then roll it in the cinnamon sugar until it's "coated in a nice layer of deliciousness," as Madeleine says. Place enough of the balls in the bottom of the Bundt pan to cover the bacon pieces, then cut the rest of the bacon and fill the pan by adding an appropriate mix of dough balls and bacon.

7. Cut the butter into tablespoons into a medium microwave-safe bowl and add the brown sugar. Microwave on high for about 45 seconds, give it a stir, and microwave a few more seconds as needed, until the butter is just melted. Whisk up to 60 seconds to melt the sugar and butter into a rich-colored sauce that looks like gravy. Pour it evenly all over the dough balls.

8. Bake until a deeply baked brown crust forms on the exposed dough, 55 to 60 minutes. Remove from the oven, invert a plate or platter on the pan, and flip—very carefully, as some of the melted sugary butter may run out. We leave the pan on top for a couple minutes so the buttery sugar inside the pan can drip down onto the bread. If it's still stuck, give it a tap or two, then slowly lift off the pan.

9. Let the monkey bread rest a few minutes, then serve. Sweet, savory, and spectacular!

FULL IRISH BREAKFAST NACHOS

ONE OF THE BEST WEEKS OF MY LIFE WAS WHEN I TOOK MY FATHER AND HIS BROTHER, my uncle Phil, on a trip around Ireland where we traced our Irish roots—which were not deep. They could not find any Doocy family records in their National Archives—and years later when I did a DNA test, it turned out I'm only 17 percent Irish. But for that week with my dad and uncle I felt 100 percent Irish—especially as I'd affect a fake Liam Neeson accent every evening after a pint at the pub.

It was an epic week—so years later Kathy said she'd like to visit Dublin for a family vacation. She booked us in the heart of the city, and each day we'd venture out and do touristy things involving castles or Guinness. Then at the end of the day we'd go to a different pub for the atmosphere and of course adult beverages . . . it's what you do in Ireland. You ever hear of people going to Ireland for the hurling? I'm talking about the sport. *Note to self: Never refer to pub-drinking and hurling in the same paragraph of a cookbook.*

Anyway, we fell in love with the pub life *and the food*—boxty, coddle, colcannon, and champ—and every morning Kathy and I had the Full Irish breakfast of bacon and eggs, Irish pork sausages, beans, potatoes, and tomatoes. Presented compartmentalized on a platter, it was great. One night at a pub we spotted Irish nachos on the menu, and it included the same basic ingredients as the Full Irish. Once home we made our own version, adding our own twist: a perfect cheese sauce that we drizzle on top.

This is delicious, filling, and quick to make—perfect when you're *Dublin down* on breakfast.

Nacho breakfast!

Makes 4 servings

One 22-ounce bag frozen waffle-cut French fries

½ pound traditional Irish breakfast links (we use Tommy Moloney's), casings removed

4 Campari tomatoes, halved

Table salt and freshly ground black pepper

4 ounces Velveeta, cubed

2½ tablespoons whole milk

4 large eggs

2 green onions, dark green parts only, snipped into ¼-inch rings

1. Preheat the oven to 450°F.

2. Bake the waffle fries on a sheet pan according to the package directions. Turn off the oven but leave them in to keep warm.

3. Meanwhile, in a nonstick medium skillet cook the sausage over medium-high heat, breaking it up as you go, until browned and cooked through, 7 to 10 minutes. Move the sausage to one side and place the tomatoes cut side down in the pan. Lightly salt and pepper the tomatoes and grill them undisturbed until the cooked sides are substantially softened, 3 to 5 minutes. Remove from the heat and set the pan aside to stay warm.

4. Meanwhile, for the nacho cheese sauce, in a medium microwave-safe bowl, combine the Velveeta cubes and milk. Cover and microwave in 30-second increments, stirring after each, until perfectly smooth. Set aside to keep warm.

5. In a nonstick skillet, fry the eggs sunny side up, according to your preference for yolk-doneness (we like them firm but still a little runny, looking almost poached).

6. Now let's assemble these Irish nachos! Pull out the sheet pan of waffle fries and sprinkle them with salt and pepper, then divide them among four plates. Top each serving with sausage, grilled tomatoes, green onions, and cooked eggs. Drizzle cheese sauce on top of everything and serve promptly.

Two trips with three generations . . .

. . . of Doocys in Dublin.

JOLT IN A JAR

AS I MENTIONED BEFORE, WHEN I WAS A KID IN THE BOY SCOUTS, ONCE EVERY COUPLE of months we'd go on a campout. They let us throw hatchets at stumps and jackknives at outhouses. We'd jump directly into the Smoky Hill River after lunch and swim in the deep brown water for an hour without life preservers. And the ultimate—for years in my school desk I kept a paper target to remember the bull's-eye I got from one hundred paces with an actual .22 caliber rifle. That was the most dangerous thing I ever did—until I got married.

One night after dinner one of the adult leaders called the boys to gather around the leader's campfire because he wanted us to watch him cut a Schlitz beer can in half—which he'd apparently just finished. There was a TV commercial on at that time where a guy took a very sharp knife and slashed one in half in a single slice. But this poor guy was sawing back and forth with his Swiss Army knife, and it was nothing like the commercial. I was positive he was going to lop off a finger. Luckily we all had first-aid merit badges. Finally he hacked all the way through, a cheer went up, and he celebrated his amazing feat by throwing the can as far as he could into a thicket of tall grass behind the tents.

It was about 3 a.m. when we all woke up to an earsplitting scream. We learned later our scout leader with the knife had been searching for the outhouse in total darkness but had instead located half the severed beer can with his bare foot. The scream woke us all up—it sure sounded like he shrieked Schlitz. He was not at breakfast the next morning.

At those campouts we ate the same breakfast every morning: a cup of uncooked oatmeal in a paper cup with raisins and brown sugar, doused with air-temperature Carnation evaporated milk. My brain would tell me that oatmeal was supposed to be hot, which is why I was jealous of the Scout dad who poured hot coffee in his. Game changer.

I never forgot that guy who put coffee in his Quaker Oats, and fifty years later, when the overnight oats craze started, Kathy and I came up with this smooth and delicious recipe that's reminiscent of the clever Scout dad. The primary flavor is Nutella, but the secondary flavor is coffee! That's why we call this *Jolt in a Jar*.

This recipe is a happy memory of my days in uniform. Of course now that I'm an adult, I've realized that guy probably didn't say Schlitz after all.

Makes 1 serving

Young scout Doocy.

¾ cup unsweetened almond milk

1 teaspoon instant coffee

1 tablespoon chocolate-hazelnut spread (we use Nutella)

1 tablespoon chia seeds

3 tablespoons Craisins (sweetened dried cranberries)

⅔ cup rolled oats

Fresh blueberries or strawberries, for topping (optional)

1. We serve these in Ball jars because they've imprinted the ounces on the side of the jar and you can skip using a measuring cup for the milk. Otherwise, mix it all in a 2-cup glass measuring cup. Combine the almond milk and instant coffee in the jar or cup and whisk with a fork until the coffee dissolves. Add the hazelnut spread and whisk until it's dissolved into a lovely smooth mocha color (because the milk is cold, this takes more stirring than you'd think). Stir in the chia seeds and Craisins. Add the oats and mix until combined.

2. Screw on the jar lid or transfer the mixture to a large glass and cover it with plastic wrap. Move it to the fridge and keep it there overnight.

3. Next day, when it's time to eat, it's perfect as is, or if you have some blueberries or sliced-up strawberries on hand, sprinkle them on top. Grab a spoon and enjoy this delicious and nutritious jolt in a jar!

SALLY'S EGGS BENEDICT BOWLS

ONE SUMMER MORNING AFTER I'D MADE A BATCH OF SCRAMBLED EGGS AND BAKED THEM in bread bowls, Sally said, "You know, Dad, I don't want to be critical, but this would be a lot better with hollandaise sauce." We had some hollandaise mix on hand, so I whipped it up and added some diced ham, and this easy version of eggs Benedict was born.

The Doocys have been a bread bowl family for fifty years. It started with something my mom made in the 1970s. She'd buy a loaf of fresh pumpernickel bread, then lop off the top and hollow out the innards, which she'd fill with an unbelievably delicious and creamy dip with something green in it that I could not identify. Eventually one of my bubble-bursting sisters asked what the green ingredient was, and my mom answered, "It's spinach."

Wait, what? Who ate spinach other than Popeye? I hoped none of the neighbor boys found out I liked something healthy. The cynical eight-year-old Stevie wondered if it was a clever trick by the USDA to get kids to eat spinach. But if it was, it worked!

Fast-forward to modern times, and great places like Panera Bread and Tim Horton's have made bread bowls very popular. At our house Kathy and I have used bread bowls to serve soups and chili, lasagna, and even a couple different casseroles, but this is now an easy brunch favorite. We started making it during the pandemic, when everybody was trying to have individualized portable portions. The best parts—cleanup is a snap because you eat the bowl . . . and there's no spinach!

Makes 3 servings

3 wide round rolls from the bakery department (Kaiser rolls work great)

One 0.9-ounce package Knorr Hollandaise sauce mix

4 tablespoons (½ stick) unsalted butter

1¼ cups whole milk

4 large eggs

Table salt and freshly ground black pepper

1 tablespoon olive oil

½ cup diced cooked ham or Canadian bacon

1. Adjust an oven rack to the center position and preheat the oven to 325°F.

2. Using a sharp knife, carefully cut a circle in the top of one of the rolls, starting about ¾ inch from the sides. Pull off that top piece and then pull out the bread inside to create a bowl, leaving about ½ inch of bread in the bottom. Set the roll aside on an ungreased sheet pan. Repeat to carve out the other bread bowls. (You can reserve the top crust and bready interiors to dry out and make bread crumbs.)

3. In a small saucepan, make the hollandaise sauce according to the package directions, using the 4 tablespoons butter and 1 cup of the milk.

4. Meanwhile, in a medium bowl, crack the eggs, add the remaining ¼ cup milk, give that a shake of salt and pepper as you would for scrambled eggs, and whisk until smooth.

5. In a medium nonstick skillet, heat the olive oil over medium heat, swirling to coat the bottom of the pan. Add the eggs and use a silicone spatula to keep the eggs moving until just set. Move the eggs to one side of the pan, add the ham, and stir a bit to warm it up. Mix the ham into the eggs.

6. Spoon about 1 tablespoon of the hollandaise sauce onto the bottom of each bread bowl. Divide the eggs among the bowls, filling them slightly above the top. Set the bread bowls on their sheet pan in the oven to warm up the rolls, 2 to 3 minutes.

7. Place the bread bowls on plates and spoon hollandaise sauce on top as you like. Serve immediately.

3

SANDWICHES AND SOUPS

WHEN YOU'RE MAKING BREAKFAST IN THE morning, just know that because of my hours working decades on a morning show, I never experienced the chaos of the carpool lane or made breakfast for my kids. And while I was never home for the Eggo Hour, they still loved my job because sometimes *if they were good* I would take them to work or a Hollywood event and they would meet some of the most famous people in the world.

Kathy, who hosted a celebrity magazine on ESPN, had grown up in Encino, a Los Angeles suburb where her neighbors were some of America's biggest boldface names. John Wayne and the actual Walt Disney lived not far away, and Michael Jackson was in her high school. She invited Michael and his brothers, then known as the Jackson 5, to her sweet sixteen, and they came!

Celebrities have never been a big deal to Kathy, and when the kids would go with me to work to meet the famous folk, she offered some advice on courtesy: "Shake hands, introduce yourself, and be a good listener." And that's what our kids did over the years in the greenroom and on red carpets, when they met dozens of movie and TV stars, authors, and sports icons who had projects to promote.

When our daughter Mary was eight years old, she started reading the Harry Potter books. One summer when she was in high school she applied to study at Oxford University because she was an English major and England invented English. As a bonus—Oxford was also the actual filming location for some of the Harry Potter movies' interiors. You know that big spooky dining hall from the movies where the kids from Hogwarts ate? That was her actual cafeteria! We

have plenty of photos of the kids smiling in the big room with the floating candelabras that were magically added by Hollywood's computers.

By the time Mary was in college, all the Potter books had been released, and she'd read every one of them at least once. It was her favorite series of all time—so when I asked her if she wanted to go to the world premiere of *Harry Potter and the Half-Blood Prince*, she actually *screamed*.

We arrived a little late to New York's Ziegfeld Theatre, and Mary got to see a couple of the less famous stars walk the red carpet. We'd missed the biggest star, Daniel Radcliffe, who played Harry Potter. We went inside and loved every minute of the movie. Having been to a million of those premieres, just as they started to roll the end credits, I whispered, "Mary, let's go," and we exited toward the back. Nobody else was moving during the credits because the people who had made the movie didn't want to miss their names.

But I wanted to beat the rush to the parking lot. Down the stairs and through an empty lobby, I opened the door in the direction of our parked car—and suddenly we were on the red carpet. "Dad, this is amazing!" Mary said, just as a security guard started racing toward us. I assumed he would tell us we were trespassing, but his very authoritative voice instructed, "Follow me, I'll escort you to your car."

What I didn't tell Mary earlier was that the minute when they started to roll the credits was when the movie studio's security team would whisk the stars out the door so they wouldn't be bothered by nine hundred fans asking for selfies.

Judging by the small talk I had with the guard, he recognized me as a guy from TV and thought I was in the movie. He said he would walk us to our car (which was actually five blocks away) and ushered us to the first in a long line of brand-new white Audi SUVs. As we approached,

Mary Potter.

Harry Potter's cafeteria.

a driver popped out and opened the rear door, so I did what every person in New York who needed a ride would do—I started to climb in the car. "Dad?" Mary asked, "What are you doing?"

What was I doing? Apparently they were going to drive us to the after-party, which we were not invited to. Mary looked confused, and the little voice in my head said it was time to confess. Just as I turned to the driver, Daniel Radcliffe—Harry Potter himself—walked up behind Mary and said, "Hi guys. Are we all riding together?"

I looked at Mary, and she had that same slack-jawed and stunned look one associates with being tasered.

"Daniel, you were terrific in the movie," I gushed, "congratulations!" as I stuck out my right hand for a shake. I turned and introduced Mary instinctively and she politely shook hands and introduced herself, just as her mother had instructed. I was amazed Mary was still upright, because she'd stopped breathing when the biggest movie star in her world tried to carpool with the Doocys.

"Daniel—you take our car. We'll walk," I said, and he happily hopped into our Audi and drove off with a wave—which was a better ending than us getting charged with grand theft auto.

When Peter was at Villanova doing his undergraduate studies in political science, I called him and asked him if he'd like to accompany me to the White House, where I was hosting a veterans group event. Peter was studying political science and immediately said yes. I told him to meet me at the Philadelphia Amtrak station the next day at the designated hour and he could hitch a ride with me to DC.

Kathy had reminded me to ask him, "Do you have a proper suit?" He said he did, and that it was definitely clean because he hadn't worn it in years. Next day I was on the 9:30 Acela when we pulled into 30th Street Station and there he was—oddly bundled up on a pretty warm day. Nobody else was wearing a coat—but most important, I could see he was wearing a suit underneath it.

I waved him in and he walked to my row and whispered, "I can't sit down."

I gave him the "confused dad" look (I had it down pat), and he opened his coat to show that the top button of his pants was not buttoned. "They don't fit anymore."

No kidding! He looked like my dad, who was famous for unbuttoning his top pants button after every Thanksgiving feast.

Peter hadn't worn his suit since the opening ceremony on his first day at Villanova, when he apparently started on his freshman fifteen, which he accomplished with flying colors.

"I'll be fine," he assured me. "I just can't take off my coat."

At the White House, the president's staff invited us for a personal tour of the Oval Office by the commander in chief. George W. Bush was very friendly and kind and directed the entire conversation toward Peter, about what he'd do in the future and the importance of public service. As Peter was listening, all I could think of was the fact that Peter was politely listening to POTUS while sucking in his gut as much as he could, because he'd taken off his coat. And Peter would surely bust out of those britches if he had to bend over to tie his shoes. Thankfully he was wearing loafers.

After the president gave us the history of the carved wooden Resolute desk, I asked, "Mr. President, have you seen the new *National Treasure* movie?" He had—so I continued. "Then

Peter smiling and sucking in his gut.

you know in the movie they reveal that there's a secret compartment on the right side of your desk." I walked over to the exact spot at the desk where Nicolas Cage had knock-knock-knocked to pop open a secret door. Standing resolutely—but a little too high—I did what Peter couldn't; I got down on my hands and knees in the Oval Office and started tapping the desk like the Terminix guy looking for termites.

"Maybe if I push on this medallion," I said, hoping I wouldn't trigger the panic button that would bring the Secret Service guys in. "You saw the movie, Mr. President. You know there's a carving in here someplace that leads to the Book of Secrets, which shows how to get to the Lost City of Gold."

"Get up, Steve—we already checked and I can't find it either," the president said with a smile. He turned to Peter and said, "Is he always like this?" Peter nodded, and just then the White House photographer snapped some shots of Peter and POTUS and me in front of that historic (and briefly hysterical) desk.

At the world premiere of *Anchorman 2,* I was invited onto the red carpet—because I was an anchorman, too. At twenty-four, Mary was my perfect plus one because she was young enough to recognize everybody famous. I'd stopped learning celebrities' names about the time Tom Selleck retired from *Magnum P.I.*

"Dad—there's Paul Rudd!" I vaguely recognized him and remembered that Mr. Rudd and I had both attended the University of Kansas, and we had a nice chat about how at graduation we'd both stiffed the university with substantial library fines. Brooke Shields was floating around being fabulous, and then Mary pointed over toward a group and whispered cryptically, "Dad, look . . . it's you." It could have been the complimentary *Anchorman*-themed cocktail, but I was completely confused—*It's me? What?*

"Dad—it's the guy who plays you on *Saturday Night Live.*"

Really? Didn't look like him to me, because *that* guy who'd mercilessly spoofed me for years had blond hair and the guy she was pointing at had brown hair.

"Are you one hundred percent sure?" She was, so I grabbed her hand and tugged her in his direction. "Let's go. By the way, what's his name?"

"Taran Killam." *Okay, Taran Killam, I've got something to say to you, mister!* When the actor realized *who* was rushing his way he appeared to tense up, probably anticipating that I was going to punch him in the jaw.

Instead I surely stunned him, saying, "I want to shake the hand of fake Steve Doocy!" He said something to the effect that he thought I might be steamed, and I responded that I was actually

Mary on the red carpet.

Real and Fake Steve Doocy.

flattered. "I love the fact that they chose you—a funny twentysomething guy—to play me on TV!" I was fifty-eight at the time, and the only thing that would have been better would have been if Brad Pitt played the phony Steve Doocy—sorry, Steve, one dream sequence at a time.

I told him that I was flattered by the attention and reminded him his show wasn't going to do a cold open with people that nobody's ever heard of.

The next day Taran Instagrammed a photo of us side by side at the party and wrote, "Steve Doocy is a good-ass sport." We became texting friends, and he wrote, "Thank you, Steve! It's a privilege playing you!"

I responded, "You are the best fake Steve Doocy—ever."

I was glad Mary got to see that civil celebrity interaction, and just like all our kids, she'd been polite, introduced herself to everybody, and most important, gave them all a good, firm handshake.

Those were the same instructions seven-year-old Peter Doocy had when we took him to Radio City Music Hall for the 1994 remake of *Miracle on 34th Street*.

The evening was absolutely magical. When we walked in, Kenny G was playing Christmas music on his clarinet, the Rockettes did a dance number, and then it snowed—indoors. And the actual movie was terrific. Kathy and I both said Sir Richard Attenborough was the best Santa in the history of Christmas movies. As the credits rolled, the guy in the row behind us, John Hughes—yes, that John Hughes, who wrote and directed the movie—leaned in to say he watched Peter the whole movie to see if he laughed in the right parts.

"And?" I asked.

"It's gonna be a hit with the kids," he said, patting the head of his one-child focus group.

Even though it was a school night, we had to go to the after-party at the glamorous Sea Grill restaurant, across the street at Rockefeller Center. We made a lap around the room, chatted with a few friends, and as it was approaching 10 p.m., we could tell the novelty of being around those Hollywood types had worn off and Peter was running out of gas.

"Dad, I have to go."

"Home?" I asked.

He shook his head no, and I knew party time was over and potty time had begun. I accompanied him into the very fancy restroom, featuring gold-plated everything. We were alone as Peter did his business. Just then the door swung open and in walked the guy with the white beard—Sir Richard Attenborough as Santa Claus. I could tell Peter was confused, the image every kid has of Santa is him going down a chimney or driving his sleigh—but there was the jolly old elf making a pit stop in a Rockefeller Center men's room.

Santa is of course the most famous celebrity in the world to a seven-year-old, and yet with great restraint Peter said nothing until we got outside—and he immediately apologized.

"Daddy, I'm sorry," he said with big sad eyes. "I remember what you and Mommy said, but right then I didn't think it was a good time to shake hands with Santa."

Smart kid. Can't teach that.

LASAGNA GRILLED CHEESE
SANDWICHES

MY MOM USED TO SAY, "RAINY DAYS ARE FOR NAPS." SHE SAID IT SO MANY TIMES THAT if I woke up and it looked like a damp day ahead, I'd think, *Rainy days are for naps*. And after lunch I'd take a nap. Now that I'm a parent I recognize that my mother was programming me like Pavlov with his dog. On showery days she was stuck inside the house with five kids hopped up on A&W root beer, so to minimize the craziness, she'd say, "Rainy day, time for a nap," and we'd all take a nap. We'd wake up and she'd be watching Gene Rayburn on *Match Game*. My mother was a genius.

By the way, on rainy nap days she'd always make us tomato soup and grilled cheese sandwiches. Don't know why—maybe one element of that combo was sleep inducing. I fondly remember helping her in the kitchen put a Kraft Single between two slices of Wonder bread, then butter the outside with Fleischmann's margarine, and she'd grill it until it had a gorgeous golden crust on each side. I'd dunk mine in the tomato soup and then ketchup, which is a lot of tomato—but I was a kid, and it's what kids do.

Last year as I was preparing a batch of our lasagna soup from our *Happy in a Hurry Cookbook*, as I was mashing the Parm and mozzarella with the ricotta for the topping, I tasted it and some neurons misfired and I thought, *This would be great as the cheese in a Lasagna Grilled Cheese Sandwich!*

My son-in-law, Ali, said, "It doesn't sound like it'll work."

I made it the next day, with Italian sausage, marinara, and that three-cheese mixture inside buttered bread grilled to golden-brown perfection. "Best darn sandwich of my life!" Sally complimented the chef, but I knew she also wanted to borrow my car.

"When you said you were making a pasta dish into a sandwich, I thought you'd lost your mind," Kathy observed. "Like the time you voted for Ross Perot."

If you love grilled cheese sandwiches and/or lasagna, please try this amazing amalgamation. We make a single batch and have plenty of leftovers for lunch the next day. Best part is, you don't have to wait for a rainy day.

By the way, now that I'm in my sixties, forget *rainy* days, *every day* is for naps!

Makes 6 sandwiches

___

1 cup whole-milk ricotta cheese

½ cup shredded mozzarella cheese

¼ cup shredded Parmesan cheese

¼ teaspoon table salt

1 tablespoon olive oil

1 pound bulk mild or sweet Italian sausage (or links with casings removed)

2 garlic cloves, thinly sliced

2 cups jarred marinara (our favorite is Rao's)

12 bread slices (we use Pepperidge Farm Farmhouse Butter Bread)

Butter, at room temperature

1. In a medium bowl, combine the ricotta, mozzarella, Parmesan, and salt and mix well. Set aside.

2. In a nonstick skillet, heat the olive oil over medium-high heat. Add the sausage and garlic and cook until browned and thoroughly cooked, about 10 minutes. Drain any excess grease. Reduce the heat to low and stir in 1 cup of the marinara to warm it up.

3. To make one sandwich, spread 2 or 3 tablespoons of the cheese mixture on one slice of bread. Spread about ½ cup of the marinara-meat mixture on another slice of bread and smooth it out. Close the sandwich, then repeat to assemble the rest.

4. To cook the sandwiches, heat a large nonstick skillet over slightly warmer than medium heat. If it's too hot it will toast the outside before the cheese mixture is warmed, so make sure the pan is at the Goldilocks temperature—not too hot, not too cold, just right.

5. Butter the outsides of the sandwiches. Cook on one side until it's a deep beautiful golden brown, about 5 minutes. Flip and do the same for the other, about 10 minutes total. Depending on the size of the pan, you can cook more than one sandwich at a time. Just watch them carefully so they don't burn!

6. Meanwhile, warm the remaining 1 cup marinara in the microwave and divide it among small bowls, one for each sandwich.

7. Slice the sandwiches in half and serve them with the bowls of marinara for dipping. Wow, that's good! Who knew lasagna could be a showstopping sandwich?

KATHY'S CLEAN-OUT-THE-PANTRY CHICKEN POSOLE

KATHY IS A GREAT SOUP MAKER, AND THIS POSOLE IS ONE OF HER BEST. I LIKE TO TELL her, "Your soups take my broth away!" She never laughs at that one, but it still cracks me up.

During the pandemic, certain foods were hard to get, but we could always pull this one together because it's a very flexible recipe—you can clean out the pantry with this one. You can make it with pork or chicken, or make it vegetarian. When we couldn't get chili powder and cumin, we substituted a packet of fajita seasoning, and that stuck. When we couldn't find hominy, which is processed field corn, Kathy went rogue and used a can of sweet corn kernels. It was tasty, but when you can use hominy, that makes it amazing.

This recipe is now a Doocy family tradition on Cinco de Mayo. If we're marking the occasion with a happy hour margarita (or two), this recipe is a dream because it's started in the slow cooker long before our blood alcohol reaches an actual number and spends the afternoon on the counter pumping deliciousness into our air supply.

Our whole family adores this recipe. In fact, if Kathy ever opened a restaurant, people would line up and pay good money for her savory soups and brilliant broths—I wouldn't be surprised if someday she'd become a *bouillonaire!*

#DadJokesRule

I'll be here all week, try the posole.

Makes 6 to 8 servings

Cooking oil spray

1 large red onion, roughly chopped

4 garlic cloves, roughly chopped

2 pounds boneless, skinless chicken thighs, cut into 1-inch chunks

1 cup chicken stock

1 tablespoon olive oil

One 1.12-ounce packet fajita seasoning mix (we use McCormick)

One 19-ounce can mild red enchilada sauce

One 10-ounce can Ro-Tel mild diced tomatoes and green chilies

One 20-ounce can white hominy, drained

Sour cream, for garnish

1. Mist the inside of a slow cooker with cooking spray (to make cleanup easier). Place the onion, garlic, and chicken in the slow cooker. In a small bowl, combine the chicken stock, olive oil, and fajita seasoning and mix to combine, then pour the mixture slowly over the chicken. Add the enchilada sauce and Ro-Tel and stir.

2. Cover the slow cooker and cook on high for 4 hours.

3. Add the hominy, stir thoroughly, cover, and cook on low for 90 more minutes, until it thickens a bit and the flavors combine.

4. Serve the posole in bowls. A spoonful of sour cream on top smooths out the flavors. *Delicioso!*

SAUSAGE AND PEPPER PULL-APARTS

WHEN OUR YOUNGEST CHILD, SALLY, WENT TO SMU IN DALLAS, WE HAD NO IDEA IT HAD one of the most elaborate football-season tailgates in America. They call it the Boulevard, because it's centered on Bishop Boulevard in the heart of campus. At her first tailgate, deep in the heart of Texas, Sally stood out like a non-Texan in her preppy New York shoes.

A frantic post-tailgate phone call was made to her mother to talk about her footwear situation. Kathy told Sally not to worry, and with a few keystrokes Mom had found a custom pair of cowboy boots in Sally's school colors, with an SMU logo, and their beloved pony mascot on the boot—to boot! As she added them to her cart she realized the boots were *one thousand dollars*. That's $500 a foot! Dr. Phil's sons went to college there, and he'd told me that "SMU stands for Southern Million-aires University." Suddenly those boots made sense. Remove from cart!

Sally eventually graduated, moved to New York, and got married to her boyfriend from SMU, Ali Sadri. They've since moved back to Dallas. Reliving their college glory days, they are back most weekends for the Boulevard tailgate. But now that Ali and his college pals all have jobs, they can tailgate in style. They've rented their own spot where every home game they park their tricked-out trailer with the school's logo on the side.

Some of the school's high-roller tailgaters go epically crazy, with flat-screen TVs, white-gloved waiters, bartenders serving top-shelf hooch in real crystal, and in some of the larger tent structures—chandeliers! At a tailgate!

The fanciest thing Sally and Ali have at their tailgate is a big YETI cooler—because the food is the main attraction. Kathy and I came up with this delicious sausage and pepper taste of New Jersey that Sally can make and tailgaters can eat with one hand. When people see it, they say, "What is it?" And when they take a bite they say, "That is unbelievably good!"

By the way, in college Sally did eventually find a lovely $200 pair of cowboy boots, but they required an hour-long car ride outside Dallas to an authentic Western wear shop. Sally wore them all four years, and she still wears them at the Boulevard, where just like during her college years her many enthusiastic friends continue to tell hilarious stories at high volume, and they still spill Shiner Bock on her boots.

Makes 12 slider-size sandwiches

---

1 pound bulk sweet Italian sausage (or links with casings removed)

1½ tablespoons olive oil

1 red bell pepper, finely diced

1 medium yellow onion, finely diced

1 large garlic clove, minced

1. Adjust an oven rack to the center position and preheat the oven to 350°F. Line a 9 × 13-inch baking dish with enough foil to over the bottom of the dish and enough extra foil on one side to cover the entire dish later for baking.

2. Divide the sausage into 12 equal portions and roll them into balls, then squash them a little so they're about as wide as your biscuit cutter. Place them on a nonstick sheet pan and bake until they read 165°F on an instant-read thermometer, 20 to 25 minutes.

1 cup jarred marinara sauce (we use Rao's)

One 12-pack slider buns (we love potato rolls)

6 to 8 deli mozzarella slices

1½ tablespoons unsalted butter, melted

Garlic powder

1½ cups shredded mozzarella cheese, or more as desired

NOTE: This recipe uses a 1¼-inch or 2-inch biscuit cutter (the smaller the better). If you don't have a set, buy one online; they're less than $10 and we use ours all the time! You can use a knife to cut the holes, but it takes longer and they won't be as uniform.

3. Meanwhile, in a medium skillet, heat the olive oil over medium-high heat. Add the bell pepper, onion, and garlic and sauté until the onion has softened and has golden highlights, about 10 minutes. Mix in the marinara and heat to serving temperature, then remove from the heat and keep warm.

4. Keeping the 12 slider buns connected to one another at the sides, carefully lift the tops from the bottoms, keeping the tops and bottoms in two large pieces. Place the bun bottoms cut side up in the prepared baking dish. Completely cover those bun bottoms with the mozzarella slices, then evenly spoon the marinara mixture on top and spread it almost to the edge of the pan.

5. Lay the bun tops on a cutting board. Use the biscuit cutter to cut a hole in the center of each bun top and carefully remove the bread circles (set them aside to toast as croutons later). Set the connected bun tops over the marinara mixture. In a small bowl, combine the melted butter and a dusting of garlic powder. Brush the garlic butter on the golden tops of the buns (not in the holes). Gently place a sausage ball in each hole, pressing carefully until it hits the marinara. It's not far!

6. Cover the pan with the extra foil you left on one side and crimp it tightly closed. Transfer to the oven and bake until the cheese inside has melted, about 15 minutes.

7. Remove the pan from the oven and turn on the broiler (make sure the oven rack is at least 6 inches from the heat). Roll back the foil and scatter the shredded mozzarella over the buns and sausage balls, lightly covering the sausage balls and covering most of the buns. If you want a little more cheese, feel free! Broil the rolls to quickly melt the cheese—it should take less than 1 minute. Keep an eye on it or you'll burn the bread!

8. If you're taking these to a tailgate, replace the foil on top to keep them warm. Or serve right away with the sliders in the pan, or lift them out of the pan by the foil liner. If they're hot when you serve them, there will be an epic cheese pull every time you pull one apart!

THE TWO MARYS' SCRUMPTIOUS SHRIMP ROLLS

WHEN THE KIDS WERE GROWING UP, HALF OF OUR FAMILY VACATIONS WERE SOUTH IN Florida and half were up north in Cape Cod. Our daughter Mary loved New England so much she wound up going to Boston College. Of course her dining hall had to serve lobster—once a semester on Surf 'n' Turf night. With fishing nets, lanterns, and lobster pots for decoration, the semiannual nautical-themed night gave some of Mary's wisecracking pals an excuse to spend the meal talking like a pirate. *ARRRG!*

A member of the BC varsity crew team, Mary made a number of friends for life because she would let them use her meal-plan card. They'd run out of money on their cards early in the semester and were terrified to ask their parents for more cash, so St. Mary fed the hungry.

One kid was the child of the CEO of one of the biggest restaurant chains in America—so while that father's franchise was feeding America, the Doocys were feeding his child—pro bono. Mary did not reveal this to me until ten years *after* graduation. She couldn't tell me how many times I bought that kid a dinner. I'd call the father, but the statute of limitations on meal-plan pilfering expired last April.

When Kathy and I would visit on parents' weekend, Mary would take us to one place famous for its epic lobster sandwich. It featured the clever amalgamation of arugula and crispy prosciutto—and *wow* was it good! Today, however, the price of lobster is *sooo* high—but luckily we have a way to replicate the same taste at a fraction of the cost.

Our great friend Mary Wiatr is famous in our neighborhood for her shrimp roll recipe. My daughter Mary and I have combined our favorite parts of Mary the neighbor's shrimp rolls with that Boston restaurant's entree to make this zesty showstopper that should be called *I CAN'T BELIEVE IT'S NOT LOBSTER!*

This recipe from Mary & Mary will have you feeling like you're at a cozy spot somewhere in New England or, at the very least, talking like a pirate. *Shiver me timbers—that's good, Cap'n!*

Mary the neighbor always serves wavy potato chips with this, but she warms them on a sheet pan in the oven for about 10 minutes, and people think she made them from scratch! But now all our neighbors will know Mary just rips open a bag and pops them in the oven. Try it yourself!

If you're counting carbs, skip the bun and the arugula—just scoop the shrimp salad onto a romaine spear or two.

Makes 8 rolls

2 tablespoons sour cream

2 tablespoons mayonnaise (we use Duke's)

1 lime

¼ teaspoon table salt

¼ teaspoon freshly ground black pepper

½ cup finely diced celery

½ cup finely diced red onion

1 pound cooked and cleaned frozen extra jumbo shrimp (16/20 count), thawed and tails removed

One 4-ounce package diced prosciutto

Wavy potato chips, for serving (optional)

8 split-top hot dog buns

Butter, at room temperature

Baby arugula, for garnish

1. First let's make the zesty lime mayo. In a medium bowl, mix the sour cream and mayo. Directly grate the zest of the lime into the mix, then squeeze all the juice from that lime into the bowl. Add the salt and pepper and whisk until smooth. Mix in the celery and onion. Preheat the oven to 200°F.

2. Now to the main event—the shrimp. Shrimp give off a lot of water as they thaw, so give them a gentle squeeze and pat them dry with paper towels. Next, chop the shrimp—we aim for pieces that are about ½ inch wide. I cut the shrimp in half lengthwise, then slice the halves crosswise nice and small. Drop the chopped shrimp into the mayo bowl and stir to completely coat every piece with the lime mayo, then cover and refrigerate.

3. In a small nonstick skillet, sauté the prosciutto over medium-high heat until just crispy. Set aside.

4. On a sheet pan, warm the wavy chips in the oven for about 10 minutes.

5. Lightly butter the insides of the buns. Heat a large nonstick skillet over medium-high heat, add the buns butter side down, and pan-toast until golden brown and delicious looking, working in batches as needed.

6. Time to assemble! Place a bun on a plate and sprinkle some arugula inside. Use a slotted spoon to lay shrimp down the middle, then sprinkle with crispy prosciutto. Hinge the bun closed like a book and enjoy!

Mary, Mary, not contrary . . . in the kitchen!

SUSAN'S SLOPPY JOES

REMEMBER WHEN IT SEEMED LIKE EVERY FAMILY IN AMERICA ATE SLOPPY JOES AT LEAST once a week? My mom's recipe was a squirt of ketchup and half a squeeze of French's mustard into some cooked hamburger scooped between a couple slices of super-soft Wonder bread—and that was it. Then Manwich came along and revolutionized the Sloppy Joe world.

But then we all grew up, and Sloppy Joes kind of faded away.

So it was a pleasant surprise one night when our friend Susan invited Kathy and me over to have dinner with her and her husband, Bill, and the main course was *Sloppy Joes!* They were absolutely perfect—the best I'd ever had. Fabulous comfort food served on a super-soft potato roll, it was a warm taste of my childhood. And Susan's childhood, too, as this recipe has been a Ritchie family staple for decades.

The family was from Michigan, and Susan would make these for impromptu suppers when their family and friends would come in after cross-country skiing in the Stoney Creek Apple Orchard. When she hosted a neighborhood dinner, this was the main course. And when her son, Bob Ritchie, also known as Kid Rock, was celebrating his birthday, they didn't go to the fanciest steakhouse in town—nope, his mom made the family's famous Sloppy Joes.

At the end of that birthday dinner, Susan brought out a sheet cake from Costco, and we all sang "Happy Birthday." As I was singing, Bob was glaring directly at me. I assumed he was offended by my energetic yet off-key singing, but when I got home I realized he was probably staring at a giant Sloppy Joe stain down my shirt. #ShirtHappens

These are delicious, but there's a reason they call them Sloppy Joes.

Simmering Susan.

Makes 20 sandwiches

2 pounds ground beef (or buffalo—Susan often uses it because it's leaner)

1 cup roughly chopped yellow onion

½ green bell pepper, cut into medium dice

½ cup medium-diced celery

One 15-ounce can Campbell's condensed tomato soup

½ cup ketchup

2 tablespoons apple cider vinegar

1 tablespoon Worcestershire sauce

1 tablespoon sugar

2 teaspoons table salt

½ teaspoon freshly ground black pepper

20 hamburger-size buns (we love Martin's potato rolls)

Coleslaw (optional)

1. In a large skillet, brown the ground beef over medium-high heat. Use a slotted spoon to transfer the meat to a bowl, leaving any grease in the pan. Add the onion, bell pepper, and celery to the pan and sauté until they turn a little soft and are just starting to get some brown highlights on some edges, 7 or 8 minutes. Return the meat to the pan over medium-low heat and add the soup, ketchup, vinegar, Worcestershire, sugar, salt, and black pepper. Stir well, bring to a simmer, and cook until the sauce is the desired thickness and the scent is driving you crazy, 15 to 20 minutes.

2. To serve, scoop the Sloppy Joe mixture onto soft hamburger or slider buns. Susan sometimes serves this with a side of coleslaw, and some guests reportedly put the slaw on top of the meat.

THE NEXT DAY . . .

We use the leftovers to make Sloppy Joe dip! Warm up the Sloppy Joe mixture in the microwave to a good serving temperature. Spread it in a small baking dish, level out the top, and scatter on a healthy layer of shredded Cheddar. Heat it in a 350°F oven until the cheese is completely melted, 3 to 5 minutes. Serve with chips or baguette slices. *Mmmmmm good.*

SUPER-SIMPLE SPANISH GAZPACHO

WE ARRIVED IN BARCELONA, SPAIN, FOR A FAMILY VACATION AND DISCOVERED THAT wherever we went to eat they were only serving appetizer-size plates, or tapas. They were beautifully prepared and often stuck together with toothpicks, and the kids were terrified because most were made with food they had not experienced in their young lives—like barnacles, squid, and octopus. A few featured whole fish heads with open eyes that freaked us out because wherever we were in the restaurant, dinner was watching us.

Sally ordered her default childhood meal: chicken fingers. But something got lost in her eighth-grade English-to-Spanish translation and the waiter brought her an entire chicken—and adding insult to injury, there were no fries, but there was a roasted green pepper, which her brother finished after he ate his entire whole chicken.

Luckily we didn't starve, because most places served a zesty, refreshing, and healthy cold soup called gazpacho, which the kids enjoyed and we continued to make when we went home to New Jersey. This recipe is for our current very quick version. We add corn to the recipe because during the summer in the Garden State we have plenty on hand. And it's a lovely memory of that great trip and how that soup was the only food from Spain that didn't keep an eye on us as we walked across the dining room.

Makes 6 cups of soup

---

1 dinner roll–size piece of bread, roughly torn (day-old bread is great)

⅓ cup roughly chopped sweet onion

3 medium tomatoes, cored, halved, and cut into ½-inch slices (we use tomatoes on the vine)

2 cups V8 Spicy Hot vegetable juice

1 tablespoon olive oil

3 celery stalks, finely chopped

½ medium cucumber, finely chopped

1 ear of corn, kernels sliced off the cob, or 1 cup thawed frozen corn kernels

Sour cream, for serving (optional)

Cooked bacon crumbles, for serving (optional)

1. We use the blender to make quick work of most of the vegetables, then fold in the rest. In the blender, combine the bread, onion, tomatoes, and V8. Briefly pulse a few times, until any large chunks are processed and it's well blended into small but visible pieces.

2. Add the olive oil, celery, cucumber, and corn kernels to the blender—but don't blend them. Use a rubber spatula and give them a stir so they remain whole pieces. That's it—you're done!

3. Cover and refrigerate a couple hours before serving.

4. When it's time to serve, give a stir, then pour into bowls or coffee cups. If you'd like the gazpacho a little creamier, stir in a drizzle of sour cream to smooth out the flavors. Then, if you like bacon (who doesn't?), add some crumbles on top and serve.

CAST-IRON CABERNET CHEESEBURGERS

IT'S . . . WINE O'CLOCK!

You know how you sometimes stand outside at your BBQ grill and you're drinking an adult beverage and you're thinking about all the big issues of the world . . .

So one day I was doing some burgers in a cast-iron pan on the grill, and because it was after 5 p.m., I had an adult beverage in hand. As I was waiting to flip the burgers, I was thinking about our longtime friend Kevin Kohler at Cafe Panache in northern New Jersey, who had just passed away.

One night after dinner at his restaurant, I'd complimented him, saying, "That was the best steak I've ever had—how do you make that wine sauce?" And you know what he did? He took me in the kitchen and showed me how he did it. He gave that recipe to us for our first cookbook. It's called World's Best Steak, because it simply is. Kevin shared many of his clever cooking techniques with Kathy and me, and for that we are eternally grateful.

So there I was, grilling and chilling and thinking about this great chef and friend as I waited for the burgers to finish, and boom! Out of nowhere this idea for a cabernet cheeseburger hit me. Clearly I had a guardian angel that day . . .

So—if you adore the taste of delicious meat prepared in wine, such as beef bourguignon or coq au vin—try this. In our humble opinion it makes one of the best cheeseburgers we've ever tasted . . . but then again when was the last time you had a cheeseburger cooked in red wine and topped with cabernet-infused sautéed mushrooms? Exactly!

Makes 4 cheeseburgers

One 8-ounce package mushrooms, thinly sliced (we use Baby Bellas)

1 large shallot, cut into medium slices

2 tablespoons unsalted butter, plus more for buttering the buns

Table salt and freshly ground black pepper

1 cup cabernet wine

2 tablespoons balsamic vinegar

Four 6-ounce hamburger patties

Montreal steak seasoning

4 burger buns (we use brioche buns)

Goat cheese crumbles, for serving

1 medium tomato, thinly sliced, for serving

Baby arugula, for serving

1. We cook this in a large cast-iron skillet on the outside grill, so we don't have to clean up any burger spattering. Preheat a grill to 500°F, and place an ovenproof skillet (preferably cast-iron) on the grill to preheat for about 10 minutes.

2. Add the mushrooms, shallot, and 2 tablespoons of the butter to the pan; it will instantly melt. Salt and pepper the mushrooms and shallot, give them a stir, close the lid, and cook for 90 seconds. Open the lid and you'll see the mushrooms are releasing their liquids. Stir again, close the lid, and cook 2 to 3 minutes to let the liquid cook off a bit. Open the lid, move the pan away from the heat, and carefully pour the wine from a measuring cup into the center of the hot pan, then return to the heat. Mix and cook for about a minute, until the liquid stops bubbling around the outside rim. Stir in the balsamic vinegar and cook 2 minutes, as it quickly thickens and reduces. These wine-infused mushrooms are the MVPs of this recipe—you'll love them! Use a slotted spoon to remove the mushrooms and shallots to a bowl. Cover and keep warm for later.

3. Give a stir to the red wine reduction. Lightly season the hamburger patties with Montreal steak seasoning and gently squeeze the center of the patty with your thumb and fingers to create a slight indentation in the middle on both sides (this keeps the patties from bulging too much when cooking). Place the patties directly into the wine pan, taking care not to splash! Close the lid and cook the patties on one side for 6 or 7 minutes, until the bottom half of the burger is a deep brown from the wine reduction. Then flip and cook to your preferred level of doneness. (The USDA says 160°F is the safe minimum internal temp—check with an instant-read thermometer if you have questions.)

4. Set the burgers aside to rest, then lightly butter the burger buns and briefly toast them cut side down on the grill grates.

5. To build a burger, place some goat cheese crumbles on a bottom bun and fork-smash them into the toasted bread. Set a burger on top, add some more goat cheese crumbles, and spoon some wine-infused mushrooms and shallots on top. Add a few thin slices of tomato and finally some arugula. As a wild card, I will sometimes drizzle a little ranch dressing on the arugula for a little creamy goodness. Close with the toasted bun top and you're done!

6. Check your watch, it's a *winner* at wine o'clock!

BUFFALO CHICKEN
FRENCH TOAST SANDWICHES

I KNOW SHE'S ONE OF AMERICA'S MOST BELOVED COOKBOOK AUTHORS, BUT KATHY Doocy told me on our first date that when she lived in New York City, every morning she would call the coffee shop downstairs and have them deliver her breakfast: coffee and toast.

"You paid for toast?" I asked.

"I didn't have a toaster," she said, and added, "or the recipe."

As soon as we were married, we got a toaster, and her take-out days were over.

Fast-forward thirty-five years, and during a visit to Washington to see Peter and his wife, Hillary, the younger Doocys took us out to lunch at Lyon Hall, a place near their home in Virginia, where they featured a dish Peter had told me about before: a spicy chicken sandwich served on French toast. We all ordered it and it was amazing! A perfect combination of sweet and savory, and it came with dill pickles to boot—it was off-the-charts fantastic!

The next day, the whole family brainstormed our version of that sandwich. We initially made the French toast from scratch with eggs and Texas toast the way my mom made it—and it was terrific. Then our daughter Mary, who is responsible for the Buffalo sauce glaze, said, "Dad, if you're writing *The Simply Happy Cookbook*, let's make it simpler." And she showed me Eggo French toast on her phone. We went to the store, bought a box, and saved 10 minutes of kitchen time—which made me *simply happy*. Thanks, Mary! My sister Lisa—who used to work at a great chicken restaurant—suggested using frozen chicken patties to save time, and Hillary's idea was to put the all-important pure maple syrup on the inside so that you could pick it up with your hands and not wind up with fingers that smelled like Vermont.

Sometimes it takes a village—to make a sandwich.

This morning after *Fox & Friends* I made one of these sandwiches, and I've gotta say, the French toast makes it breakfast-y and the Buffalo chicken makes it lunch-y . . . meaning it's the *perfect* quick brunch, unless you're waiting for some guy to deliver your toast.

Makes 2 sandwiches

---

2 fully cooked frozen chicken patties (we use Tyson Spicy Chicken Patties)

2 tablespoons unsalted butter

¼ cup Frank's RedHot Wings mild sauce (or RedHot Wings Buffalo sauce, if you like it hot)

4 slices Eggo Thick & Fluffy Classic French toast

Maple syrup, warmed, for serving

Dill pickle slices, for serving

1. Bake the chicken patties on a sheet pan according to the package directions.

2. Meanwhile, to make the sauce, in a shallow microwave-safe bowl, melt the butter in the microwave. Add the wings sauce and whisk with a fork to blend. Set aside.

3. Toast the Eggo French toasts in your toaster. For best results, toast each slice twice, or until nicely browned!

4. Time to put it all together! To make one serving, lay 2 slices of the French toast side by side on a plate and then drizzle about ½ tablespoon of maple syrup on each piece. Use a butter knife to spread it up to the edges. Warm the Buffalo sauce for 15 seconds in the microwave and stir. Pour it into a saucer and coat a chicken patty in the sauce on both sides. Set it on one piece of French toast, then on top of the chicken add as many pickles as you like. Top with the other piece of French toast with the syrup side facing *inside*, so you don't get your hands messy! Repeat to make the second sandwich.

5. Serve with more maple syrup or the remaining warmed wings sauce for dipping purposes. We have family members who'll add some syrup or sauce to *every bite*! What can I say . . . we're sweet and spicy people . . .

French toast goes with chicken? Yes!

GRANDMA'S GREEN GARDEN AND BEAN SOUP

I REMEMBER WHEN I WAS GROWING UP MY MOM WOULD POUR A BAG OF DRIED NAVY beans into a pot and cover them with water, and it meant we'd have her bean soup the next day. My sister Lisa and I were talking about how much we both loved our mom's navy bean soup and how she had to soak the beans for half a day or overnight, which was torture because when kids start thinking about a food, they want it *now*. Once, we complained and she made the soup even though the beans hadn't soaked nearly long enough, and the beans weren't tender; they were like bullets. That was the last time we asked Mom to rush physics.

Lisa reminded me of the best accompaniment for the soup—Wonder bread. We would each slather a piece of Wonder bread with bright yellow margarine—it was the seventies. Then we'd stick the super-soft bread into the hot soup and the margarine would melt off, leaving a little golden oil slick on the top of the soup.

This recipe captures that bean-y taste, but we use canned beans, which require zero soaking, and we've updated it with extra flavor from lots of fresh vegetables. It makes great leftovers—we actually think it tastes better the next day!

Makes 8 to 10 servings

2 tablespoons vegetable oil

1 large yellow onion, cut into medium dice

2 garlic cloves, thinly sliced

3 carrots, peeled and sliced into thin coins

3 celery stalks, medium-sliced

1 small head cauliflower, broken or cut into bite-size florets

Two 15.5-ounce cans navy or cannellini beans, undrained

One 10-ounce can Ro-Tel mild diced tomatoes and green chilies

4 cups (32 ounces) low-sodium vegetable stock

½ teaspoon table salt

½ teaspoon freshly ground black pepper

One 5-ounce bag baby spinach

Grated Parmesan cheese, for serving

Wonder bread and butter, for serving

1. In a large soup pot, heat the oil over medium-high heat. Add the onion and sauté until the onion softens and the edges start to turn golden, about 5 minutes. Add the garlic, carrots, celery, and cauliflower, stir, and sauté 2 to 3 minutes to give them a little flavor. Add the beans and their liquid, the Ro-Tel, vegetable stock, 4 cups water, and the salt and pepper. Give a good stir, bring to a boil, cover, and simmer for about 30 minutes to thicken it a bit and blend the flavors.

2. When ready to serve, turn off the heat, stir in the spinach, and let it wilt; it will quickly turn a very deep green.

3. To finish with a flourish of flavor, top each bowl with a sprinkling of grated Parmesan. Let it sit a moment to get a little melty. Serve with Wonder bread and butter on the side, then enjoy!

4

SIDES

SALLY, OUR YOUNGEST, STOOD AT THE FRONT OF OUR church in a stunning white imported Italian lace gown that she'd waited a year to finally wear. I couldn't believe I was looking at Daddy's little girl. I glanced over at Kathy and saw a tear in her eye, and my waterworks started—but unlike at work, I wasn't wearing my waterproof mascara.

Sally kept looking back at her parents, smiling as she stood near the altar with a young man we'd *just met*. But that was fine with us . . . it wasn't like she was getting married. It was Sally's first Holy Communion, and she was seven.

First communions are very big things in our town, and Kathy wanted Sally to look like a million bucks. Which is why one year earlier, at the end of Communion season, Kathy had gone to Daffy's, whose slogan was "Clothing Bargains for Millionaires." Marked down from $375 to $49, her dress was a steal.

One year later, at her first Holy Communion, Sally looked beautiful. As I contemplated her standing there, I thought to myself, *Someday—maybe in this church—she's going to get married* . . . and that's when I wondered if it would be to one of the boys in her class. We'd always assumed she would marry either the boy whose family owned the fancy grocery store where Peter was a stock boy, or his cousin. Either way, she'd marry into that family and we'd get a price break on tomahawk steaks for the rest of our lives.

Sally was without a doubt our most mischievous child—and so it was wonderful to see her looking like an absolute angel as she received her first Communion. After she got the sacrament, we expected her to return to her seat—but in typical Sally fashion she made a beeline for the Eucharistic minister holding the chalice full of wine. Sally stuck out her hands and took the chalice. Glug, glug, glug.

Because Sally was the first in line, everybody lined up behind her for the wine; she was the pied piper of Piper Sonoma. After she appeared to glug, glug, glug, chug it, she turned to Kathy and me and gave us a thumbs-up and a little wink, as if she'd just signed on as a sommelier at Kendall-Jackson.

Of course my first reaction was *Sally drinks wine?* Then I was horrified that she was sharing a communal cup with twenty-seven kids during the flu and croup season. Meanwhile Kathy was terrified she'd spill red wine on her $49 pint-size wedding dress before the reception at the home of the grocery store family, where Sally had to make a good impression if she was ever going to marry one of those seven-year-old boys who'd just shared the holy rosé with her.

An hour later, at the grocery store family's party, the hooch must have gone to Sally's head because while throwing caution to the wind inside the bouncy house, she ripped her brand-new imported-lace practice wedding gown. Absolutely crestfallen, she vowed right then and there that she would never touch alcohol ever again. Fine with us—that meant we didn't have to worry about her going from Tang to Tanqueray.

Sally's first Communion day.

And we did not. Sally had a happy childhood, but there was one time when something was bothering her and we could not figure out what it was. At that time she was the captain of the high school varsity swim team, and she was up early for school and swimming at the YMCA until eleven some nights. Sundays she would sleep in . . . very late. Because I got up so early for my job, I would often go to church before anybody else in the house was awake. One Sunday morning at 7:15, just as I was about to drive to the 7:30 mass, Sally came downstairs, completely dressed. I told her I'd be back in an hour and she announced, "Dad—I'm going to church *with* you," and she did. And I loved the company.

The next Sunday, same thing—she got up very early and went to church with me. Next Sunday, same thing. After a month of early rising, as we were walking toward the car at the end of the service, I asked her why she wanted to suddenly go to church with me. She said nothing. I didn't follow up, because she obviously had a reason and didn't want to share it.

Just as we pulled into our driveway she blurted out, "Dad—I went because I wanted to pray," and tears started to well up in her eyes. She continued, "I was praying that I get into college."

"What college?" I asked.

"*Any* college," she whispered.

High school had been very challenging for Sally, who was diagnosed with dyslexia when she was in third grade. School was hard—but tests like the SAT were ten times harder. We both said many prayers, hoping *any* school would let her in.

Peter and Mary had both applied to a slew of schools, but none had ever accepted a Doocy on early decision. With her dyslexia, Sally worked three times harder than anybody

in her class—on every paper, every project, everything. Then out of the blue, a few days after our Sunday morning church service, Sally was admitted *early action* to both of the colleges she applied to. The power of prayer.

As I've mentioned, she chose SMU in Dallas, where the mascot is the mustang, and she liked being Mustang Sally. She absolutely thrived there and found an area of interest that would become her vocation. Because she was Daddy's precious little girl, it never dawned on me that in college, during her off hours, she would be around lots of young men who were looking for dates. At a freshman party she met a smooth-talking young man who told her that she was the most beautiful girl in the world. They started going out and next thing we knew, that young man, Ali Sadri, proposed—seven years after they started dating. (Coincidentally, Sally was seven when I saw her in her first wedding dress.)

Sally and Ali were planning a May 2020 wedding of their dreams. The invitations for almost two hundred people were mailed, every detail was determined, the dinner, the music, the pictures, the priest—all signed up to make sure that our first Doocy family wedding would be one nobody would ever forget. As the father of the bride, with a wife and daughters who love rom-coms, I always identified with Steve Martin, who played George Banks in the movie *Father of the Bride*. And just like Steve Martin's character, I knew that as the father of two potential brides, someday I was going to finance a couple of blowout weddings that would require me to rob a bank or sell a kidney. Luckily I had two daughters *and* two kidneys.

Then Covid hit. Their wedding was optimistically moved ninety days into the future, but things didn't get better and for safety's sake the big wedding was canceled and ultimately

Sally's second wedding dress, first wedding.

downsized to only ten—with just immediate family members attending. A few weeks before the service, the priest who was going to officiate suddenly died. In his place Sally's brother, Peter, was asked to officiate; he'd been Internet-ordained earlier to perform a civil wedding ceremony for his producer. Then at 5 p.m. on August 1, 2020, the official start time of the twice-canceled wedding, we were at a hotel in Palm Beach, Florida—just as Hurricane Isaias shut down the entire town.

After everything we'd been through we were not going to let a measly Cat 1 hurricane derail the blessed event. As the hurricane outside howled, I did offer my father of the bride toast and observed among other things that "life is short." When given the chance, I suggested they order dessert. "Go for the leather interior. Have the dream wedding with two

hundred people and top-shelf booze, unless there's a global pandemic and the ultimate dream wedding is the one with just the people in this room—sheltering in place—together."

The week before, I'd asked Sally and Ali why they didn't postpone their wedding and offered them a big blowout party the next year. They both said no, because who knew what the world was going to be like in a year? It turned out to be a very wise choice.

Their wedding hashtag was #WhenAli MetSally, so at their wedding I quoted a line from *When Harry Met Sally.* "When you realize you want to spend the rest of your life with a person, you want the rest of your life to start as soon as possible. So," I said, "it starts right now."

And with that they were married. During dessert they got a text that their dream honeymoon in the Bahamas was Covid canceled, but it didn't even faze them. They'd gone through

The father of the bride toast.

so many ups and downs, *why wouldn't it get canceled?* Besides, all they really wanted was to be with their families and each other. It was a perfect night.

When Sally was seven, I had her whole life figured out—right down to which of the boys from second grade she would marry—but none of it happened. Some days we think we can see into the future, but don't waste your time—it will make you crazy. Take it one step at a time, and don't be in such a hurry to get to the next thing—because when you spend your life running to the next thing, you miss a lot.

Erma Bombeck wrote, "Seize the moment! Remember all those women on the *Titanic* who waved off the dessert cart."

Sally did not wave off the dessert cart at her wedding. She enjoyed carrot wedding cake, and despite her early indulgence with sacramental wine, she had only one single champagne flute parked in front of her, which she picked up only for the toast. She took one ceremonial sip. Perhaps it was memories of the bouncy house?

Ali's favorite planet.

Sally may not have married into the grocery store family, but Ali's family has a wonderful chain of upscale beauty product stores. So instead of unlimited lamb chops, she now gets waterproof mascara for life—which her father could use occasionally.

MELANIE'S SWEET POTATO CRUNCH CASSEROLE

"FIRST TIME I HAD IT, I WAS LIKE A LABRADOR PUPPY—I ATE IT AND ATE IT—I COULDN'T get enough of it." That is American hero Marcus Luttrell recalling the first time his wife, Melanie, made him this recipe for Sweet Potato Crunch. "It's just joy—from the time you put it in your mouth until it hits your belly."

You've heard people say, "In Heaven I'm going to eat this every day." This is one of those recipes they're talking about. And Marcus should know because nobody on this planet has come closer to Heaven than he did—after his one-day trip to Hell. Remember the amazing movie *Lone Survivor?* Mark Wahlberg played Marcus in the film based on his gripping real-life account of a Navy SEAL mission in Afghanistan that went horribly south and everybody was killed—except Marcus. Somehow he made it out alive, and he's now retired on a ranch in Texas, where he regards every day as a gift—that's why they call it the present.

Today he spends most of his time with his family—and the best part of the day is when they're all gathered around the supper table. When Melanie made this dish the first time, it got such stellar reviews that it became an instant Luttrell family fixture. "We only have it at Thanksgiving and Christmas—and I look forward to it all year," Marcus told me. But so does the whole Luttrell family,

and a couple of years ago by the time the serving dish got around to Marcus on Christmas Day, it was empty! What did he do, having been looking forward to it for months? In his exact words: "Went outside and *ugly cried* for five to ten seconds."

The next year, Marcus got his man-size portion—and it was so worth it. That time he was third in line, after his wife and his momma.

Marcus's mother, Holly, has a prime rib recipe that was in our *Happy in a Hurry Cookbook* and seemed to be America's favorite Christmas main course in 2020. I'm equally confident that Melanie's Sweet Potato Crunch Casserole will become an instant comfort-food classic, too; it's one of the most delicious holiday side dishes I've ever made. Make sure you don't miss your portion, or like Marcus, you might wind up *ugly crying* outside the dining room.

Authentic American hero.

Makes 12 servings

CASEROLE

½ cup (1 stick) unsalted butter, melted, plus 1 tablespoon for the pan

5 large sweet potatoes (about 5 pounds)

1¼ cups granulated sugar

1 teaspoon table salt

4 large eggs, whisked

1 cup heavy cream

1 teaspoon pure vanilla extract

1 teaspoon ground cinnamon

TOPPING

2⅓ cups packed light brown sugar

⅔ cup all-purpose flour

⅔ cup (1⅓ sticks) unsalted butter, melted

2 cups chopped pecans

Half of a 10.5-ounce bag mini marshmallows

1. To make the casserole: Adjust an oven rack to the center position and preheat the oven to 400°F. Line a sheet pan with foil. Butter a 9 × 13-inch baking dish.

2. Arrange the sweet potatoes on the sheet pan and roast until—as Melanie says—"You can poke a fork through 'em," about 1 hour 15 minutes. Slice the potatoes in half lengthwise and let them cool. Leave the oven on and reduce the temperature to 350°F.

3. Peel off and discard the sweet potato skins (they'll come off easily) and put the sweet potatoes in a large bowl. Use a potato masher to mash them to an even, smooth consistency. Add the granulated sugar, salt, eggs, cream, vanilla, and cinnamon and mix with a spoon until nice and smooth. Pour the potato mixture into the prepared baking dish and spread it out evenly.

4. To make the topping: In another large bowl, combine the brown sugar, flour, melted butter, and pecans. Mix with a wooden spoon until evenly combined, breaking up any brown sugar clumps as you stir. Spread the topping evenly over the sweet potato mixture.

5. If the rack is not already in the middle of the oven, adjust it to that position. Slide the casserole in and bake until the topping has baked into a sensational sweet and crunchy crust, about 30 minutes. Spread a single layer of mini marshmallows over the crust, pop the dish back into the oven, and bake until the marshmallow tops turn a deep tan, 5 to 10 minutes longer. They will melt into the other marshmallows, forming another crispy layer that adds to the sweet potato crunch!

6. Serve to your happy guests—and wonder why you can't have this every day!

PICKLE AND PASTA GARDEN SALAD

THIS IS A CASE OF EVERYTHING OLD IS NEW AGAIN. OVER THE LAST YEAR MACARONI salad has taken off, with seventy-eight million hits on Google. But for our version we're getting into the Wayback Machine for my grandma Doocy's macaroni salad recipe. I found it in her recipe box, written on the back of a bank statement from Bancroft Iowa.

Every time I have a bite of this salad it takes me back to Sunday lunches at Grandma's house. It's great! It has a ton of fresh vegetables in it, and Grandma cleverly infused the macaroni with a zestiness that you taste in every bite. It comes from a clever French dressing marinade for the noodles. (Grandma made her own French dressing, but we know you're busy, so we'll go with a good bottle from the condiment aisle—where you'll also find pickles.)

Grandma *loved* pickles. I can't think of a single meal at her house at which she didn't have a plate of home-cured pickles on the table. She had seven different pickle recipes in her recipe box. Turns out she was on to something . . . according to Harvard, pickles can help your gut health by giving a dose of healthy probiotics. This is also true for kimchi and sauerkraut. If you don't have a grandma to make homemade pickles, then you want to buy "naturally fermented" pickles. Given the perks of pickles and the fact that they're just so darn tasty, we've upgraded their prominence in Grandma's recipe by putting *pickles* prominently in the title. In fact, we *relish* that. Yes, that's a dad pickle joke, so just dill with it.

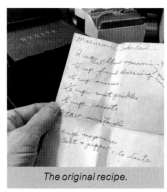

The original recipe.

Makes 10 servings

---

2 cups uncooked elbow macaroni

½ cup French salad dressing (we use Ken's Creamy French)

1 cup mayonnaise (Grandma used Miracle Whip)

2 tablespoons Dijon mustard

½ teaspoon table salt

½ teaspoon freshly ground black pepper

½ cup finely diced sweet pickles (we use sweet gherkins)

¼ cup finely chopped red onion

2 medium carrots, peeled and coarsely shredded

1 long celery stalk, cut into medium dice

1 medium tomato, cut into small dice

1. This dish requires some refrigeration, so plan accordingly. First, cook the elbow macaroni according to the package directions. Drain and place in a medium bowl. Add the salad dressing, mix well, cover, and refrigerate so the dressing is absorbed and infused into the noodles. Grandma did this overnight, but if you're in a big rush, an hour or two will do in a pinch.

2. In a large bowl, whisk the mayonnaise, mustard, salt, and pepper. Add the pickles, onion, carrots, celery, and tomato and mix well. Add the chilled macaroni and any dressing in the bowl and mix well. Cover and return to the refrigerator for at least 2 hours to even out the flavors.

SMASHED BROWN POTATOES

ONE NIGHT ON A BIKE RIDE IN MY TOWN I SAW OFFICER JIM MATTHEWS ON PATROL. HE asked what Kathy and I were up to, and I told him we were working on this cookbook. I asked if he had a recipe that he loved, and he told me about something he learned at the academy that works great when he's on long stakeouts. "Wrap a good-size potato in aluminum foil, open the car hood, and place the tater on top of the engine manifold—which is always hot." Brilliant! While idling, that part of the motor is probably 500°F, and you can cook a potato in less time than it takes to say "You have the right to remain hungry . . ."

I told him that was a great tip—and because it was getting dark I'd ask him more about it next time I saw him. About ten minutes later he spotted me heading home as our trails crossed again, and he pulled over to me. "By the way, at the police academy we called that recipe po-po potatoes!" *Po-po* is slang for "police," and we had a big laugh because the name was po-po-perfect.

Five minutes later I was pulling into our driveway, and it was pretty dark but I could see Kathy was talking to our neighbor Sue. Just then, third time's a charm, Jim's cruiser passed us, and I shouted, "Po-po potato!" Uh-oh. The brakes lights lit up the dark. The car door opened, the dome light popped on—it wasn't Jim, it was a new guy. "Hi, I'm on a noise call . . . did you hear anything?" Other than me heckling law enforcement? "No sir." He said good night, got back into the cruiser, and continued his dragnet, looking for the noisemaker.

Couple days later I saw Officer Matthews again and he gave me an update on what the new cop, Officer Steve Huskisson, told him at the shift change. "Mr. Doocy yelled 'po-po potato' at me! I get the po-po part, but the *potato*?" Bursting into laughter, Officer Jim said, "Case of mistaken identity—Mr. Doocy thought you were me." And he proceeded in Joe Friday granular law enforcement detail to tell the tale of the tater.

Making a meal on a motor.

This smashed potato recipe is much like the way Jim mashes his engine-baked potato with a fork once it's done and he has some downtime to enjoy it in his cruiser. But we smash little ones and then fry them until they get to the crunchy goodness of hash browns. And just like Jim, we like to load these up with sour cream, and bacon bits, and green onions . . . and *ketchup*.

Yes, I know, ketchup doesn't go on a baked potato. But trust me, it's delicious, so please don't report me to the potato police . . . or this cookbook author might wind up serving *thyme*.

Makes 6 servings

1½ pounds small potatoes

2 tablespoons olive oil

Table salt and freshly ground black pepper

½ cup shredded Cheddar cheese

Crumbled cooked bacon

1 or 2 green onions, dark green parts only, cut into ¼-inch rings

Sour cream, for serving

Ketchup, for serving

1. In a large microwave-safe bowl, cover and microwave the potatoes on high for 9 minutes.

2. In a large nonstick skillet, heat the oil over medium-high heat, swirling it across the pan to coat. Add the cooked potatoes and use something sturdy with a flat bottom—like a measuring cup—to firmly smash the spuds down to ¾ inch thick. Lightly salt and pepper the potatoes and let them fry undisturbed until deeply golden on the bottom, 5 to 7 minutes. Flip them and cook the other side for about the same amount of time. When they have about 2 minutes left to brown on the second side, scatter shredded Cheddar over each potato. When the cheese is melted and the bottoms are golden, transfer them to a platter or plates and top them like a baked potato with bacon bits, green onions, and a drizzle of sour cream and/or ketchup.

The long arm of the law's lunch.

BROSOTTO
BRUSSELS SPROUTS AND CAULIFLOWER RISOTTO

AT THE BEGINNING OF EACH *FOX & FRIENDS* SHOW, AFTER WE READ A FEW SCRIPTED introductory remarks to set up that hour, the teleprompter will say simply *ADLIB,* and that's our cue to chat freely about the news of the day. One of the show's former producers, Stephanie Freeman, was often in the control room and would ask us to ad-lib when a satellite feed went dead or the guest wasn't in the chair ready to be interviewed. We'd talk until they worked out the bugs in the control room, and nobody watching would have ever suspected that the guest overslept (it happens all the time).

One day after work, Stephanie was in her kitchen looking in the vegetable crisper, pondering how to use up a head of cauliflower and a half pound of Brussels sprouts; it was about the last day they'd be good. She was like a contestant on *Chopped* trying to visualize a recipe using all the ingredients in the basket. She decided to make shaved Brussels sprouts and cauliflower rice, lightly sauté them, and cheese-ify it all with grated Parmesan. You know what Stephanie was doing? She was *ad-libbing*!

But she's good at it . . . her parents used to run a restaurant, and she is a great cook. One morning when I was talking about recipes for this cookbook, she offered this one, and I immediately started making notes. When I asked her what we should call it, she listed the ingredients in order. It was kind of a long list, so I suggested, "What about bro-sotto, you know—Brussels sprouts and cauliflower risotto? She thought about it for three seconds and said, "Sounds good to me!" There I go, ad-libbing again.

We make this at least once a week! It's my favorite side in the cookbook, and it makes great leftovers.

Makes 6 to 8 servings

---

4 tablespoons olive oil

2 garlic cloves, minced

½ pound Brussels sprouts (see page 102) or store-bought fresh pre-shaved Brussels sprouts

1 cup frozen mixed vegetables (we use a medley of carrots, corn, green beans, and peas)

Table salt and freshly ground black pepper

1 medium head cauliflower, processed into "rice" (see page 102), or 4 to 5 cups store-bought fresh or thawed frozen riced cauliflower

½ cup shredded or grated Parmesan cheese

1. In a large skillet, heat 2 tablespoons of the olive oil over medium-high heat. Add the garlic and cook for a quick minute to flavorize the oil. Add the shaved Brussels and frozen vegetables. Salt and pepper them the way you like your vegetables seasoned and sauté until you start to see some light golden highlights on the edges of the sprouts, about 5 minutes.

2. Use a spatula to move the sprouts and vegetables to one side of the pan, then add the cauliflower rice to the bare spot. Drizzle the remaining 2 tablespoons olive oil over the cauliflower rice, add ½ teaspoon of salt and ½ teaspoon of pepper, give everything a stir and cook, stirring occasionally, until the sprouts are wilted and the cauliflower is cooked, 8 to 10 minutes.

3. Sprinkle the Parmesan on top and stir to coat. Let the veggies sit for a minute to melt the cheese, then serve and enjoy.

CAULIFLOWER RICE AND SHAVED BRUSSELS SPROUTS

You can buy premade riced cauliflower from your produce department, but we like to make it at home because it's so easy and we know it's fresh. Same with the shaved Brussels sprouts. Here's a quick lesson in making both.

CAULIFLOWER RICE

Wash the head of cauliflower, cut off any green parts, and break it into florets. All the florets from a medium head will fit perfectly in a food processor, but if you have a big head (of cauliflower), process in two batches. Pulse the cauliflower until you have pieces the size of large grains of rice.

SHAVED BRUSSELS SPROUTS

Wash the sprouts, trim the ends, and remove any damaged leaves. Run the Brussels sprouts through the slicing disc on the food processor. That's it!

FRESH CORN CHIP SALAD

WHEN I WAS PROBABLY TEN, MY DAD AND I WOULD SPEND SATURDAY AFTERNOONS AT Reilly's gas station, in rural Industry, Kansas, just shooting the breeze with the local guys who were done with their chores. Conversation topics were all over the map: crop yields and livestock production, the Kansas City Royals' lousy bullpen, and occasionally town gossip. But everybody seemed to know what everybody was doing, which coincidentally was back when everybody had a party line.

Today a "party line" is a political concept, but back in the 1970s and earlier, it was what you called it when you shared your phone circuit with three or four or five different parties (our neighbors). Can't tell you how many times I'd pick up the phone and somebody was talking. I'd immediately hang up out of courtesy, but some people would listen on the line until we'd say, "Time to hang up, Snoopy!" Then we'd hear a click and they were gone. There was no privacy on the party line.

Which could explain why everybody at the gas station knew everybody's stories. It might also be because everybody told the same stories week after week. During these gas station gabfests, I'd just listen, happy as a clam with an ice-cold Coke and a bag of the greatest chips ever created— Fritos corn chips. I was born in Iowa—America's largest producer of corn—so eating Fritos was my way of supporting my home state. Truth be told, I just loved them, with that crunchy texture and salty kick. So good!

I have fond memories of my mom making fresh sweet corn salad using corn my dad grew out back in his garden patch. My contribution was that I had to shuck it and get every piece of silk off, or my sisters wouldn't touch it. Somewhere along the way Fritos were added to this Doocy family favorite, and when it's sweet corn season there's no tastier or easier side dish.

Hope you like it—and wish I could be listening in on the party line tonight for your reviews!

Makes 8 servings

4 or 5 ears of yellow sweet corn, unhusked

½ cup sour cream

1 cup finely shredded Cheddar cheese

One 4-ounce can diced green chiles, undrained

2 celery stalks, cut into ¼-inch slices

1 cup grape tomatoes, quartered

Corn chips, for serving (we always use Fritos original corn chips)

1. Place the corn still in its husks in a single layer in the microwave and cook for 7 minutes. Remove and carefully pull open one side of the husk so the corn starts to cool. When cool enough to handle, shuck the husks and silk off and carefully cut the kernels off the cob into a medium serving bowl.

2. Add the sour cream, Cheddar, chiles, celery, and tomatoes to the bowl and mix well with a rubber spatula.

3. When it's time to serve, crumble corn chips on top. They'll get soggy in the fridge overnight, so only top with the amount of chips you'll eat at that meal.

CAULIFLOWER MASHED TRIO

DR. ARTHUR AGATSTON, THE CARDIOLOGIST BEHIND THE HIT *THE SOUTH BEACH DIET*, came on *Fox & Friends* often to promote his books. Kathy and I loved the books, and on the first day I met him we started making his cauliflower mashed potatoes. We fell in love with them.

During one trip to New York, Dr. Agatston and his wife, Sari, invited the show hosts and producers to lunch with them, and we went to a famous midtown lunch spot called Michael's. When we walked in, heads swiveled around because everybody knew who he was—and these were famous people doing the swiveling.

Everybody was fascinated to see what *the most famous diet doctor in the world* would order off the menu. I overheard someone tell the waiter, "I'm having whatever the doctor ordered . . ."

After analyzing the menu, Dr. Agatston ordered a healthy-sounding salad (of course), and I got the chicken paillard, my usual order, in part because it was served with a mountain of fantastic French fries. About five minutes after our meals were delivered, I was having an insightful conversion with Dr. Agatston when he leaned in to me and whispered, "Is anybody looking at us?"

People had been gawking the whole time, but at that *exact* second I scanned the room. "No."

And with that he instantaneously reached across the table, grabbed about four fries, and immediately inhaled them. I waited ten seconds, then burst out laughing. "You might make Page Six with that, Doctor!"

This basic recipe is our very quick and easy 2022 version of that mashed cauliflower, using a bag of frozen cauliflower and a couple other ingredients. This recipe is so versatile that we're sharing three different ways we make them: the basic creamy version; a horseradish version, for something that tastes straight out of a fancy steakhouse; and a blue cheese version that pairs with a lot of terrific foods. Try our trio of tastes . . . you'll love them!

A final note—after the very famous doctor swiped my fries, he got a great big grin on his face and said, "They were driving me crazy . . ."

Don't tell anybody, but these days I actually like these cauliflower dishes as much as those French fries the doctor lifted. Just saying.

SIMPLE CREAMY MASHED CAULIFLOWER

Makes 4 servings

One 20-ounce bag frozen cauliflower

4 ounces cream cheese

¼ **cup shredded Parmesan cheese**

¼ **teaspoon table salt**

¼ **teaspoon freshly ground black pepper**

1. Place the cauliflower in a large microwave-safe bowl and add 1 tablespoon of water. Cover and cook about 10 minutes on high, stirring after 5 minutes so the cauliflower doesn't burn in one spot.

2. Place the cream cheese and Parmesan in a food processor. Drain the cauliflower and add it to the food processor. Run on high about 10 seconds, then remove the lid, add the salt and pepper, and pulse to blend in the seasoning. Serve immediately.

HORSERADISH MASHED CAULIFLOWER

Makes 4 servings

One 20-ounce bag frozen cauliflower

¾ **cup sour cream**

1½ **tablespoons prepared horseradish (we use Reese brand)**

1. Place the cauliflower in a large microwave-safe bowl and add 1 tablespoon of water. Cover and cook about 10 minutes on high, stirring after 5 minutes so the cauliflower doesn't burn in one spot.

2. Place the sour cream and horseradish in a food processor. Drain the cauliflower and add it to the food processor. Pulse until the mixture reaches the mashed tater-like smoothness you love.

BLUE CHEESY MASHED CAULIFLOWER

Makes 4 servings

One 20-ounce bag frozen cauliflower

¾ **cup sour cream**

⅓ **cup blue cheese crumbles, plus more (optional) for serving**

1. Place the cauliflower in a large microwave-safe bowl and add 1 tablespoon of water. Cover and cook about 10 minutes on high, stirring after 5 minutes so the cauliflower doesn't burn in one spot.

2. Place the sour cream and blue cheese in a food processor. Drain the cauliflower and add it to the food processor. Let the hot cauliflower sit on top of the blue cheese for at least 30 seconds to get it a little melty, then pulse until all the large pieces of cheese are processed. Run on high until you get the smooth mashed potato consistency you love. If you're a big lover of blue cheese, lightly sprinkle it on top as you serve the hot mashed cauliflower. Let it melt a bit, stir it in, and enjoy!

SWEET CORN BRÛLÉE

IN THE FIRST FIVE YEARS OF OUR MARRIAGE, WHENEVER KATHY AND I ATE OUT, WHEN the waiter would wrap up the meal and give us that "Dessert, anyone?" look, I'd always ask, "Do you have crème brûlée?" It was always a happy treat when they did—it's crunchy, it's creamy, it's really dreamy. The magic part was the crunchy sugar crust on top.

For one birthday Kathy bought me a butane kitchen torch so I could make brûlées of my own. Some people might be intimidated by holding a 1,430°F flame thrower in their kitchen, but not me. One summer in college my dad got me a job working with a plumber, learning how to use a torch to sweat and solder pipes . . . a skill I'd use later to artfully burn sugar on top of my fancy French custard!

Fast-forward almost thirty years, for Kathy's birthday we went to one of her favorite restaurants, 1000 North in Jupiter, Florida. She didn't know I'd called Ira Fenton, who runs the place, to secretly order her favorite birthday carrot cake from her favorite bakery. When we arrived, the staff discreetly gave me *the nod* that signaled the cake was in the cooler. *Shhhhhh!*

Towers of seafood, 36-ounce tomahawk rib eyes . . . their menu is amazing. But that night they had something new on the menu that immediately caught my eye.

"Corn brûlée?" I asked our waiter, "Is that a side dish, like crème brûlée—with corn?"

It was! Of course I ordered it. Not only was it delicious, it was downright *brilliant*. The corn was creamy, like crème brûlée, and the crunchy sugar on top made the sweet corn a little sweeter. Win-win.

On our way out I complimented Ira on the corn brûlée. "I have it every meal," he said. If I were the boss, I would, too! He sent me their recipe for this dish, which was pretty involved, because they're one of Florida's best restaurants and they're able to spend all day making it perfect. So Kathy and I came up with this easy version—one that doesn't require a butane torch to make the crunchy top. All you have to do is turn on the oven!

Thanks for the great idea, 1000 North! We went for the cake and fell in love with the corn.

Happy brûlée to you!

Makes 8 servings

2 tablespoons unsalted butter

½ cup finely diced sweet onion

2 large garlic cloves, sliced

½ cup whole milk

1 tablespoon all-purpose flour

1 teaspoon granulated sugar

½ teaspoon table salt

¼ teaspoon freshly ground black pepper

¼ cup shredded Cheddar cheese

1 large egg, whisked

Two 15.25-ounce cans whole kernel corn, drained

One 4-ounce can diced chiles, drained

Turbinado cane sugar, for topping

1. Preheat the oven to 325°F. Grease a 1-quart baking dish (a 6 × 9-inch dish works great).

2. In a large skillet, melt the butter over medium-high heat. Add the onion and garlic and sauté until they have some golden highlights, 5 to 8 minutes.

3. Meanwhile, measure the milk in a large measuring cup, add the flour, granulated sugar, salt, and pepper, and whisk well.

4. When the onion and garlic have those golden highlights, pour in the milk mixture and whisk to create a roux. Whisking constantly, let it bubble for about a minute, then remove from the heat. Quickly mix in the Cheddar and then mix with the egg for a moment. Once completely incorporated, quickly add the corn and diced chiles and mix well.

5. Pour into the prepared baking dish and level it out smoothly. Make sure there are no errant kernels sticking up or they will burn in the oven. Clean up the sides with a paper towel.

6. Bake until you see bubbling up along the sides of the dish and the top of the casserole has taken on a dull glossiness, about 30 minutes. Remove from the oven and let it rest 30 minutes to cool down.

7. To make the brûlée magic happen, sprinkle turbinado sugar over the casserole to form a thin but consistent layer. Make sure every kernel is covered; poke them under the sugar if needed or they will burn a little. Set the dish on the top rack of a *cold* oven and turn on the broiler. Broil for 6 to 9 minutes, checking very often by opening the door to make sure nothing is burning. You'll know you're getting close when you can smell the sugar as it brûlés. It will caramelize unevenly in the beginning; quickly and carefully rotate the baking dish and keep it under the broiler until the entire top of sugar has turned deep golden.

8. Remove from the oven and let it sit about 5 minutes to harden the brittle sugar crust. If you notice a few dark spots form on the top, that's okay. Some of the corn kernels are going to poke their heads out—it happens!

9. When cooled, serve it up! Just know this is best the day it's prepared, because the sugar brûlée crust on the top will soften overnight and the effect won't be the same. So enjoy it at once— it's sweet and savory and oh so tasty!

SMOKED BRUSSELS SPROUTS WITH BACON

WHEN PETER DOOCY ACCOMPANIED PRESIDENT BIDEN TO THE 2021 NATO SUMMIT IN Brussels, I forecast what every restaurant's menu would prominently feature. "Peter, you're gonna get sick of Brussels sprouts." Which is fine—he loves them. But after days in the Belgian capital, he reported back, "Didn't see a single sprout in Brussels, not once!"

So what was the big food trend? "Everybody told me I had to get the *mussels in Brussels*!"

So instead of an eponymous entree, the locals were pushing foods that rhymed. *Mussels in Brussels* . . . sounds like a heavyweight prize fight, am I right? Now I'm rhyming—stop me before I do it again.

Maybe what the people of Brussels need is a good recipe! This is a delicious dish that's so worth it. We cut the cooking time in half via the miracle of the microwave, so it's quick and easy, and it's deeply satisfying with a creamy, dreamy bacon taste that doesn't *muscle the Brussels sprouts'* natural flavor.

One late report from our son, who was on an expense account that trip: "They were big on Belgian waffles and Belgian beer, but you know me, Dad—can't drink on duty." I'm pretty sure he had his fingers crossed.

Makes 5 servings

¼ **pound thick-sliced bacon (3 or 4 slices), cut into 1-inch pieces**

1 large shallot, cut crosswise into medium slices

1 pound Brussels sprouts, ends trimmed and tatty leaves removed

1 tablespoon olive oil

1 teaspoon smoked paprika

½ cup heavy cream

½ cup low-sodium chicken stock

1 teaspoon cornstarch

½ teaspoon freshly ground black pepper

1. In a large skillet, fry the bacon pieces over medium-high heat. After a couple minutes, add the shallot and sauté until it softens with golden highlights and the bacon is crisped and cooked, another 6 to 8 minutes. Scoop the bacon and shallots onto a plate, leaving the grease in the pan.

2. Meanwhile, in a large microwave-safe bowl, combine the Brussels sprouts, olive oil, and smoked paprika. Toss to coat, then cover and microwave on high until tender, 5 to 7 minutes.

3. Drain the sprouts and add them into the skillet with the bacon grease. Turn the heat to medium-high and cook, stirring occasionally, until the sprouts are caramelized, about 5 minutes.

4. Meanwhile, in the emptied bowl, combine the cream, stock, cornstarch, and pepper. Give that a good whisking.

5. Pour the cream mixture into the skillet, bring to a quick boil, and cook, stirring often, until thickened, about 1 minute. Reduce the heat to medium and return the bacon and shallots to the pan to warm them up.

6. When heated to serving temperature, serve up the sprouts and enjoy. The sauce is off the charts!

CRUNCHY CABBAGE SALAD

LEE LEWITTES IS ONE OF OUR TOP PRODUCERS ON *FOX & FRIENDS*—SHE'S BEEN WORKING the Dawn Patrol longer than almost anybody on the program. When I get to work at 4 a.m., Lee's already there. When I leave, she's still at her desk. She is the quintessential TV producer, who answers my quesions 24/7 within 3 minutes—and she's also a loving mother with young kids and a husband. I have *no idea* how she works full-time for us and full-time for her family—so I asked her.

Lee says she knows the importance of the family gathering together at the end of the day and sitting down at dinnertime, and that's why she's always home to make the evening meal. She's essentially done a cost-benefit analysis about what is crucial and what is not and has calculated ways to streamline everything both at work and at home, including getting supper on the table as quickly and efficiently as possible.

We asked Lee if she'd share some of her kitchen shortcuts that are quick, easy, and delicious—and this is one of them. "This is the salad that makes me feel that at least I'm getting a vegetable on the table." That's right—this is a salad kids love! And so do I, because it has a sweet and zesty dressing and a surprising crunch, and Lee has turned simple little Craisins into salad flavor bombs. And because the kids toss the salad, you wind up with a great meal and memory!

"Mom . . . Mr. Doocy texted you again."

"Benjamin—I'll answer him after we eat . . . in three minutes!"

Makes 6 servings

DRESSING

⅓ cup vegetable or canola oil

¼ cup red wine vinegar

2½ teaspoons soy sauce

¼ cup sugar

½ teaspoon table salt

⅛ teaspoon freshly ground black pepper

SALAD

One 3-ounce package ramen soup (in the square package)

½ cup slivered almonds

One 8-ounce bag shredded red cabbage

3½ cups shredded green cabbage (packaged coleslaw mix works great, too)

1 cup reduced-sugar Craisins (sweetened dried cranberries)

1. Preheat the oven to 400°F. Line a sheet pan with foil.

2. To make the dressing: In a small bowl, combine the oil, vinegar, soy sauce, sugar, salt, and pepper. Give that a *really* good mixing, cover, and place it in the fridge. The longer it chills, the better it tastes.

3. To make the salad: Crumble the ramen noodles into very small pieces and scatter them on the lined sheet pan. (Toss the spice packet, or save it for another use.) Add the almonds and give the whole sheet a gentle shake so everything is evenly distributed. Bake until the noodles are just slightly golden, 5 to 8 minutes. Set the pan aside to cool.

4. Time to assemble the salad! In a large serving bowl, mix both cabbages, the Craisins, and the cooled almonds and noodles. Remove the chilled salad dressing from the fridge and whisk it really well until it's a uniform color. Pour about half the dressing over the salad and toss very well. Give that a taste to gauge whether you'd like to add more dressing. Some days Lee uses all of it and some days less. Sometimes less is more, you know what I mean?

5. Toss again and serve.

I CAN'T BELIEVE IT'S NOT POTATO SALAD—IT'S CAULIFLOWER!

EVERY COUPLE OF WEEKS IN THE SUMMER MY MOM WOULD MAKE POTATO SALAD, WHICH was great because it was tasty—but the effort cost was high. I was the eldest child, and I had good hand-eye coordination and motor skills, which meant I was Mom's designated potato peeler. When I'd ask Dad why he couldn't help, he'd say, "I peeled potatoes for Uncle Sam for three years, Stephen," reminding me of his public service in the US Army protecting America, which would immediately send me back to solo potato duty.

Years later, when Kathy and I first got married, we were invited to a dinner with people from the neighborhood and Kathy graciously offered to bring something. The host said, "Like what?"

Kathy said, "Lasagna!" Which early in our marriage was her best dish.

But the host was already planning an entree and instead suggested, "How about potato salad?"

Kathy wholeheartedly agreed it was a great idea, although she'd never made it in her life.

She consulted an elaborate cookbook and found a recipe that sounded amazing, but it turned out to be labor-intensive, with about thirty-five ingredients and several obscure herbs that she didn't realize would require visits to two different supermarkets and a farm market. And guess who had to peel the potatoes? That's right.

By the time we were going to the neighbor's house, Kathy was exhausted, but the potato salad was off-the-charts delicious. For years after that, people would boldly ask Kathy if she would make another batch of that potato salad. Over the years she figured ways to make it faster, and our Perfect Potato Salad recipe was in our first cookbook. But now, with so many people wanting to eat fewer carbs, this recipe is the great alternative. You get the taste of her Perfect Potato Salad, but it's made with cauliflower. And you don't need a potato peeler! Now that's *appeeling* . . . right?

Makes 5 or 6 servings

One 20-ounce bag frozen cauliflower

¾ cup mayo (we use Duke's)

¼ cup sour cream

3 tablespoons Dijon mustard

½ teaspoon freshly ground black pepper

1 large or 2 medium carrots, peeled and coarsely grated

2 celery stalks, cut into medium dice

2 green onions, dark green parts only, cut into ¼-inch rings

1. Place the cauliflower in a large microwave-safe bowl and add 1 tablespoon of water. Cover and cook about 10 minutes on high, stirring after 5 minutes so the cauliflower doesn't burn in one spot. Set aside to cool.

2. Meanwhile, in a small bowl, mix the mayo, sour cream, mustard, and pepper. Set aside.

3. In a large serving bowl, combine the carrots, celery, green onions, and eggs.

4. Place the cauliflower on a cutting board and cut any larger pieces so that nothing is larger than ½ inch. The smaller the florets are, the more it tastes like real potato salad. Add the cauliflower to the serving bowl.

2 hard-boiled eggs (see page 13), cut into ½-inch chunks

3 fresh dill sprigs

5. Add the sour cream and mayo mixture to the bowl and give everything a good mixing to coat it in dressing. Cover and refrigerate until it's time to serve—the colder it is the better. A couple hours is dandy.

6. Just before serving, use kitchen shears to snip some fresh dill on top and enjoy!

BABYSITTER BUTTERNUT SQUASH SOUFFLÉ

OUR DAUGHTER MARY IS NOW A PERSUASIVE LAWYER IN DC, BUT JUST TO SHOW HOW much of a negotiator she already was, in *third grade*, she convinced ten-year-old Peter and five-year-old Sally to allow Kathy and me to leave the house for three hours on a Friday night and leave them with a sitter—as long as they could have a "make your own pizza" contest. That was the only alone time Kathy and I would get during the week, and we liked the idea of having a quiet meal where perhaps I could order an adult beverage that could, in the event of an emergency, be used to clean a knife or bullet wound.

This was shortly after Boboli introduced a line of premade pizza crusts, which made it easy to be creative. Mary was going through her pink phase—everything she wore and ate was pink—so she made pink sauce. Peter would take an entire pack of processed meat and create a single Leaning Tower of Pepperoni. And Sally would simply pile a mound of mozzarella in the middle of the crust. It looked like an igloo, and it never melted. On the bright side, pizza night was the only way our kids would sit for a sitter.

Our friend Lee worked as a sitter in high school for a family who paid her $5 an hour and let her study her AP chemistry. But that wasn't the best part—any leftovers in the fridge were fair game. The mother would make a butternut squash soufflé as a shabbat dish, and they always had leftovers on Saturday nights, when Lee would hustle the kids off to bed early so she could watch the biggest large-screen TV she'd ever seen in a private home. She became good at using the remote to scan the channels for a Matthew McConaughey movie or a *Full House* marathon starring the always-dreamy John Stamos.

Mary's prize pizza.

All grown up with a family of her own, today Lee makes this once a week, because her kids love it. They've lived their whole lives in Manhattan and think that butternut squash soufflé is a naturally occurring phenomenon, spouting straight out of the ground—already in a pie pan and dusted with cinnamon. I miss that age.

A soufflé is French and spelled with an accent, but this dish is so easy and positively delicious, so don't be intimidated! And the sooner you make it, the sooner you can search for John Stamos on Netflix. I'm sure he's in there somewhere . . .

Makes 1 pie

Cooking oil spray

One 12-ounce box frozen cooked butternut squash chunks

1 cup whole milk

3 large eggs

4 tablespoons (½ stick) unsalted butter, melted

½ cup all-purpose flour

⅓ cup sugar

½ teaspoon ground cinnamon, plus more for garnish

1. Adjust an oven rack to the center position and preheat the oven to 350°F. Mist a 9-inch round baking dish or a 9½-inch pie plate with cooking spray.

2. First, make sure the butternut squash is good and thawed or it won't bake properly. We thaw it overnight in the refrigerator—but if you're in a hurry, put it in a freezer bag and hold it under running water until it's thawed.

3. In a large bowl, with an electric mixer, combine the squash, milk, eggs, butter, flour, sugar, and cinnamon. Beat on medium speed to get the ingredients blended, then turn the speed to high and mix until the mixture is smooth, with no lumps. It won't take more than a minute or so. Scrape the mixture into the prepared baking dish or pie plate (but don't overfill it). Shake a smidgen of cinnamon on the top.

4. Transfer to the oven and bake until you see little bubbles around the edges of the dish or plate, the crown has risen and is a beautiful gold color, and when you gently move the pan back and forth, the top doesn't jiggle, 50 to 60 minutes.

5. Let the soufflé rest for a few minutes, then slice it like pie and serve it up. Just know it's delicious when served cold. So after a warm meal today, it'll make great leftovers tomorrow, served straight out of the fridge. By the way, cover any leftovers and refrigerate, but you knew that . . .

Peter and a pack of pepperoni.

RICE COOKER COCONUT RICE

ONE SUMMER VACATION IN HAWAII, WE WERE AT AN EPIC RESTAURANT FACING THE PACIFIC when the kids alerted me that they weren't going to finish their $45 entrees because the mahi-mahi was only so-so. Hungry and almost five thousand miles from home, they had to eat something, so they turned to the side dish, and Mary proclaimed, "Dad, this is the best rice I've ever had . . . it's coconut-y!"

We hadn't even ordered the rice; they threw it in with the entree. Realizing it could be the highlight of the trip, I asked the waiter how they made it. "One can," he said, locking eyes as I nodded—not having the foggiest idea what he was talking about. My second mai tai is probably the reason that despite being a curious correspondent for forty years, I didn't ask the obvious question: One can of what? I nodded, assuming it was a can of some sort of tropical alcoholic beverage, which would explain why the kids loved it.

We left, but the kids kept requesting *that* rice—so I called the place and asked how they made it, and they told me they use *one can* . . . of coconut milk.

The easiest way to make fluffy rice is with a rice cooker, which you can find for $20 on Amazon. Our cooker has paid for itself many times over—for making this simple recipe and for any other dish where rice is required. When we brew up a batch of this coconut rice and stir in toasted coconut flakes, after just one bite we're right back in Hawaii, without the jet lag or the mai tai hangover.

Makes 6 servings

1¾ cups uncooked jasmine or basmati rice

One 13.5-ounce can unsweetened lite coconut milk

¼ teaspoon table salt

½ cup sweetened shredded coconut or coconut flakes

To surf, with love.

1. The key to this recipe is *rinsing the rice—THRICE!* There's naturally a starchy residue on the surface of rice, and rinsing it three times makes sure the rice won't be sticky. I use a colander with a fine mesh so the rice doesn't just go through the holes. I put the rice under running water and use my fingers to make sure all the rice gets a wash, and then allow it to briefly drain. Rinse and repeat. By the third time, the water that runs through the rice will no longer be cloudy. Sometimes I'll put the colander over the sink and rinse it with the sink hand sprayer. Do whatever's easiest for you!

2. Place the rinsed rice in the rice cooker. Pour in the coconut milk, ½ cup water, and the salt. With a rubber spatula, blend everything together, then let that sit for 10 to 15 minutes. Stir again, cover with the lid, and hit the cook button. The cooker will magically stop when the rice is ready, usually 25 to 30 minutes.

3. Meanwhile, in a small dry nonstick skillet, toast the shredded coconut over medium heat, stirring with a silicone spatula until about one-third of the coconut has tinges of gold. Remove to a plate to stop it from cooking.

4. When the rice cooker light has switched from cook to warm, it's done, so remove the lid, stir in the toasted coconut, and serve.

CASSEROLES AND SLOW-COOKED CLASSICS

*W*HEN SALLY AND ALI GOT MARRIED, OUR NEIGHBORS across the street, Leanna and Chip, gave them the just-starting-out wedding gift every house needs, the kitchen's MVP: the Dutch oven.

"There could be no more important item on your kitchen wish list," Leanna wrote to the newlyweds. "We have *three*. One was Chip's mom's. One was from my aunt Biddia, who taught me to cook, and the third I got in France from a friend who had used it for years. I actually hauled it back in my carry-on, before they thought things like that were a danger."

I can just see Leanna standing in the air-port screening line as the US Customs X-ray operator hits the panic button and they send in US Customs. "Red alert—somebody's packing a Le Creuset!"

I guess you could clunk somebody over the head—but if you really wanted to hurt somebody, make them eat an in-flight meal—and those little bottles of wine? How are they not against the Geneva Conventions?

But Leanna's larger point is right—the Dutch oven is useful for almost everything, and Sally and Ali will have it their entire lives. In fact, I'm told that French grandmothers have been known to specify in their wills which heir inherits their Dutch ovens, so in a way they can keep cooking in the afterlife.

Sally and Ali use their Dutch oven for soup, chili, Bolognese, and the appropriately iconic Doocy family Engagement Lasagna Soup. As readers of our cookbooks know that lasagna soup (featured in *Happy in a Hurry*) is based on Kathy's lasagna that she made me on our first date—when after a couple of drinks I told her

Sally's wedding Dutch oven.

one day we'd be married—and she immediately said, "It's getting late, you've gotta go."

Since then we've dubbed it *Engagement Lasagna*—and featured it in *The Happy Cookbook* because it's a happy story. Long before Sally and Ali were married, Kathy said, "Sally—if you're serious about Ali, *long term* . . . it's time you learned how to make *the lasagna*," as if it had proven matrimonial powers.

She did and barely two weeks later Ali popped the question! The legacy of the lasagna.

I'm a little envious of Leanna's Dutch ovens because I don't really have a kitchen heirloom from my family. If we had one, it would have come from one of my grandmas, both of whom cooked in northern Iowa restaurants and were loved for their fried chicken. My grandma Sharp fried hers in Crisco. Grandma Doocy used lard.

Note to Dr. Oz: Do not read the next line.

The lard chicken was *EPIC*!

With the last name of Sharp, I sometimes wondered if one day a probate attorney would show up at our door to reveal that my grandfather Sharp—about whom I knew little—was actually the founder of Sharp Electronics. Then the lawyer would hand me a check for a bazillion dollars—but then a gust of wind would blow it into the river, the ink would run, the check would be worthless, and we'd be back to clipping coupons. Then I'd wake up from the dream. Robitussin does that to a guy.

On the Doocy side, Grandma Helen pretty much ran one of the world's largest family-owned chicken hatcheries, back when it was unusual for a woman to have such an important job. But there's a lot we don't know about her, and it wasn't until I was well into my thirties that I heard an amazing story about her.

Grandma at Christmastime.

We have no idea where Grandma was born, who her parents were, not even her nationality. Let me tell you all we know.

Starting in the 1800s and running through the early twentieth century, some big orphanages in places like New York found themselves with thousands of homeless children. My aunt Helen Doocy told me that at that time there were a lot of immigrants coming to the United States who found themselves with children but no money to raise them. So they sent these children to the Midwest, hoping to give them a better life.

Frank and Ida Butterfield, my great-grandparents, had one child and wanted to adopt another, so they got up early one day, put on their Sunday best, and went to where everybody in their town adopted children—the train depot. The Orphan Train brought thousands of children to live in America's heartland—kind of like the Polar Express but with real kids. It would make brief whistle stops in towns along the train line as the children were paraded in front of the potential parents. They were all dressed in new clothes, courtesy of the organizers, and each was given a Bible. That day in Iowa the Butterfields were looking for someone who would fit into their family. We don't know why Frank and Ida finally selected the young girl who would someday be my grandma—but they did. They took her home that night, and she started her new life in Iowa.

Grandma never talked much about the Orphan Train. She'd arrived too young to remember much, and when she was older had no interest in learning who her parents were. As she'd say, "They were folks who either didn't want me or couldn't keep me," both heartbreaking scenarios. Grandma died at eighty-eight, never knowing where she was from.

I spoke to my surviving Doocy aunts and uncle about Grandma, and nobody knows in what city that train originated, let alone what country her immigrant parents had come from. So when we try to fill out her family tree, there's not much to it.

In doing research for this cookbook, I asked some of my cousins about Grandma

Grandma with my aunt Patty.

She was a great grandmother.

and the wonderful yet simple recipes they remembered from when we were all growing up. About a week after a conversation I had with my cousin Angi Nemmers in South Dakota, a small cardboard box arrived via the US Postal Service. When I opened it, I realized I was holding—for the first time in my adult life, an honest-to-goodness *family heirloom*.

Angi was the custodian of two of Grandma's recipe boxes and had some of our family's recipes. When she described them over the phone I thought she'd photocopy and mail them to me; I didn't realize she'd send me the actual boxes, which I clearly remember sitting in Grandma's kitchen cupboard. I'm looking at them right now—sitting on my writing desk.

The idea behind our cookbooks is that we all have foods that inspire happy memories. As I thumbed through the 3 × 5 cards of Grandma's iconic recipes—including monkey bread, rhubarb torte, macaroni salad, and the snow-white divinity she'd faithfully make at Christmastime—those memories came rushing back to me. I was ten years old again, standing in the kitchen of her big house on the corner,

wondering when she'd be momentarily distracted so I could sneak a treat from the cookie bucket she kept in the freezer. If she saw me, I'd get a stern *Stephen James!* But with Grandma being Grandma, I'd still get to keep the cookie. I was the firstborn grandchild, and she spoiled me pretty good.

Grandma set out a plate of pickles at every lunch and supper. But until I opened her recipe boxes, I didn't realize how many different kinds of pickles she made. I don't have as much patience as she did, but I've read the instructions on how to make her famed bread-and-butter pickles, Texas dill pickles, split pickles, and 6-day and 14-day sweet pickles. Obviously they're easier to buy in a store, but the taste isn't even close. After Grandma died, my aunt Helen picked up the pickle mantle using Grandma's recipes and is now legendary for her sweet pickles. The last time I spoke to Helen, she had eight gallons of them in her fridge, which she will dole out to the grandkids one pint at a time.

Today Grandma's recipe cards are yellowed and worn from being used hundreds of times over the last fifty years or more. For months after they arrived I'd carefully remove them from their boxes and try to remember which of these recipes made up the meals that made our family happy. Every time I'd notice a new detail. Like the amount of oleo in baked goods or alum in her prized pickles. And then one day I noticed there was a ten-digit phone number on one of the cards. Back then people in that town had to dial only four numbers. So I texted my sisters to see if they recognized the number, and one of them immediately responded that I'd been away from Kansas too long, because it was *our* phone number growing up!

Tasty treasure chest.

A lifetime of family favorites.

And just next to our number, in Grandma's perfect cursive handwriting, she'd written *Steve*.

Not gonna lie—I got goosebumps.

Grandma had seven kids, dozens of grandkids, and great-grandkids. With such a big family, I don't know why ours was the only phone number mixed in with the recipes. And why was *Steve* the only family name on any piece of paper?

I found it by accident, half a century after she jotted it down. It's probably just a cosmic coincidence—but then again, if you're a spiritual person, as I am, Grandma is still talking to me. *I hope you still enjoy these recipes, Steve . . . have a cookie from the freezer.*

When I was in high school, my favorite writer was Kurt Vonnegut, who once said, "Enjoy the little things in life, because one day you'll look back and realize they were big things."

In the grand scheme of things, these recipes aren't *that* important—but they are to me today. They're a time capsule to my childhood, when the most important thing in Grandma's kitchen was the five-quart ice cream pail full of cookies that she kept in her freezer. And I can make them today—because I have her recipes.

Grandma's gone, the freezer's gone, the house is gone . . . but the memories are right there in my heart. All I have to do is close my eyes and I'm back in that house on East Ramsey Street in Bancroft, Iowa, and Grandma's wearing a lacy apron frying chicken in lard.

It was a simple, wonderful life . . . one that started at a train station.

Grandma and four of her kids.

IOWA CAUCUS CASSEROLE

IN THE MOVIE *FIELD OF DREAMS***, SHOELESS JOE JACKSON WALKS OUT OF THE CORNFIELD** and asks Kevin Costner, "Is this Heaven?"

Costner tells him, "No, it's Iowa."

Costner's wrong—it *is* Heaven to me—but then again I was born there.

The East Coast Doocy who's spent the most time in Iowa in the last couple of years is our son, Peter, covering the Iowa Caucuses. You may remember that in 2016 Peter took a live camera into the caucuses during primetime so people could understand exactly how the process worked.

I was a little envious. Peter was sent to events in *my* hometown, drove by the hospital I was born in, hung out with my aunts and uncle, and came away with a greater appreciation for his family and Iowa's home cooking. Most of the presidential campaigns had limited budgets early in the process, and to defray costs, events were often held in the living rooms of supporters, who would try to convince caucus-goers to vote for their candidate.

"Dad, what's that baked dish with all the Tater Tots on top?" That, Peter, is Iowa's ubiquitous corn and chicken casserole. Baked with a starch, a meat, some canned soups, and vegetables, my favorites are always topped with golden-brown Tater Tots from the local Hy-Vee.

He encountered one of those casseroles at a staffer's event near Dysersville, Iowa, the location where they filmed the movie *Field of Dreams*. In a TV standup, Peter walked out of the ball field's cornfield (like Shoeless Joe Jackson) to explain that Bernie Sanders was using the iconic Iowa diamond for a campaign event. It would have been amazing if Kevin Costner had showed up to tell people to "vote for Bernie," but this was real life, not a movie, and Mr. Costner wound up campaigning in Iowa—for Pete Buttigieg.

Peter has received an education in both hardball politics and impromptu potluck dinners in his visits to the state of my birth. This recipe, which we're calling the Iowa Caucus Casserole, is a combination of the favorite casserole dinners Peter spotted and taste-tested during the caucus season. To me, it tastes like home.

Makes 8 servings

Kevin Costner on the campaign trail.

If you bake it, he will eat it.

1 pound ground beef (80/20)

Table salt and freshly ground black pepper

1 yellow onion, cut into medium dice

One 15.25-ounce can whole kernel corn, drained

One 10.5-ounce can condensed cream of mushroom soup

One 10.5-ounce can condensed cream of chicken soup

2 cups shredded Cheddar cheese, plus more for garnish

One 32-ounce package frozen Tater Tots

⅓ cup sour cream, for garnish

1 green onion, dark green parts only, cut into ¼-inch rings, for garnish

3 or 4 grape tomatoes, quartered, for garnish

Hot sauce, for serving (optional)

1. Adjust an oven rack to the center position and preheat the oven to 450°F.

2. Set a 10-inch ovenproof skillet (we use a Lodge cast-iron skillet here, because it's exactly the right size for the entire bag of Tater Tots!) over medium-high heat. Add the ground beef and crumble with a spoon, then sprinkle lightly with salt and pepper and sauté until just browned and cooked through, 8 to 10 minutes. Move the meat to one side of the pan, add the onion, and sauté in the fat until just softened, 5 to 7 minutes. Mix in with the beef and cook a minute or two. Remove the pan from the heat, and if there's any grease in the pan, spoon it out.

3. Add the corn, both of the soups, and ½ teaspoon pepper to the pan and mix well with a silicone spatula. Smooth out the top. Scatter 1 cup of the Cheddar over the top, then, starting along the edge of the pan, place the Tater Tots with their ends sticking up. Make concentric circles until you get to the center. Wow, that's pretty!

4. Slide into the oven and bake until the Tater Tots are crispy and the soup mixture is bubbling up between the Tots, about 30 minutes. Scatter the remaining 1 cup Cheddar on the Tots and return to the oven for 3 to 5 minutes, until it melts completely.

5. For a little flair, add a thin round layer of sour cream in the center and top with a sprinkle of green onion, a few quartered grape tomatoes, and a little more shredded Cheddar. Get a big spoon and serve pronto! We like to add a little extra oomph with some hot sauce—if you do, too, please do!

DUBLIN PUB POT ROAST

WHEN I WAS YOUNG, I COULDN'T IMAGINE ANY OTHER MEAL ON THE PLANET THAT COULD possibly be better than my mom's pot roast, which she made with Lipton onion soup mix and cream of mushroom soup. To this day, just thinking about it brings back such happy memories. Her pot roast is where we got the original inspiration for our series of Happy Cookbooks.

Kathy had been making an exact replica of my mom's pot roast for twenty-five years, until we went on a family vacation to Ireland—and everything changed. Being typical tourists to Dublin, we had to tour the Guinness Storehouse and Plant and walk the hallowed halls of hops to pay homage to Ireland's most iconic beer.

At the end of the tour we wound up in their legendary top-floor Gravity Bar, where they poured all four members of the Doocy family a glass of Draught, which Guinness describes as "sweet smelling with a coffee and *malty nose* . . . smooth, creamy and balanced." I love anything with a *malty nose;* Kathy thought it was uniquely refreshing; Mary, who was in college, observed, "Interesting . . . "; and Sally took one sip and announced, "That's gross!" But she would—she was only thirteen, and until then the only *beer* she'd ever sipped was *root*.

In the days after our informative tour, we noticed how many Dublin dining establishments proudly announced ways they were cooking with Guinness Draught. And why not—it's a national treasure! I saw beer soups and stews, a creamy mac and cheese, beer brownies, beer bread, and even an intoxicating chocolate ice cream! But my favorite was Guinness pot roast, which reminded me of my mom's pot roast—*but with beer*. Why didn't we think of that before?

It's draughty in here.

Back at home, Kathy and I came up with this version, which we think is our best pot roast recipe. Why did we wait so long to start cooking with beer? After all, there's no fat or cholesterol! And who knows . . . if Mom had cooked with beer when I was a kid, I might never have left home for the University of Kansas, where I majored in Advanced Coors Studies.

Since this recipe is so delicious, our next cookbooks should consist only of recipes made with beer: *The Hoppy Cookbook,* followed by *Hoppy in a Hurry*, and finally *The Simply Hoppy Cookbook*. You heard it here first!

Makes about 6 servings

Cooking oil spray

One 3-pound boneless beef roast (chuck is our favorite)

½ cup all-purpose flour

3 tablespoons vegetable oil

Table salt and freshly ground black pepper

One 14.9-ounce can Guinness Draught Stout (or 2 cups dark beer), at room temperature (beef stock is a good substitute)

One 1-ounce packet Lipton onion soup mix

One 28-ounce can crushed tomatoes (we use San Marzano)

1 large sweet onion, quartered

5 medium carrots, peeled and cut into 2-inch chunks

4 celery stalks, cut into 2-inch chunks

Mashed potatoes or Horseradish Mashed Cauliflower (page 107)

1. Set a slow cooker to low and lightly mist it with cooking spray.

2. Cut out any gristle or big fat deposits from the roast and cut the meat into 3-inch chunks. Put the flour in a zip-top bag and add the meat, a couple pieces at a time. Shake-shake-shake, adding more beef until all is coated in flour.

3. In a Dutch oven (to keep it from spattering too much on the stove), heat the oil over medium-high heat. Working in batches so not to crowd the pan, set the chunks of beef in the pot, salting and peppering as you put them in, and sear the beef on all sides, about 15 minutes total. As the meat is browned, place it in the slow cooker.

4. Add the beer to the Dutch oven; it will start boiling immediately. Use a silicone spatula to deglaze the pan, scraping the flavor nuggets off the bottom. Stir in the packet of onion soup and 1 teaspoon pepper. Pour this mixture over the roast in the slow cooker.

5. Top the meat with the crushed tomatoes, snuggle the onion into the meat, and add the carrots and celery on top. Cover and cook on low for about 8 hours, until meat is tasty and fall-apart tender. To test that it's done, shred a little off one side with your fork.

6. To serve, plate or platter the meat and vegetables. We use the cooking liquid as gravy over mashed potatoes or our easy Horseradish Mashed Cauliflower.

ANGI'S CRISPY AND CREAMY CHICKEN CASSEROLE

"I AM THE PRESIDENT OF THE UNITED STATES," GEORGE HERBERT WALKER BUSH ONCE said, "and I'm not going to eat any more broccoli!" He would have fit right in at the Doocy house. My mom's supper was always a big piece of meat, next to a pile of potatoes with pan gravy and a tablespoon or two of marble-hard green peas or kernel corn heated briefly right out of the can. Honestly I think my mom included vegetables just in case somebody from the Kansas Child Welfare Department burst in our door and did a plate inventory. "Why are there green marbles on the children's plates, ma'am?"

Because nobody ate vegetables in the 1970s. Maybe Jane Fonda.

My cousin Angi has similar flashbacks to her childhood. "Why waste stomach space on vegetables?" she remembers. But then a funny thing happened on the way to adulthood.

Angi was visiting a friend's house and made a magical discovery.

"What is this green stuff?"

The mom said, "Honey—that's broccoli, do you hate it?"

"Are you kidding? I adore it!"

To this day, broccoli is one of Angi's favorites, and it's a cornerstone in this recipe, which she's been tweaking for the last thirty years. Comfort food? Yes, it is. Angi will take any comfort she can get at the end of the day—a nurse for decades, now she works in a hospice. After providing comfort to so many as an unsung hero, she enjoys this casserole as a nice and great-tasting end to her workday.

I just like to remind her that she was the first Doocy cousin who discovered the health benefits of fresh vegetables. Not only are they delicious—vegetables are a ripe source of humor in the family. Angi says I'm a little corny in my old age, which is better than a dead beet. If you feel the same way, lettuce know. But please romaine calm and don't disturb the peas.

I could do this all day, but that won't get dinner on the table. Try this—it's great!

Makes 6 to 8 servings

Cooking oil spray

2 boneless, skinless chicken breasts (about 1¼ pounds)

1½ cups chicken stock (we use Better Than Bouillon roasted chicken flavor)

1 large head broccoli, cut into 1-inch florets

4 tablespoons (½ stick) unsalted butter

One 6.5-ounce can sliced mushrooms, drained

1. Adjust an oven rack to the center position and preheat the oven to 325°F. Mist an 8 × 8-inch baking dish with cooking spray.

2. Place the chicken breasts in a small saucepan and pour in the chicken stock, which should cover the chicken. Bring to a boil over medium-high heat, cover with a lid, and reduce the heat to a good simmer (don't let it boil over or you won't have enough stock for later). Cook for 20 minutes, then check for doneness; 165°F is chicken's target temperature.

3. Place the chicken on a cutting board, reserving the stock in the saucepan. When the chicken has cooled, cut it into bite-size chunks and spread them evenly in the prepared baking dish. Top with Angi's beloved broccoli and set aside.

½ cup slivered almonds

½ cup all-purpose flour

1 teaspoon table salt

½ teaspoon freshly ground black pepper

2 cups whole milk

One 2.8-ounce package French's Crispy Fried Onions

Green side salad, for serving

4. In a medium nonstick skillet, melt the butter over medium-high heat. Add the mushrooms and almonds and fry just a couple quick minutes. Add the flour, salt, and pepper and stir, then whisk in the milk and 1 cup of the reserved chicken stock. Bring the milk-flour mixture to a simmer; at first it will come to a boil around only the outer edge of the pan and it will still be very thin. Keep whisking; after a couple more minutes it will bubble energetically and suddenly turn *very thick*. Whisk for a minute, then pour the sauce over the chicken and broccoli and stir to coat completely.

5. Scatter the crispy onions on top and bake until you see that the sauce between the broccoli is bubbling and the onions are starting to turn a much deeper brown, about 30 minutes. Which means the *crispy* part of my cousin's crispy and creamy casserole is now complete!

6. Remove the pan from the oven and let the casserole rest a couple minutes. Serve with a big green side salad—heavenly!

CORN BREAD-CRUSTED TAMALE PIE

OUR SON, PETER, PLAYED BASEBALL IN HIGH SCHOOL, BUT HE REALLY HAD NO CHOICE; the baseball field was literally in our backyard on the other side of our property line. During his four years at third base, a regular midgame conversation between Peter in the dugout and Kathy, who was always in the stands, went like this: "Hey, Mom, what's for dinner?" To which she'd often reply, "It's taco night!" Which was code for *Because I'm here, I won't have time to make anything but tacos after this game . . . so hurry up!*

While Kathy tried to make the tacos interesting, switching between hard and soft shells, beef and chicken and even carnitas, taco night eventually got a little repetitive, so she branched out into other dishes from south of the border. This recipe for tamale pie is one of our favorites; it comes together fast and has an amazing corn bread crust on top. As a bonus, we've included our favorite exotic taco tastes from growing up eating Taco Bell—sour cream and black olives!

Incidentally, when Kathy would announce to Peter it was taco night, other parents would say, "Sounds great—I'll be over at 6:30!" But nobody ever dropped by at dinnertime—even though our house was literally three hundred feet away.

There was one time, though, when we returned from a family vacation during hot weather and a group of the boys told Peter, "We all jumped in your family's pool . . . please thank your parents."

Peter smiled and honestly reported, "We don't have a pool."

Suddenly Taco Tuesday sounded like Trespassing Tuesday.

Enjoy this tamale pie . . . it's terrific!

Makes 6 servings

Cooking oil spray

1 pound ground beef (80/20)

1 small red onion, cut into small dice

One 1-ounce packet taco seasoning

One 15.25-ounce can whole kernel corn, drained

One 2.25-ounce can black olives, drained

1 large egg

⅓ cup whole milk

One 8.5-ounce box Jiffy corn muffin mix

1 large jalapeño, seeded and cut into very thin rounds (see Note)

1. Adjust an oven rack to the center position and preheat the oven to 375°F. Mist a 9½-inch pie plate with cooking spray.

2. Set a large skillet over medium-high heat, add the ground beef, and break it up. Add the onion and cook, stirring often, until the beef is browned and completely cooked and the onion is softened, about 15 minutes. Add ⅔ cup water and the taco seasoning, mix well, and bring to a quick boil. Add half of the corn and half of the black olives and cook until any liquid is gone.

3. Meanwhile, in a medium bowl, combine the egg, milk, muffin mix, and the rest of the corn kernels and stir just until it's no longer grainy (do not overmix).

4. Scoop the meat mixture into the prepared pie plate and level it out. Top the meat evenly with the muffin mixture. On top of that corn bread crust, make a concentric circle with the jalapeño slices midcrust, then scatter the rest of the black olives over the rest.

¼ cup shredded Mexican or Cheddar cheese blend

¼ cup sour cream, plus more (optional) for serving

¼ cup diced fresh tomatoes (we use grape tomatoes)

Taco sauce, for serving (optional)

Guacamole, for serving (optional)

NOTE: We wear gloves when slicing jalapeños, because it's hard to get the pepper oil off your hands, and it can burn—so be careful!

5. Bake until the top crust is a deep golden color and the meat juice is bubbling up on the sides, 22 to 25 minutes. Sprinkle the shredded cheese on top and bake 2 to 3 minutes to melt.

6. Set the tamale pie aside to rest for 5 minutes. Spread the ¼ cup sour cream over the middle third of the top. Scatter the diced tomatoes over the sour cream for a colorful flair. If you'd like, drizzle with taco sauce and serve with guacamole and more sour cream. This tamale pie was always a grand slam, even when the baseball game was not!

"Put me in, Coach."

Peter in the playoffs.

HEIFER IN A HAYSTACK CASSEROLE

I'VE MENTIONED MY COUSIN ANGI NEMMERS, WHO'S A REGISTERED NURSE. SHE TOLD ME once about a job working in the intensive care unit of a busy hospital in the Midwest. The ICU unit was adjacent to the emergency room, making that one floor ground zero where lives were saved and lost every day. A very hard and challenging job for anybody—and everybody took their jobs very seriously.

If one shift was really rough, someone might pick up a Stretch Armstrong toy that a child patient had left behind and quietly walk through the ICU and ER with Stretch in hand. Every staff member knew that was a silent signal that after work they'd be hitting the bar . . . just like on *St. Elsewhere*! And here's the epic aspect—their shifts ended at 7 a.m., so they'd go to whatever place was open and selling adult beverages that were often strong enough to clean a wound in a pinch while helping them forget what they'd seen that day.

To mark special events and holidays, the staff would throw a potluck party. Because people would come in at different times, to keep the food hot they'd borrow a blanket warmer from the ICU, a brilliant idea. But it makes you wonder if it was approved by the FDA.

"Nurse, why does this patient smell like goulash?"

At one impromptu potluck, somebody brought this recipe, and Angi fell in love with it. She's tweaked it for years and has made it even more delicious. As for the name, she has no idea where Heifer in a Haystack originated. A heifer is a young cow, and that clearly refers to the recipe's hamburger, but haystack is a head scratcher. Angi thinks the hash browns are the haystack, I think it's the potato chips, maybe it's a combination. The good news is that no actual hay is used. It's topped with wavy potato chips, which were probably the only actual food they had at that Iowa bar serving the hospital heroes. I wonder if they ever took the ambulance home after a morning of celebrating? They would on *St. Elsewhere* . . .

Makes 10 to 12 servings

Cooking oil spray

2 tablespoons vegetable oil

1 medium yellow onion, roughly chopped

2 pounds ground beef (80/20)

1 teaspoon table salt

1 teaspoon freshly ground black pepper

½ teaspoon garlic powder

One 30-ounce bag frozen shredded hash browns, thawed

One 8-ounce package cream cheese

1. Preheat the oven to 350°F. Coat a 9 × 13-inch pan with cooking spray.

2. In a large skillet, heat the oil over medium-high heat. Add the onion, ground beef, salt, pepper, and garlic powder. Cook, stirring often to break up the meat, until browned and cooked through, about 15 minutes. Drain the fat from the meat.

3. Meanwhile, place a layer of the thawed hash browns in the prepared pan. Spread the meat over the hash browns and set aside.

4. In a medium saucepan, melt the cream cheese and Velveeta over medium heat. Keep a silicone spatula moving on the bottom of the pan to make sure it doesn't scorch. When the mixture is

One 8-ounce package
Velveeta

One 15-ounce can condensed
cream of mushroom soup

Half an 8-ounce bag wavy
potato chips

½ cup shredded Cheddar
cheese

Ketchup and/or Frank's
RedHot Original sauce, for
serving (optional)

Green salad, for serving

NOTE: The frozen hash
browns for this recipe must be
thawed, so plan accordingly.

smooth, add the cream of mushroom soup and give the works
a good stir to combine the flavors. Carefully pour that creamy
sauce evenly over the hamburger layer.

5. Now it's time to create the tasty top! Roughly crush the chips,
but don't go crazy and make the pieces too small. Scatter the
chips evenly over the casserole.

6. Bake until the chips on top are a deep golden brown, about
45 minutes. Scatter the shredded Cheddar on top and bake for
5 minutes to melt.

7. Maybe it's because of the hash brown layer, but our family
likes to serve it with the option of ketchup and/or hot sauce. I
know it's confusing Heifer and Buffalo, but just telling you—it's
great! We serve this with a big green salad.

BOURBON BRISKET IN A BISCUIT

I SAW A DOCUMENTARY THAT SAID THE REASON SOME WHISKEY IS CALLED "BOURBON" is people in New Orleans would ask for "that whiskey they sell on Bourbon Street." Which (if true) makes you wonder what we'd be calling it if it was sold on Elm Street.

During the pandemic, I decided I was going to start drinking bourbon, even though I'd never really liked the taste. I asked my kids and some of their friends, "What's the best bourbon in the world?" One answer was immediate: "Pappy Van Winkle!" Googling it, I found that the cheapest bottle was $1,099.99. Throw in the bottle deposit and that's still out of my price range, so I stopped thinking about bourbon.

A couple of days later a box arrived at my door, and inside was a carefully wrapped bottle of Blanton's Straight from the Barrel Bourbon. Online that exact bottle started at $800, and I started to pack it up to send it back when the bourbon sender called and assured me that the actual price was less than a hundred, so I decided to keep it.

Then I noticed that the bourbon was 129.2 proof! Which scared me—it was without a doubt the most flammable thing in the house. So I did the only thing a responsible adult who's worried about fire safety would do: I poured a drink and started sipping. It was delicious, but *very* strong. When I drank faster than one atom at a time, I had the thought, *This is what a Molotov cocktail would taste like if it were an actual cocktail.*

Not exactly my cup of 129.2 proof tea! So I switched to Bulleit bourbon, with its crooked label

Zero carbs in bourbon.

on a bottle that looks like a Depression-era medicine bottle my grandma used to have in her cupboard. It's a satisfying drink, and you don't need to see a loan officer before they let you take a bottle home from the adult beverage store.

For this bourbon brisket recipe, we use a store-bought sauce with bourbon that has been meticulously measured and metered and built into the sauce (see our suggestions, opposite). We also add a little extra, not just for medicinal purposes (ha), but because bourbon is reportedly a great meat tenderizer!

You can also put that bottle of fancy bourbon to good use by pouring a shot in a cut glass tumbler with a single big ice cube and sipping it slowly as you stare at the slow cooker.

But don't have too many—the pot may be crocked, you shouldn't be.

Makes 8 servings

Cooking oil spray

One 18-ounce jar barbecue sauce with bourbon (we use Sticky Fingers Sweet Kentucky Bourbon Barbecue Sauce or Stubb's Hickory Bourbon Barbecue Sauce)

One 2½- to 3-pound brisket, trimmed but leaving a ¼-inch-thick fat cap

2 sweet onions, such as Vidalia, peeled and quartered

1 cup beef stock (we use reduced-sodium Better Than Bouillon roasted beef flavor)

2 airline bottles bourbon or ⅓ cup bourbon

4 tablespoons (½ stick) unsalted butter

2 tablespoons all-purpose flour

8 homemade biscuits (or buttery brioche rolls are easier)

Shredded Cheddar cheese, for serving

Fresh Corn Chip Salad (page 105), for serving

129.2 proof.

1. Mist the inside of your slow cooker with cooking spray (to make cleanup easier). Pour in about ¼ cup of the barbecue sauce and spread it around the bottom, then place the brisket in the sauce fat side down. Place the quartered onions in the cooker at the ends. Mix the beef stock with the bourbon and pour that on top of the meat, then add the rest of the barbecue sauce on top of the brisket. Stick a spoon in there and swirl it as best you can to combine the liquids, then cover the slow cooker and cook on low for 8 to 9 hours. The brisket won't be falling apart— it's too dense—but it should be fork-tender.

2. When you're about to serve, make an easy gravy. In a small saucepan, melt the butter over medium-high heat. Stir in the flour to create a roux. Because the cooking liquid around the meat will have separated a bit during the cooking, stick a fork in the slow cooker and whisk the liquid so it's nicely blended, then ladle out 2 cups of the liquid and pour it into the butter-flour mixture. Whisk until smooth and cook, still whisking, until warmed to a serving temperature.

3. Carefully move the brisket to a plate or platter to rest. Strain out the onions and put them in a bowl.

4. Slice the brisket against the grain, place it on the biscuits (or rolls), top with some of the onions (if you're an onion person), and top with a little of the gravy and a scattering of Cheddar. Put on the top of the biscuit or roll and enjoy!

5. We serve this with a side scoop of our veggie-packed Fresh Corn Chip Salad. You will have brisket leftovers, which are great for brisket tacos, brisket grilled cheese, brisket quesadillas . . . and of course another bourbon biscuit with brisket!

BUFFALO CHICKEN POT PIE

GROWING UP I SPENT A LOT OF TIME WITH MY DAD. I LOVED BEING WITH HIM, BUT I honestly think he felt like he had to make up for lost time with me. When I was born, he was in the US Army, deployed to Germany. The family-friendly army of the 1950s made sure he got home to his wife and new baby—when I was a year and a half old. I was already talking and walking. But my mom was just relieved to have him home—she'd waited eighteen months for him to show up so he could kill a big scary spider in the bathroom.

Those early days of our family were challenging; we didn't have a lot of money. But we did have a lot of frozen pot pies—because they were priced ten for a dollar. I loved them—as soon as they'd come out of the oven my mom would say to let them cool down a couple minutes, but I couldn't wait. I'd pierce the top of that wonderful flaky crust with my fork and take a big bite of one-million-degree chicken. Then I'd grab the nearest cold beverage and Mom would shoot me that "You never listen, Stephen" look—the one moms are taught at mom school.

Fast-forward to today, and this is our idea of the perfect pot pie. We use puff pastry crust on top—an idea we got in Ireland, where they baked lots of things into pies. I can't tell you how many times we'd see somebody at a pub impatiently bite into a one-million-degree meat pie and immediately try to put the fire out with a giant swig of Guinness. Not a workable solution for a kid, but I'm typing this at 6 p.m. and it actually sounds pretty good about now . . .

Makes 4 servings

---

4 tablespoons (½ stick) unsalted butter

2 celery stalks, finely diced

1 cup medium-diced sweet onion

¼ cup all-purpose flour

1½ cups chicken stock

1 large boneless, skinless chicken breast, cooked and shredded

One 15-ounce can peas and sliced carrots, drained

¼ cup Frank's RedHot Original sauce

1 sheet frozen puff pastry (we use Pepperidge Farm), thawed according to package directions

1. Adjust an oven rack to the center position and preheat the oven to 400°F.

2. In a medium skillet, melt 1 tablespoon of the butter over medium-high heat. Add the celery and onion and sauté until the onion softens and you start to see some golden edges on it, 7 to 9 minutes. Add the remaining 3 tablespoons butter, and as it melts, whisk in the flour, coating the vegetables evenly. Stir in the chicken stock, mix well, and cook a few minutes, whisking often, until there are bubbles across the center of the pan and the mixture thickens up.

3. Stir in the chicken, peas and carrots, and hot sauce and mix well. We think that's the perfect level of spiciness, but if you'd like more, knock yourself out—these are your pot pies! Cook to serving temperature.

4. We serve these pot pies in four 3½-inch-wide ramekins. Place the thawed puff pastry on a sheet of parchment paper and invert one of the ramekins over one corner of the dough. Run a sharp

4 tablespoons blue cheese crumbles

1 large egg, whisked

Green salad with ranch dressing, for serving

NOTE: For this you will need four 3½-inch-wide ramekins (or similar containers for individual serving).

knife around the edge of the dish to cut out one pot pie "lid." Repeat to cut out 3 more lids. (You can bake up the puff pastry trimmings as a separate treat—sprinkle on a little cheese or some spices and toast them up!)

5. Divide the chicken mixture among the ramekins; the filling should go right to the top of the dishes. Smooth it out with a spatula, then sprinkle 1 tablespoon blue cheese crumbles over each portion. Use a paper towel to clean the top edge of each ramekin, then place a puff pastry round on top of each and use your fingers to gently press the outside edges into the top of the dish.

6. In a small bowl, whisk together the egg and 1 tablespoon of water to make an egg wash. Brush the egg wash over all the top crusts. (If you don't have a brush, a finger works fine.)

7. Set the ramekins on a sheet pan and bake until the puff pastry is perfectly golden brown, 15 to 18 minutes. As the pastry puffs, you may see chicken mixture starting to bubble out.

8. Let the pot pies cool for 10 to 15 minutes before serving. Serve with a green salad with ranch dressing and you've broken the Buffalo chicken pot pie code!

GI Jim Doocy.

These Irish eyes love pies.

CORN AND CRACKER SQUASH CASSEROLE

GO OUT IN OUR GARAGE RIGHT NOW AND YOU'LL FIND TWO CARS WITH NEW YORK CITY press plates that entitle me to park on the streets of New York City *for free*! Of course it has to be in a legit press plate zone, and those are as easy to find as authentic Hermès purses sold out of a Hefty bag on a Times Square corner.

On the bottom of the press plates is the official nickname of New Jersey: the Garden State. Where's the garden? Madison Square Garden is across the river in New York City. New Jersey is the most densely populated state in the union, so where do they get off pretending it's one big cabbage patch?

It's apparently historical. Abraham Browning, speaking at the Philadelphia Centennial exhibition on New Jersey Day, was describing the state's hundreds of thousands of acres of America's richest farmlands. And then, using rather odd imagery, he proclaimed that New Jersey was like a giant barrel—filled with nutritious and delicious foods, with New Yorkers near north Jersey eating out of the top of the barrel and Pennsylvanians in south Jersey eating out of *the bottom of the barrel*. The guy was not a marketing genius. Who thinks saying our foods are from the bottom of the barrel is going to help sell eggplant?

But the sentiment is correct; fresh Jersey vegetables are some of the best in the world, and every summer at our local grocery, we load up on them—that's why they call us the Garden State.

We love this recipe, which tastes like something your grandma would make. Kathy's grandma actually lived in New Jersey in a first-floor rental. To her, New Jersey was the Garden Apartment State.

Makes about 9 servings

Cooking oil spray

3 or 4 medium yellow squash (about 2½ pounds total), cut into ¼-inch slices, with the larger pieces cut in half as well

2 tablespoons olive oil

1 medium sweet onion, cut into medium dice

3 garlic cloves, thinly sliced

Kernels from 2 ears sweet corn (or 2 cups thawed frozen corn)

4 large eggs, whisked

½ cup sour cream

1½ cups shredded Cheddar cheese, plus more to taste

1. Adjust an oven rack to the center position and preheat the oven to 375°F. Mist an 8 × 8-inch baking dish with cooking spray.

2. Fill a large saucepan halfway with salted water and bring to a boil over medium-high heat. Add the squash and return the water to a boil. Parboil the squash until just crisp-tender, 3 to 5 minutes, then drain in a sieve and set aside in the sieve to get rid of more excess liquid.

3. In a large skillet, heat the olive oil over medium-high heat. Add the onion and garlic and sauté until the onion has softened, about 5 minutes. Add the squash and corn and cook until the corn is warmed and the squash releases much of its liquid, 5 to 8 minutes. Spoon out any extra liquid.

One 4-ounce can diced green chiles, drained

½ teaspoon table salt, plus more to taste

½ teaspoon freshly ground black pepper, plus more to taste

½ teaspoon garlic powder

3 tablespoons unsalted butter, melted

40 Ritz crackers, crushed

4. In a medium bowl, combine the eggs, sour cream, 1 cup of the Cheddar, the green chiles, salt, pepper, and garlic powder and mix well. Pour the mixture over the squash and corn in the pan and mix well. Scrape the mixture into the prepared baking pan and level the top layer of squash with a spoon.

5. In a large bowl, combine the melted butter and crushed Ritz crackers and mix until the crackers are evenly coated. Scatter this topping all over the squash.

6. Bake until the casserole has perfectly set and you see some tiny little bubbles coming up on the sides, about 30 minutes.

7. Remove from the oven and sprinkle on the remaining ½ cup Cheddar (a little more is okay if you're in a cheesy mood). Return to the oven for about 5 minutes to get the cheese melty.

8. Set aside to cool for about 5 minutes before serving.

Garden Staters.

Ritzy cracker casserole.

DR. KEN'S OVEN-SMOKED COFFEE-CRUSTED BRISKET

WHEN I GO TO SEE OUR FAMILY ENT, DR. KEN REMSEN, IF HE'S EXAMINING ME WITH A camera up my nose or a gizmo down my throat, I really can't talk. But that's okay, because he does—about food! Which means I can't complain about my co-pay.

He and his wife are diehard foodies, and they love our cookbooks. He always has clever culinary ideas, and this recipe is absolutely his best.

Ken grew up in a Jewish family in Brooklyn, and on all the Jewish holidays and most Friday-night Sabbath dinners, Ken's mother would make a family-size brisket. Then, for more than twenty-five years, Ken and his wife, Erika, baked a brisket in a sweet and sour sauce. It was great, but he took brisketry to the next level when his kids bought him a smoker for Father's Day. That started his personal PhD program in Advanced Meat Smoking. But during winters at their Miami condo, the doctor started to smolder, because the building didn't allow the use of smokers.

So they came up with a clever hack using their electric kitchen oven for a nonsmoker smoked brisket. They've created a subtle smoky undertone using liquid smoke to frame a flavor-packed coffee-crusted outer bark. When Kathy and I told them we wanted to include the recipe in this cookbook, the Remsens made this brisket every night for a week, slightly tweaking it each time until it was perfection. Had the CDC done some random scanning, they both would have tested positive for the brisket variant.

Dr. Brisket house call.

Dr. Brisket (as I now call him) is able to produce perfect results every time because he monitors the meat with a smart thermometer throughout the slow roasting. He swears by the Meater Plus brand, and he's gotten us hooked on it. I wouldn't be surprised if next time he's taking my vitals I ask, "Doctor—why does this thermometer taste *piquant*?"

"Baby back ribs, Steve."

Just know the thermometer is essential because the recipe involves a substantial and expensive cut of meat, and you want to make sure you don't overcook it. You don't want to *brisket*! The steaks are too high . . .

Kathy and I love this recipe. Just one bite and you're back at Ken's mother's table in Brooklyn—or if you're a snowbird, their place in Miami!

Makes about 5 servings

One 3-pound brisket

Coarse sea salt and freshly ground black pepper

1 tablespoon plus 2 teaspoons hickory-flavor liquid smoke

⅓ cup prepared yellow mustard, plus a little more if needed (French's mustard is perfect)

2 teaspoons ground coffee

½ cup barbecue meat rub (we use McCormick's Grill Mates, sweet and smoky flavor)

¼ cup brewed coffee

NOTE: This is an easy recipe, but you'll need to start it the night before, and count on 8 or 9 hours total cooking and resting the next day! Read the recipe carefully and calculate your timing for starting the roasting process.

1. The night before you're serving the brisket, season it amply with salt and pepper, then cover and return it to the fridge.

2. One hour before the meat is to go in the oven, adjust an oven rack to the upper third level and preheat the oven to 275°F. Remove the meat from the fridge so it can come to room temperature. When you're ready to start the cooking, pour 1 tablespoon of the liquid smoke in a small bowl and brush it all over the brisket, then coat it completely in a thin layer of the mustard. Finally, mix together the ground coffee and meat rub and thickly coat the brisket with it.

3. To properly cook, the brisket needs to be elevated in the pan. Cover a large baking pan or sheet pan with foil for easy cleanup, then set a wire rack on top. Lay the meat fat side down on the rack. Insert a thermometer (preferably wireless) into the thick center of the meat and place the pan with the meat on the upper oven rack. Roast until the internal temperature hits 165°F, which will be about 4 hours for a cut of this size.

4. When it hits 165°F, lay a large double layer of heavy-duty foil on a work surface (the foil should be large enough to wrap around the meat). Lift the brisket from the rack and place it fat side down in the center of the foil. Fold the foil up and around the sides of the brisket, forming a leakproof foil pan. Mix the coffee with the remaining 2 teaspoons liquid smoke and pour the mixture evenly over the meat. Now it's time to close the foil over the meat, cinching and sealing it with the thermometer sticking out.

5. Back it goes into the oven to roast until the internal temp hits 200°F, which will take 3 to 4 hours.

6. Remove the brisket from the oven and remove the thermometer. Wrap the brisket, still in its foil, in a kitchen towel for insulation and let rest at least 30 to 45 minutes. Dr. Ken says it can safely remain warm inside that blanket for 1 hour.

7. Unwrap the towel and open the foil a bit, then form a little funnel with the foil on one end and pour the juices into a heatproof bowl. Carefully remove the meat from the foil to a cutting board—it's so tender it will fall apart, so be careful! Carve the meat against the grain—Dr. Brisket makes ¼-inch-thick slices; ours are more toward caveman thickness.

8. Serve the cooking juices as a drizzle on top and enjoy! Warmed-up leftovers are amazing the next day on sourdough bread—including the warmed-up cooking juices.

HILLARY'S CHICKEN OLÉ

PETER'S WIFE, HILLARY, MADE THIS TASTY CHICKEN DISH FOR OUR FAMILY ONCE WHEN we were all together, and we fell in love with it. Growing up in California, Hillary ate a steady diet of wonderful Mexican meals; she says one version of this dish or another has been floating around her family for decades. Her grandmother would make a legendary but elaborate taco stack—from scratch. It was off-the-charts fantastic but labor-intensive and took all day. Then again, what else was Grandma going to do with her time? Facebook hadn't been invented yet.

Hillary's mom, Vicki, has been a kindergarten teacher for coming up on thirty years, and after a long day trying to keep the kids from eating the glue sticks, she didn't have a lot of time to re-create Grandma's taco stack. So she took the basic idea, streamlined the process, and came up with this recipe, which she preps in the morning.

The dish is reminiscent of Kathy's mom's Mexican Lasagna from our *Happy in a Hurry Cook-book,* with layers of meat and tortillas baked in the oven. Hillary's family makes this dish in the slow cooker, and the tortillas turn into a marvelous texture with the chicken and chiles. They like that it's a salute to Grandma—and that there aren't many dishes to do after dinner.

Now, with Hillary married and reporting from Washington, DC, this is what she preps when she needs a quick weeknight dinner and a taste of home.

Olé!

Makes 6 to 8 servings

Cooking oil spray

1¾ pounds boneless, skinless chicken breasts

One 10-ounce can Ro-Tel mild diced tomatoes and green chilies

One 10-ounce can red or green enchilada sauce

One 4.5-ounce can diced green chiles, drained

¼ cup sour cream, plus more for garnish

Six 6-inch corn tortillas

2 cups shredded Mexican cheese blend

One 2.25-ounce can sliced black olives, drained

Salsa, for garnish (optional)

Green onions, dark green parts only, cut into ⅛-inch rings, for garnish (optional)

1. Adjust an oven rack to the center position and preheat the oven to 350°F. Line a 9 × 13-inch baking dish with foil. Mist a slow cooker with cooking spray.

2. If the chicken breasts are quite thick, slice them horizontally in half making a couple of cutlets so they'll cook faster. Place the chicken in the prepared baking dish, mound the diced tomatoes on top, and bake until the chicken reads 165°F on an instant-read thermometer, about 30 minutes.

3. Shred the chicken with the Ro-Tel. The easiest and most complete way we do this is to carefully pick up the foil under the chicken, lift everything, including the tomatoes and juices, and dump it into a stand mixer with the paddle attachment. Turn the mixer to low speed and process for about 30 seconds, until the chicken is completely shredded. Stir in the enchilada sauce, diced green chiles, and sour cream and mix evenly.

4. This dish goes together like a lasagna, with three layers of chicken and two layers of tortillas. Place one-third of the chicken mixture on the bottom of the slow cooker and spread it out evenly. Lightly top with ⅓ cup of the shredded cheese, then add a single layer of corn tortillas, usually one on each end, and rip up a third tortilla to cover the sides. Now do another layer: half of the remaining chicken mixture, ⅓ cup cheese, and 3 more tortillas. Top evenly with the remaining chicken mixture.

5. Scatter as many black olives as you like evenly over the top, followed by a nice thick layer of cheese (we use 1 ⅓ cups). Cover the slow cooker and cook on high for 1 hour, until the cheese is a completely melted slurry on top, with the black olives peeking out of the melted cheesiness.

6. Scoop into bowls and top with your choice of salsa, green onions, and/or sour cream. Olé!

NANA'S GR8 POT ROAST

KATHY'S MOM, LIL, WAS A GOOD COOK WHO HAD A COUPLE OF KITCHEN SHORTCUTS I'D never seen. When she was living in Phoenix, we flew out to see her with the kids, and the minute we walked into her home we were met with open arms and the smell of Thanksgiving. It was mid-March, but she had gotten up in the middle of the night to make us a welcome meal of a sixteen-pound tom turkey. "Steve, would you take it out of the oven?" Always happy to help my mother-in-law, I opened the very hot oven—and there was a shopping bag from Safeway.

Did she buy the turkey and was just keeping it warm? She had me carry it to the table and set it on a platter, then she ripped open the bag to reveal a gorgeous turkey with the kind of perfect skin that Martha Stewart has dreams about.

"Lil, did you bake the turkey in this bag?" She nodded proudly. I asked the obvious: "Why didn't it catch on fire?"

"No idea . . . let's eat!" The turkey was juicy and delicious. The recipe involved setting the turkey in the bag, sealing it up, and not touching it for three and a half hours. Why didn't the paper bag burn? Simple science: She baked the turkey at 325°F, but paper doesn't ignite until it hits 480°F. She was about 150°F from having her neighborhood first responders drop in with lights and sirens for a very early Thanksgiving.

Now, that doesn't mean she never set her kitchen on fire—but that story is for another day.

Today we're showing you another Lil shortcut—one that creates a fall-apart-tender pot roast that, like the turkey, requires very little manpower. She used flavor-packed V8 juice in her version, and we've updated it to use V8 Spicy Hot juice, which doesn't make the final product one degree spicier; it just makes it more flavorful. And the gravy—*fuhgetaboutit!*

We don't use a Safeway grocery bag for this recipe, but rather a slow cooker, which—trust me—*is* the Safer Way.

V8 makes it GR8.

Makes 6 to 8 servings

Cooking oil spray

2 tablespoons olive oil

2 garlic cloves, thinly sliced

Table salt and freshly ground black pepper

One 2½- to 3-pound pot roast (chuck is our favorite)

One 1-ounce packet Lipton onion soup mix

One 1½-pound bag little potatoes

1. Mist the bottom and sides of a slow cooker lightly with cooking spray. Turn the cooker to low.

2. In a large skillet, heat the olive oil over medium-high heat. Add the garlic and sauté until the oil is fragrant and the garlic has golden highlights (don't let it burn!), 1 to 2 minutes. Swirl the pan to infuse the oil with the garlic, then transfer the garlic to the slow cooker (leave the oil in the pan).

3. Lightly salt and pepper the roast, set it in the skillet, and brown it on all sides, about 15 minutes total. Plunk that roast and the olive oil from the pan into the slow cooker. Sprinkle the meat with the onion soup mix, place the potatoes, onion, and carrots on the

1 yellow onion, peeled and quartered

One 16-ounce bag baby carrots

4 cups (32 ounces) V8 Spicy Hot Juice

4 tablespoons (½ stick) unsalted butter

2 tablespoons all-purpose flour

meat, and pour the V8 juice over everything. Cover and cook on low for 8 hours, until fork-tender.

4. To make a wonderful lump-free gravy, in a small saucepan melt the butter over medium-high heat. Whisk in the flour and cook, whisking often, for 1 to 2 minutes to make a smooth roux. Stick a fork in the slow cooker and whisk the cooking liquid, which will have separated; you want it smooth again. Ladle 2 cups of the cooking liquid into the saucepan and whisk with the roux until smooth, hot, and at your desired thickness.

5. Place the meat and vegetables on a platter and serve with the gravy.

6

MAINS

*W*HEN I WAS GROWING UP, MY PARENTS HAD A standard they tried to apply to all their five kids. They wanted to treat us all equally—always. They didn't want to give a compliment to one without complimenting *all* of us. This probably seemed like a thorough-enough plan to them—but a kid can never hear enough parental praise. That need for parental affirmation doesn't end at childhood—we crave it our whole lives.

Now that my parents are both gone, I miss that a lot—although I must admit that my dad, Jim Doocy, came very close to *effusive* praise . . . once, when I was in my forties.

My mom died on Christmas morning 1997. Our whole family was a wreck for the longest time because her death was completely unexpected. I tried to comfort my father (and myself) the best I could, with phone calls to him at least once or twice a day. We'd run out of things to talk about, but it just felt good to touch base, because we both knew that someday one of us would not be around to pick up the phone.

Kathy invited my dad to visit us in New Jersey for a week—with nothing on the agenda beyond having the chance to spend time together. We'd just drink coffee, talk about the news, and Kathy would send us both on honey-do errands for things I had put off doing because I needed a second set of hands. Dad was theoretically my helper, but in reality he took

Jim Doocy was a joker.

on the jobs and I was his backup man, just as it had been when he was in his thirties and I was a teenager.

One day Kathy sent us to Home Depot and the cleaners, and then we had to swing by the grocery store to pick up a few necessities. In front of the store, my dad pulled a single shopping trolley out of a long line of chrome carts—and stopped dead in his tracks.

I'd seen that look on his face before when he'd wrenched his back, and I'd figured he pulled the cart out too hard. "You okay?" I asked.

He said nothing. He swiveled his head in my direction and pointed his arm like an Irish setter toward the front of the shopping basket.

"Oh, that . . ." I saw what he was gesturing about and was a little embarrassed.

I hadn't told him that featured on the front of shopping carts across the country that month was an 8 × 10-inch full-color advertisement featuring the *Fox & Friends* crew. He stared at me with the biggest grin and rhymed "Stephen, you're the host . . . with the toast!"

Yes, in the photo I was hoisting toward the camera a piece of cinnamon-raisin swirl toast.

The Doocys of Industry, Kansas.

I was a bit uncomfortable; I may have a 6 to 9 a.m. job as a TV broadcaster, but when I'm out in the real world, such as at the grocery store, I like to be a bit anonymous. But Dad was about to make that impossible, because his father brag gene kicked in and he spent the next ten minutes doing grinning double-takes at me and the cart, trying to get random shoppers to notice that *his son* was starring on the front grill of every cart in the store.

Nobody noticed.

Think about it—if you noticed an ad on a shopping cart, would you even look closely enough to realize that a person in the ad was pushing the cart? Of course not.

In the express checkout lane, I quickly placed my items on the belt, the clerk announced the purchase amount, and I scribbled out a check and handed it to him.

"May I have your check-cashing card?" I nodded and pulled out my car keys, which had the store card on the ring. But I'd grabbed Kathy's keys by mistake. "I got my wife's keys," I said, waving them in his direction. "Lemme give you our phone number . . ."

"Sorry, sir, you have to see the manager in the convenience booth," he said, pointing at the other end of the store.

Embarrassed that this was happening in front of my father, who'd thought I was a *big star* just forty-five seconds ago, the following words left my lips for the very first time: "Don't you know who I am?" We locked eyes and he waited for me to say something, so I did. "I've been in this store every week for the last five years."

"I'm new," he said as somebody queued up their cart behind us. Because it was New Jersey, I knew they were thinking, *What the hell is taking so long? Come on, chop chop!*

Then, out of nowhere, my father spoke directly to the clerk: "Son, cut my boy some slack, he works here."

"Since when? I've never seen him."

"If he doesn't work here," Dad started, "then why is he on your cart?" He pulled the cart back so the cashier could look at me—then the cart. Me—then the cart. Yep, it was me. He was speechless.

Then, much like a Vegas hypnotist, Jim Doocy instructed him, "Now you're going to take his check and we're going to leave."

I scribbled our phone number on the check and paid. As we walked out to the parking lot, Dad pried the *Fox & Friends* ad off the fronts of three carts.

I could tell he was proud . . . but he didn't say it out loud. Damnit!

My son the TV star!

Fifteen years later, Kathy and I were in a Topeka, Kansas, ballroom where I was being recognized as the Distinguished Kansan of the Year. My dad and sisters were there with us.

"It's official," I said, starting my acceptance speech, "the State of Kansas has officially run out of people to give awards to." I gave a good-natured retrospective of my life growing up in Kansas, talking about attending a one-room schoolhouse, and how I'd had the best job in my town for somebody who would one day make a living talking—I was a salesman at a men's clothing store, where all day long I started conversations with total strangers.

I told the crowd, "I learned it was better to tell the truth than to make a sale. If somebody asked if they looked fat in those pants, I'd say,

'Yes, you look fat.' I was seventeen. Only much later, when I got married, did I discover that I'd been answering that question wrong my whole life."

At the end of my comments I shared with them that while this boy may have left Kansas, Kansas had never left the boy. I recited the principles I'd learned in my home state. "Always be humble; don't brag. There are no shortcuts; do the work. Enjoy *every minute*. Do the right thing, not the easy thing. And always tell the truth—unless it's about whether somebody looks fat in their pants."

The last one was a joke, but every one of those other principles was something I had learned from my father. I looked over at him, and he had the most sincere grin on his face. I'd seen that smile before, but the tears running down his face were new.

As they presented me with a plaque—which is hanging above my desk as I type this—a photographer asked if he could get some pictures of me with my dad. I said, "Absolutely!" I pulled Dad toward the stage and said, "Ladies and gentlemen, this is the actual Kansan of the Year." And I meant it.

After the last picture was taken, Dad leaned in close and said, with his voice cracking just a little, "Stephen, you did good . . . we're all proud of you."

Some kids wait a lifetime for that moment, and when it arrived I was so choked up the only thing I could say was "Thank you."

The next day my family gathered for a big celebratory breakfast of chicken-fried steak and eggs, the perfect capper to a wonderful weekend. As we got into our car to go to the airport, I gave my dad a hug and told him I loved him, then Kathy and I flew back to New York.

That was the last time I would ever see him alive.

Two distinguished Kansans.

Two days later my sister called me from the emergency room. Our dad was in excruciating pain, and they had no idea what was causing it—he hadn't even been sick. Scans soon showed he had a bursting abdominal aortic aneurysm, which ultimately killed him.

One year later my sister Lisa sent me some of my father's personal effects, including a scrapbook I'd never seen. The paper was yellowed and the edges were curled from being opened and closed so many times. It was full of newspaper clippings he'd saved over my entire thirtysome-year TV career.

Looking at it was like a time capsule, bringing up many memories of long-ago assignments. I turned to the last page—and it took my breath away. Taped on the page was one of the *Fox & Friends* advertisements that he'd proudly pried off a New Jersey grocery store cart.

It was a fond memory of his son—the host with the toast.

Last goodbye.

CHEESY CHICKEN IN PUFFY PASTRY

DURING THE LOCKDOWN, I HELPED OUR PAL CELEBRITY CHEF GUY FIERI GET READY FOR a virtual event where he and his son Hunter would compete head-to-head against Bill Murray and his son Homer (also a celebrity chef) in the *Nacho Average Showdown*. To prep Guy for the event, he Skyped into *Fox & Friends* from California as I was standing in the Doocy kitchen in New Jersey. Guy had clever ideas to use unconventional things from the pantry or fridge. Not gonna lie, I was only doing exactly what Guy told me to do—but he's got a gift, and they were the best nachos to ever roll out of our house. You know what he had me take out of the fridge that was the game-changing nacho ingredient? Kathy's leftover pot roast!

Before the TV segment started, Guy and I talked a bit about his new tequila brand, Santo, which he'd started with rock legend Sammy Hagar.

Just then he turned on a dime. Guy stopped talking booze and started talking blades as he watched me struggle to chop up an onion and asked, "What kind of a knife are you using?" A little embarrassed, I told him it was the sharpest knife in the drawer . . . and it was a steak knife.

"Dude, you really need some better knives!" He asked if I wanted him to send me a set of his brand-name Guy Fieri Cutlery. I had my pride, so I declined. I'd make do with a knife that was as sharp as the plastic one that used to come with the Play-Doh.

In the Guy Fieri vs. Bill Murray *Nacho Average Showdown*, the competition was hilarious and very creative, and in the end the Fieris won for their giant tostada tower with chicken nuggets, mac and cheese, and green chile queso. It was epic, but as Guy said, grinning, "We have no idea how we're going to eat this monstrosity." In the end thousands of dollars were raised for out-of-work restaurant workers, and a good time was had by all.

A couple of days later the doorbell rang and Kathy answered. At the door was a man who asked, "Is this where Steve Doocy lives?"

"Why do you ask?"

"Guy Fieri wanted me to drop something off for him." Ah, this was Guy's knife guy. Kathy said it was my house and he handed her a heavy box. Inside were two bottles of Guy's tequila, which was delicious.

"Compliments of Mr. Fieri!" Guy's guy said as he walked to his car.

Just a few months earlier at the Super Bowl, I'd worked the fryer at Guy Fieri's Chicken Guy joint north of Miami, and on the ride home Kathy and I had raved at how good the chicken was. Then we blue-skied what would be on our menu if we had our own chicken restaurant. That conversation led to this incredible recipe, which is a clever new take on our family favorite Mamie's Creamy Artichoke Chicken (page 213) combined with the world's love for anything parked in a flaky pastry.

I'm sending the recipe to Guy Fieri. I think he'd love it—and it's so tender he wouldn't even need a knife! These pastries go great served with asparagus or a colorful side salad.

Makes 6 servings

6 boneless, skinless chicken thighs

Olive oil

Freshly ground black pepper

Lawry's Seasoned Salt

2 tablespoons all-purpose flour

2 sheets frozen puff pastry (we use Pepperidge Farm), thawed according to package directions

One 6.5-ounce package spreadable cheese (we use Alouette Spinach & Artichoke)

1 large egg

Puff the magic pastry.

1. Preheat the oven to 425°F.

2. Unroll the chicken thighs and lay them flat on a sheet pan. Use chicken shears to trim any dangling chicken parts and straighten any uneven sides so that the thighs are as rectangular as possible. Drizzle the thighs with olive oil, brush to coat evenly, and lightly shake pepper and Lawry's on top.

3. Bake the thighs until they read 165°F on an instant-read thermometer, 20 to 25 minutes. Remove to a plate to cool for about 10 minutes.

4. Reduce the oven temperature to 400°F.

5. Lightly flour a work surface with 1 tablespoon of the flour. Unroll one sheet of the puff pastry and use a rolling pin to roll it out to about 13 inches square. Repeat to roll out the other piece of pastry and set that aside. Arrange the chicken pieces on one pastry sheet so they are at least 1½ inches from the other pieces and ¾ inch from the edges of the pastry.

6. Divide the spreadable cheese among the chicken pieces and smoosh it evenly across each piece of chicken. Dip your finger in a small bowl of water and run the wet finger along the pastry around the edges of each chicken piece. This will help seal the pastry.

7. Place the second rolled-out pastry sheet directly over the first. Gently press down around each piece of chicken to seal it in dough, pressing gently where you wet the dough earlier. Use a sharp knife to cut around each piece of chicken, leaving a ¾-inch rim. Discard the extra dough.

8. Drain the water bowl, break the egg into it, add 1 tablespoon of water, and whisk to make an egg wash. Brush the tops of each piece of dough with the egg wash.

9. Place the chicken pastries on an ungreased nonstick sheet pan, then use a fork to crimp the edges closed.

10. Bake until the pastry is golden brown (the chicken is precooked, so no worries about that), 25 to 30 minutes. Because of the hot cheese mixture inside, let the pastries rest at least 10 to 15 minutes.

DATE-NIGHT STEAKS

2,610—REMEMBER THAT NUMBER.

One of my clearest memories growing up was that on Fridays—aka Dad's payday—my mom would make a steak in the broiler of our avocado-green Kenmore range. That is a tradition we continue to this day, because you need something to look forward to during the week, and a big juicy steak on Friday night is still it for me. Doing the math, I estimate conservatively I've had somewhere in the neighborhood of 2,610 steaks in my life. *Worth every Crestor.*

On steak nights Kathy's family would go to the Chart House in Los Angeles for their steaks and famous sizzling mushrooms, so since we've been married I've been making steaks with mushrooms, too. We know everybody makes their steaks differently—you can use your stovetop or grill, or the broiler like my mom, but after a lifetime of eating at the world's best steakhouses, we've settled on using a cast-iron skillet on our outdoor grill, because we can crank it up to the sky-high oven temperatures of a great steakhouse.

When Kathy needs a break in the kitchen on a Friday, we'll declare it Date Night at the Doocys and I'll make her a pan-seared New York strip steak with this mushroom-wine reduction sauce. It magically makes a tough Monday, Tuesday, Wednesday, and Thursday all distant memories.

As our daughter Sally says, "Life is all about the sauces!"

Makes 2 steaks

---

2 steaks, your favorite cut (we like NY strip; see Note)

Montreal steak seasoning

One 10-ounce package mushrooms, sliced (we use Baby Bellas)

1 garlic clove, thinly sliced

1 large shallot, thinly sliced

5 tablespoons unsalted butter

Table salt and freshly ground black pepper

½ cup red wine (we use cabernet)

½ cup chicken stock (we use Better Than Bouillon)

1 tablespoon all-purpose flour

Horseradish Mashed Cauliflower (page 107), for serving

1. Here's how we make our steaks. Let the steaks come to room temperature for 45 minutes to 1 hour. Fifteen minutes before cooking, preheat the grill to high temperature, around 550°F. Place a large ovenproof skillet (we use a 12-inch Lodge cast-iron skillet) on the grill grates and close the lid.

2. When you're ready to cook the steaks, lightly season them with Montreal steak seasoning and place them directly in the screaming-hot skillet. For 1-inch-thick steaks, cook 2 minutes per side; for 1½-inch steaks I'll sear 3 minutes on the first side to form a thick crust, then sear 3 minutes on the other side. Either way gives me a good medium-rare steak. Remove the steaks and set them aside to rest on a plate and loosely cover them with foil; they'll continue to rise another 5° to 10°F in temperature before serving. Of course the times all depend on the temperature and thickness of the steak, so adjust accordingly so the steaks are done to your liking.

NOTE: The idea is for you to make your favorite cut of steak your way—and then add our sauce. So feel free to do your thing steak-wise and skip to step 3!

3. While the steaks are resting, make the sauce. Reduce the grill temperature to 500°F. Into the still-hot skillet, add the mushrooms, garlic, shallot, and 2 tablespoons of the butter, which will instantly start to brown and melt. Lightly salt and pepper the mushrooms and shallots, give them a stir, and close the grill lid. Cook for just 90 seconds as the mushrooms start to release their liquids. Open, stir, close the lid, and cook for another 90 seconds.

4. With a slotted spoon, remove the mushrooms and shallots to a plate, leaving any savory sauce in the pan. Remove the pan from the heat and carefully pour the wine from a measuring cup into the center of the pan. Give a quick stir and return to the heat. The wine will start bubbling around the outside immediately. Let the wine cook for 1 minute, stir, and cook 1 more minute as it reduces and thickens.

5. In a small bowl, combine the chicken stock and flour and whisk to blend. Pour this mixture into the wine in the pan, give it a stir, and let the sauce reduce for about 2 minutes, stirring occasionally.

6. Add the remaining 3 tablespoons butter to the pan and let it melt. Mix until smooth, then return the steaks and the mushrooms to the skillet to warm up.

7. Time to plate the steaks! Serve the mushrooms and shallots on the side or on top of the steaks and drizzle that wonderful date-night butter sauce on top.

8. We serve these with our Horseradish Mashed Cauliflower. It's better than going out to a fancy steak house, and you don't have to tip anybody to bring you your car—it's in your garage!

CURRY AND COCONUT SEARED SHRIMP ON THE GRILL

FOR OVER A YEAR OUR JEWELER FRIEND ELLEN STORMS HEADED OFF TO THE GYM BEFORE her job at the diamond desk. She'd see the same early risers most days, but one particular guy always wound up on the elliptical right next to her. And when she'd move to the StairMaster machines . . . so would he. When she went to the weight room . . . he'd follow.

Ellen quickly realized that this guy, Paul, was a potential suitor. So she stopped sleeping in her workout clothes and invested in snappy matching athleisure separates. Her new pre-workout routine involved putting on eye makeup and blush. Ellen and Paul would spend the entire hour talking and laughing, and—you've seen this movie before—he finally asked her out on a date! But Ellen said no. A persistent fellow, he kept asking, and she kept declining . . . until one day when she replied, "Okay, okay, okay . . ."

Ellen takes care of her mother in the evenings and couldn't go out to dinner, so she invited Paul over. The entree would be very expensive USDA prime filet mignons. Arriving at her door, he presented her with a fancy bottle of red wine, which they promptly opened—and that was the beginning of the end. One glass led to another, Ellen took her eye off the steaks, and they wound up charred beyond recognition. But who cared? They had a delicious bottle of powerful wine! When the wine was gone, out of nowhere the emboldened Ellen asked Paul to marry her. To this day she has no memory of proposing, but Paul does.

We can all identify with Ellen—we've all been nervous, anxious, or freaked out about something, and when there's an open bottle of courage we've been known to throw abandon to the wind and burn $35 steaks. "I'm a bad drinker," she told me a year later.

Honesty goes a long way, and the next time Ellen saw Paul at the gym she apologized. She said she thought he was terrific, but she hadn't been on a date in years and was a tiny bit tense. She also revealed she was actually a classically French-trained chef—which surprised him given her earlier performance in the kitchen. Then she invited him back over for dinner, and as part of her charm offensive, she made this recipe—and he loved it.

Months later, during an episode of *Jeopardy!* after they had both yelled the answers at the TV, Paul got down on one knee in the living room and proposed. "Ellen, will you marry me . . . someday?"

With a gigantic smile on her face, Ellen said, "Yes, I will . . . someday."

Someday. They're both in their sixties, he's divorced, and she's taking care of her mom, who still really needs her. Neither is in a hurry, so *someday* works for both of them. Paul has a reliable, fun person he can enjoy life with—who also happens to be an amazing cook. This recipe is one of his favorites—and ours as well.

And our jeweler friend is no longer a little wistful when she works with future brides. "I love wearing an engagement ring . . . I have a lot of them!" She laughs as she pulls open a drawer full of diamond solitaires.

Enjoy this dish *someday*—it's an absolute gem.

Makes 4 servings

One 13.5-ounce can unsweetened full-fat coconut milk

1 jalapeño pepper, seeds and ribs removed, finely diced

1 large shallot, cut into medium dice

1 cup chopped fresh cilantro

2 garlic cloves, finely chopped

1 tablespoon curry powder

1 teaspoon ground turmeric

1 pound peeled, deveined, tail-on jumbo shrimp (16/20 count)

Vegetable oil, for the grill grates

Rice Cooker Coconut Rice (page 119), for serving

NOTE: This is an easy dish, but it does require 2 hours in the fridge to marinate.

The jeweler and my gem.

1. Pour the coconut milk into a large bowl. Because it tends to be very thick just out of the can, mix it with a fork until smooth. Add the jalapeño, shallot, cilantro, garlic, curry powder, and turmeric and stir well. Add the shrimp and stir until every piece is coated. Refrigerate for at least 2 hours.

2. When you're ready to cook the shrimp, heat the grill to high heat and place an ovenproof skillet on the grill over direct heat.

3. While the grill and pan heat up, one at a time, remove the shrimp from the marinade, shake any excess marinade back into the bowl, and place the shrimp on a plate. Next we'll turn that beautiful marinade into a sauce, but we have to cook it thoroughly to make it safe. Pour the marinade into the very hot skillet on the grill, bring it to a rolling boil, and keep it boiling, stirring occasionally, for 2 minutes to make it safe to eat. Remove from the heat and keep warm.

4. Meanwhile, prep the hot grill grates for the shrimp. Pour a small amount of vegetable oil on a paper towel, then with tongs, rub that oily paper towel on the hot grill grates where you'll be grilling the shrimp, so they won't stick.

5. Carefully place the shrimp on the oiled grill grates over direct high heat and cook 2 to 3 minutes per side, until just opaque in the center and firm when you push on it with your finger. Remove the shrimp to a clean platter and keep warm.

6. Using an insulated glove, pour the sauce from the very hot pan into a clean (and heatproof) serving bowl.

7. To serve, drizzle the sauce over the shrimp. We serve this with our coconut rice; Ellen also loves to add haricots verts (green beans) or julienned carrots to the plate as well.

CUBAN RICE AND BEANS

PETER CALLED ME ONE DAY IN 2016 AND TOLD ME THAT HE AND HIS THEN GIRLFRIEND (now wife), Hillary, were going on vacation—to Cuba.

"Why, Peter? Is the North Korea Club Med closed for renovations?"

"Come on, Dad, they've lifted the restrictions—it'll be an adventure!"

So they went, and it's a good thing they took pictures, because they're never going back—unless it's to Gitmo.

Communist countries are not known for their warm welcome of foreigners. Authoritarian regimes monitor their own citizens, and when American journalists like Peter and Hillary visit, they are reportedly quietly surveilled by government minders. That never occurred to these tourists, who were off the clock and just wanted to soak up the sun and drink a couple of Cuba libres.

Correspondent in Cuba.

But they felt somebody was watching from the moment they landed. And on the way to their hotel, just like in the movies, it appeared that somebody was tailing them. After freshening up in their room, they walked out the front door of the hotel and got into a waiting cab. Bang, bang, bang! The valet in a classic four-pocket guayabera shirt was hitting his hand on the roof of their car, "Sorry, you can't take that taxi. We'll call one for you . . ."

That was odd—other tourists walked out the front door after them and jumped right into a cab from a line of waiting cars. But the valet insisted that Peter and Hillary wait for an approved car, and fifteen minutes later a 1965 Chevy Impala pulled up with a driver who would never win a Havana's Most Helpful award.

"Can you take us to the Hemingway House?" Hillary asked.

"Hmmmm, never heard of it."

"You know, the home of Ernest Hemingway—the writer? The drinker? The guy with the cats?" Finally the driver spoke: "I don't like cats." Okay . . . so they asked the cat-hater about other landmark sights to see—but the driver had never heard of a single one of them. It just seemed so odd. Positive there was a microphone in the car and they were being eavesdropped upon, they gave up and returned to their hotel for lunch.

They surveyed the menu at the hotel restaurant, and Peter knew exactly what he wanted—an authentic Cubano sandwich. After he ordered it, the waiter said, "Today no pickles." They could make the sandwich, but it would be missing a critical ingredient. It arrived and it was good . . . despite the lack of pickles.

Next day, next place, he tried again and ordered another Cubano. "No mustard and no Swiss cheese," announced that waiter nonchalantly. The sandwich arrived and it was good . . . despite the lack of mustard and Swiss cheese.

Thanks to the Castros' food rationing, Peter never got a complete Cubano—in Cuba.

They wound up leaving three days earlier than planned, because it was impossible for them to relax on their vacation, with a government minder never far away.

Fox's Lawrence Jones and I were covering breaking news out of Havana one day, and during a commercial he said, "Have you ever had Cuban black beans and rice?" I had, and pointed in the general direction of a terrific Cuban place a block from Fox that had it on their menu. Next time I spoke to Peter, I asked him if he'd had black beans and rice in Havana, and he told me that was actually the most reliable thing on the menus, so he'd had it plenty of times and it was delicious. So we came up with this simple recipe with a little added pineapple as a tropical tribute to their getaway to the paranoid paradise.

By the way, Peter reported that the island's bartenders "make a pretty good Cuban mojito." Clearly the Communist government will keep the white rum flowing and the mint muddled so the buzzed locals don't notice the only way to get pickles or yellow mustard is to swim to Fort Lauderdale.

Makes about 5 servings

1 tablespoon olive oil

1 medium red bell pepper, cut into ¼-inch-wide and 1-inch-long sticks

1 medium sweet onion, cut into medium dice

1 carrot, peeled and coarsely grated

2 cups cooked rice (we use jasmine), kept warm

1½ cups diced cooked ham

One 15.5-ounce can black beans, undrained

1 cup frozen peas, thawed

½ cup chicken stock

1 teaspoon freshly ground black pepper

One 8-ounce can crushed pineapple

1. In a large nonstick skillet, heat the olive oil over medium-high heat. Add the bell pepper, onion, and carrot and sauté until the onion softens nicely, 4 to 5 minutes. Add the cooked rice, ham, black beans, peas, chicken stock, and black pepper, give a big stir to combine, and heat the mixture to serving temperature, about 5 minutes.

2. Remove the pan from the stove and stir in the crushed pineapple—it doesn't need cooking, just eating!

KATHY'S CALIFORNIA CABERNET CHICKEN SURPRISE

THIS RECIPE IS DELICIOUS—AND CAME ABOUT AS A COMPLETE ACCIDENT. BUT THAT HAPpens a lot with food.

Legend has it a restaurant customer in Upstate New York complained to the waiter that his French fries were too thick—not crispy enough—and sent them back to the kitchen. The chef made a second batch, but the customer, clearly somebody with a *chip on their shoulder*, sent them back. They were still too thick, not crispy enough! The chef didn't like people complaining about his fries, so in an act of restaurant revenge, he sliced them paper thin and left them in the fryer until they were hard as a rock, then super-salted them. The customer—who's always right—absolutely loved them. And so did chef George Crum, who'd just invented the potato chip. By mistake.

At the St. Louis World's Fair, an ice cream seller sold so many orders that he ran out of cups. The vendor next to him was selling a popular pastry from his native Syria called *zalabis*. It was a large waffle-like cookie that was baked flat between two metal plates. Apparently the two vendors talked, and the cookie maker baked a bunch of zalabis waffles and rolled them into conical shapes. Once they cooled, he handed them to the ice cream vendor, who filled the open top side with ice cream—and instantly invented the ice cream cone. History might be different had the ice cream guy been set up next to a burrito maker. Another happy accident.

This chicken recipe started with cow. One time I was making our Cast-Iron Cabernet Cheeseburgers (page 81). I was sautéing some vegetables when I opened the pre-pattied brisket burgers and immediately noticed a funny smell. I checked the date and the meat was not expired, so I walked it over to Kathy, who said to toss it, so I did. There was no zalabis vendor next door, so Kathy said, "We have some chicken breasts . . ." So I sliced them into cutlets, followed her ad-libbed instructions, and ten minutes later this star was born. We have *surprise* in the name of this recipe for a reason!

"It's hard to go wrong when you're cooking with wine," I said. Kathy paused and made that face she does right before she offers up one of her delicious bon mots. Then, with a pitch-perfect Liza Minnelli voice she belted out, *"Life is a cabernet, old chum, come to the cabernet!"*

Makes 4 servings

Bag of chips—on my lips.

2 chicken breasts, sliced horizontally to make 4 thin cutlets

Table salt and freshly ground black pepper

One 10-ounce package button mushrooms, thinly sliced

1 large shallot, sliced into thin rings

2 tablespoons unsalted butter

1 cup red wine (we use cabernet; there are no good substitutes)

2 tablespoons balsamic vinegar

Brosotto (page 101), for serving

1. Preheat the grill to high. We cook this on our outdoor grill because it gets hotter than our stove (about 550°F) and reduces the wine faster than the kitchen stove. You can make it on the stove or in your oven; adjust your times and temps accordingly.

2. Preheat a large ovenproof skillet (such as cast-iron) on the grill for about 10 minutes.

3. Meanwhile, to tenderize the chicken cutlets, use the smooth side of a meat mallet to gently pound them down to roughly a ½-inch thickness. Lightly salt and pepper them and set them aside.

4. Add the mushrooms, shallot, and butter to the skillet; the butter will melt and brown immediately. Stir the mushrooms and shallot, close the grill lid, and cook 1 minute. Open the lid and stir again and you'll see that the mushrooms are quickly releasing their liquids. Close the lid and cook another 2 minutes.

5. Open the lid, remove the pan from the heat, and carefully pour the wine from a measuring cup into the center of the pan, then return to the heat. It will quickly start bubbling. Let it simmer about 30 seconds. Stir in the balsamic vinegar and cook a quick minute, until it slightly thickens and reduces. Use a slotted spoon to carefully remove the mushrooms and shallots from the pan.

6. Place the chicken cutlets in the pan, close the lid, and cook undisturbed for about 4 minutes—just know you won't see any golden highlights on the bottom because they're cooking in a red wine. Flip and cook the other side until the chicken has taken on a deep, delicious color from the cabernet working its magic, about 4 minutes longer. That should be enough cooking time, but you really have to check with an instant thermometer to make sure the thickest part of the chicken is fully cooked to 165°F.

7. Return the mushrooms to the pan, mix to combine with the chicken, and let them quickly warm up as they glaze in the remaining sauce.

8. To serve, place the chicken on plates or a platter. Serve with the mushrooms on top. A great vegetable accompaniment is our delicious Brosotto. Enjoy!

STUFFED TURKEY TWIST

PETER DOOCY MISSED COMING HOME FOR THANKSGIVING 2020, THE FIRST TIME WE'D not all been together for that holiday as a family. That meant he'd miss his mom's turkey and trimmings, but such is life on the road during an election year; Peter and his producer, Pat Ward, were covering the president-elect's transition, pretty much living inside a rental Chrysler Pacifica that was parked as close to Joe Biden's house as they could get without being shooed away by the Secret Service.

With so many restaurants closed for indoor dining, they had very limited food choices. Then, while picking up snacks at a nearby Wawa convenience store, Peter saw a sign advertising the Gobbler. Apparently every taste of Thanksgiving—hot turkey, dressing, and cranberries—were all brilliantly served on a hoagie bun. Peter ordered one on the spot, and it was delicious. It was also the closest he'd get to his mother's turkey and stuffing that year, so he ordered one every day through Thanksgiving.

"It was Wawa wonderful," he said.

When he later told us about the all-in-one simplicity of the Gobbler sandwich, it reminded Kathy of how she used to cook an all-in-one turkey on Easter, with leeks and dried fruit, all rolled up in what was essentially a butterflied turkey breast. So when Peter announced he would bring his wife, Hillary, to our house in New Jersey for Thanksgiving 2021, Kathy and I came up with this fantastic recipe and had it waiting when they arrived the day before Thanksgiving. They loved it—and we decided to include it in this cookbook.

Turkey twistin' time.

When I asked what we should call the recipe, after some so-so suggestions Hillary proposed the Stuffed Turkey Twist, then grabbed Peter and started to dance the Twist. "When you're stuffed with turkey, you've got to do the Stuffed Turkey Twist!"

Then she added, "It's not just a dish . . . it's a dance!" The newlyweds continued to twist for about thirty seconds—until they needed to catch their breath and enjoy a piece of pumpkin pie and a whipped cream chaser.

Makes 14 to 16 slices (6 to 8 servings)

1 pound bulk pork sausage, crumbled (we use Jimmy Dean)

1 medium leek, trimmed, halved lengthwise, rinsed, and sliced into ¼-inch half-moons

1 cup finely diced celery

4 cups (32 ounces) chicken stock

2 tablespoons unsalted butter

½ teaspoon freshly ground black pepper, plus more to taste

One 12-ounce bag dried stuffing (we use Pepperidge Farm herb-seasoned classic stuffing)

½ cup Craisins (sweetened dried cranberries)

One whole skin-on, boneless turkey breast (4 to 5 pounds with both breasts)

1 large sweet onion, trimmed and sliced into 4 evenly thick rings

1 tablespoon olive oil

Kosher salt

Special equipment: Kitchen twine

NOTE: We order the turkey breast from our butcher a few days in advance. You won't need all the stuffing for the turkey roll; place the extra in a 1-quart greased baking dish and bake it, uncovered, alongside the turkey for the last 35 to 40 minutes of roasting, until it's a good serving temperature.

1. Preheat the oven to 350°F.

2. In a large skillet over medium-high heat, crumble the sausage, add the leek and celery, and sauté until the sausage is completely cooked with brown highlights and the leeks and celery have softened, about 10 minutes. Add 2 cups of the chicken stock and the butter and bring the mixture to a quick boil. Remove from the heat, then mix in the black pepper. Stir in the stuffing and Craisins and mix well. Set aside.

3. Butterflying a turkey is a snap, but if you've never done it, you can ask your butcher or watch one of the many videos online to get the picture. For this recipe, you're working with two boneless breasts, skin on, and connected in the middle. Place the area where the neck was at the top. With a long knife, start at the narrowest part of the meat and slice parallel to the cutting board *almost* the length of the breast, keeping it connected at the top/neck part. Leave about 1 inch intact at the top part. Hinge open the breast to make a large, wide single piece of turkey. Your butterflying is done.

4. Place plastic wrap over the meat and pound down with the smooth part of a meat mallet until the meat is about ½ inch thick. Remove the plastic wrap, then top the turkey with a ¾-inch-thick layer of the stuffing, leaving about 1½ inches empty around the edges (see Note). Using your hands, firmly press the stuffing into place.

5. Starting at the top end, carefully roll the turkey toward you until you get all the way to the bottom. To keep it from unrolling while cooking, use kitchen twine to tie up the bird about every 2 inches. Tie the ends closed as well for even cooking.

6. In a 9 × 13-inch roasting pan, line up the 4 onion slices in a row, then lay the turkey roll skin side up on top of the onions. This keeps the meat slightly elevated while adding flavor. Pour the remaining 2 cups chicken stock into the pan. Drizzle the olive oil over the skin and use a brush (or your fingers) to distribute it evenly. Lightly season with kosher salt and pepper.

7. Roast until the internal temp reads 165°F on an instant-read thermometer, about 2 hours, basting every 30 minutes. Check the center and both ends of the turkey roll with the thermometer, to make sure the whole roll is at least 165°F.

8. Let the roll sit for about 10 minutes, then snip and remove the string. Cut the roll into ¾-inch-thick slices. Stir up the pan liquids and use as a light gravy. We plate about 2 slices per serving.

FULLY LOADED TACO PIE

YOU KNOW HOW IT IS—ONCE YOU TURN ON THE STOVE, THERE'S NO GOING TO THE STORE for missing ingredients, especially if you have a glass of wine parked next to the range to assist with your dinnertime preparation. One night I'd started frying hamburger and an onion for Taco Tuesday, and when I opened the yellow box of taco shells, I discovered there was only one left in the box. I immediately blamed Sally, until Kathy reminded me I'd broken up half a dozen shells after she'd made fresh guacamole because I'd assured her we had tortilla chips. We did not.

It was too late to go out and buy more, so I became a contestant on *Guy's Grocery Games* as we surveyed the cupboards and fridge for substitutes. The half a bag of Fritos *I didn't eat the night before* and a single Pillsbury pie shell in the icebox were the only things approaching a taco's crispy or crunchy shell. That's when Kathy suggested making a taco pie with two different crusts—soft and crunchy—kind of like the Crunchwrap at Taco Bell.

As we blind-baked the bottom pie crust, I had a flashback to a taste from my childhood. Do you remember when Taco Bell put sliced black olives and sour cream on their Burrito Supreme? Kathy and I both *love* that taste, and because we had both of those ingredients on hand, they're in here, too!

The family review for the final product: "Tasty, Dad!" And that's how that Taco Tuesday turned out terrific!

From that day forward, not only would we check the cupboards for the necessary ingredients, we'd also shake the boxes to make sure there was actually something inside. Then again, I don't know why I'm complaining—because I once used taco shells for tortilla chips, we wound up with a new family favorite recipe!

Makes 6 to 8 servings

---

1 refrigerated or thawed frozen pie crust, at room temperature

1 pound lean ground beef

1 small onion, finely diced

One 1-ounce packet taco seasoning mix

½ cup taco sauce or salsa

1 cup sour cream

One 2.25-ounce can sliced ripe black olives, drained

2½ cups Fritos Original Corn Chips, or similar brand

1 cup shredded Cheddar cheese

Guacamole, for serving (optional)

1. Adjust an oven rack to the center position and preheat the oven to 450°F.

2. Roll out the pie crust to fit an ungreased 9-inch pie plate. Press the crust firmly in place on the rim and on the bottom so that it won't pull away from the pan while baking. Jab the bottom and sides of the crust with a fork to keep it from puffing up when baking.

3. Bake about 10 minutes, or until the crust is a lovely light golden brown. Set the crust aside.

4. Reduce the oven temperature to 350°F.

5. Meanwhile, in a large skillet, crumble in the ground beef, add the onion, and sauté over medium-high heat until the meat is completely cooked and the onion has softened, 12 to 15 minutes. Spoon any fat out of the pan. Add ⅔ cup water and the taco seasoning mix packet and bring to a boil. Reduce the heat and simmer until most of the liquid has cooked away, then stir in the taco sauce, which adds a nice zesty dimension to the taco meat. Warm that up to serving temperature.

6. Place the taco meat in the baked pie crust and smooth it out with a spatula. Spoon the sour cream over the meat and spread it out to form an even layer (don't worry if it mixes in a bit). Top with the sliced black olives.

7. Next, let's make the crunchy top. Place the Fritos into a zip-top bag. Crush the chips into ½-inch pieces (don't go overboard— we don't want corn-chip powder). Add the Cheddar to the bag and shake to completely combine. Sprinkle the mixture over the pie to form an even but not too thick layer (you may have a little left over).

8. Line the edge of the crust with foil so it doesn't overbake. Bake the pie for 8 to 10 minutes to melt the cheese into the chips.

9. Let the pie rest for at least 5 minutes to firm up a bit, then cut into wedges and serve. You can garnish with guacamole if you like, but pretty much every taco ingredient is already installed in the pie—it's fully loaded!

LEMON-DILL SALMON PICCATA

IT SEEMS LIKE EVERY TIME WE VISIT ONE FRIEND IN THEIR NEW YORK CITY APARTMENT around dinnertime, the instant the elevator doors open on their floor, it hits us right in the face . . . *somebody's cooking fish*. I'm sure the fish is delicious for whoever is polluting the apartment building, but come on, unless we're invited to that apartment to share the goodness, I don't want to smell it! And that smell seems to linger . . . for days. Am I right?

But *we love salmon*, and if we can't cook it outdoors on the grill, Kathy and I have come up with a simple way to minimize that odor while maximizing the flavor. We bake the salmon quickly at a high heat—but not so hot it spatters in the oven and makes a mess.

My family say it's a restaurant-quality salmon dish, which every cook loves to hear. And that makes me simply happy. A side of asparagus is always a good companion to this recipe.

Makes 4 servings

---

4 skin-on salmon fillets, 1½ inches thick

Table salt and freshly ground black pepper

½ cup white wine or chicken stock

½ cup chicken stock

1 teaspoon brine from a jar of capers

2½ tablespoons capers, undrained (brine included)

Juice of ½ lemon

2 tablespoons unsalted butter

Fresh dill, for garnish

1. Preheat the oven to 450°F. Top a sheet pan with a double layer of foil (for quick cleanup).

2. Place the salmon fillets skin side down on the foil. Lightly salt and pepper the fillets and bake until cooked to your level of doneness (the USDA calls for 145°F at the thickest part of the salmon), 15 to 18 minutes.

3. Meanwhile, make the piccata sauce. In a medium skillet, bring the wine to a boil over medium-high heat. Let it bubble across the pan for about 2 minutes, until it reduces by half. Add the chicken stock and bring to a boil for 1 minute. Add the capers (and caper brine), and stir to blend the flavors. Reduce the heat to keep warm until the salmon is done.

4. Just before the salmon comes out of the oven, increase the heat under the sauce to medium-high and add the lemon juice and butter. When the butter melts, set the pan aside off the heat.

5. Now let's remove the cooked salmon from the pan—and from its skin. At one end of a fillet, push a spatula through a little bit of the meat to the bottom of the pan and then slide the spatula all the way under the salmon. Lift the spatula and the skin will be stuck to the foil. Magic!

6. Place the salmon fillets into the hot piccata sauce in the pan, glazing them with the sauce.

7. Transfer the salmon to plates and spoon the sauce and capers on top. With kitchen shears, snip the wispy tips of dill fronds over the salmon. Serve promptly—and toss out that foil!

EASY CAPRESE CHICKEN

THE SUMMER OF 2003 WAS THE HOTTEST ON RECORD IN EUROPE, AND THAT'S WHEN Peter and his cousin Dane studied at England's Oxford University. At the end of the term we flew to pick up Peter and make a little holiday of it, so we checked into the nicest hotel in Oxford—but our room was like a sauna. I called the front desk to help me locate the thermostat to turn on the air conditioning. The desk clerk told me to walk toward the window.

"Okay, I'm at the window."

"Good, now open it."

We found out that summer that a lot of northern Europe isn't air conditioned. Luckily a very good friend had made a recommendation for where to stay in Rome. "It's a hidden gem," he said. Kathy booked it immediately. When the taxi driver pulled up to the hotel, we told him it was the wrong place. "That's not the hotel in the photos," Kathy said, and I nodded in agreement, but the kids were already out of the car because it had been an hour-long trip from the airport and the Fiat's AC was busted. The driver knew his business; that was our hotel. But it was not the place in the picture—this was a dump. It did have air conditioning, but it made a constant scary metal-on-metal screech of the kind one generally associates with a disaster movie in which a jam-packed airliner is going down in the middle of the Pacific and the only one who can save them is Dwayne Johnson, the Rock, who luckily is air marshaling that flight.

We were still seriously jet-lagged, but with the noisy AC nobody got a good night's sleep. On the third day of doing tourist things, Sally made an announcement regarding a tour we had reserved later that afternoon: "Mary's too pooped for the pope." She was, but we still went—because we assumed the Vatican was the one place in the Eternal City that would have whisper-quiet air conditioning.

That night we had dinner at a place called Il Pomodorino on the Via Campania. I asked the waiter what the house specialty was, and he asked, "What foods don't you like?" That was easy, so we all told him, and he said, "We will make you dinner. Trust us."

Of course that's what the online hotel company had said and we'd ended up in a firetrap, but we trusted him and he brought out the greatest meal anybody had that night in Rome—perfect for a hot summer night. First he brought us freshly sliced prosciutto from a giant ham displayed in the middle of the dining room with a spotlight over it like a featured performer. It was super fresh and delicious, like the hunks of aged Parmesan he brought just before our first-ever bites of bruschetta. An array of entrees followed that included this chicken caprese, which they made with fresh pesto and a balsamic glaze. The desserts were perfectly ripe melon, scoops of gelato, and squares of tiramisu, all of which were chilled, unlike our hotel rooms.

It was a showstopping meal, and then the best part was when the bill came. They'd given us a *big* discount, probably because the waiter liked us. Next morning, after the chianti wore off, I realized the bill was in euros.

Enjoy this chicken from that night. Buon appetito!

Makes 4 servings

---

2 boneless, skinless chicken breasts

Table salt and freshly ground black pepper

Garlic powder

2 tablespoons extra-virgin olive oil

4 deli slices mozzarella cheese

½ pint grape tomatoes, quartered

Store-bought refrigerated basil pesto, for drizzling (we love Giovanni Rana brand)

Balsamic glaze, for garnish

1. First, a little prep work: Slice both breasts horizontally in half to make 4 similar-size cutlets. Cover the chicken with plastic wrap to avoid splattering, then use the smooth side of a meat mallet to gently pound the breasts to about ½ inch thick. They'll cook faster, and it really does tenderize the meat. Sprinkle the cutlets lightly with salt, pepper, and garlic powder on both sides.

2. Heat a large nonstick skillet over medium-high heat. Add the oil, swirl to coat the pan, and add the chicken pieces. Cook, undisturbed, until a little browned on the bottom, about 4 minutes. Flip and cook the other side for 2 more minutes. Fold the mozzarella slices in half so that they are double thickness and place one on top of each piece of chicken. Add the tomatoes to the pan, cut side down, and lightly sprinkle with salt and pepper. Cover the pan and cook 2 more minutes to melt the cheese. Make sure the chicken is at least 165°F on an instant-read thermometer.

3. Remove the chicken cutlets to individual plates to rest. Toss and sauté the tomatoes until they've softened and have some dark highlights, another 2 minutes.

4. Top each cutlet with tomatoes, then drizzle some pesto on top. A zigzag squirt of balsamic glaze completes the caprese. Serve and enjoy!

Got gelato?

That hot summer in Oxford.

BUFFALO AND BLUE
CHICKEN AND CHEESE

I FIGURED OUR DAUGHTER MARY GOT HOOKED ON BUFFALO SAUCE AT BOSTON COLLEGE'S legendary tailgates. Nope, she told me, it's because she was up late at night (working in the library, I prayed) and there was only one food place open and they had a great Buffalo sauce'd menu. She remembered the delivery guy once said, "Mary, you remind me of my daughter," and because it was raining hard, he drove her back to her dorm.

"Mary!" I hollered. "They always say you r*emind me of somebody* until they get you in their car, knock you in the head, and steal your watch."

"Dad—I wasn't alone, I was with my friends. And he wasn't a stranger . . . I *kinda worked* there." *Mary had a job during college? Never heard this story, never not once.*

Turns out, Mary was such a regular customer at this spot that when they'd see her come in, they'd just start cooking her food before she ordered. A year later she'd become such good friends with everybody there the cooks would invite her back into the kitchen to talk as she waited for her order. Then, after Mary spent a year at University College of London—where it was tough to find anything tasty—she happily returned to this place, where the staff not only invited her into the kitchen to talk and catch up, but they told her to make whatever she wanted . . . and they'd watch. While every other BC coed was in their dorm making ramen noodles on a Waring hotplate, Mary was commanding a 25,000-BTU commercial range at one of Boston's most famous night-owl spots.

You know the expression "If you can't stand the heat, get out of the kitchen"? Mary was in the kitchen adding the heat giving a master class in Buffalo sauce. She gave us this recipe, which isn't spicy at all . . . but it's amazing. In fact, it could kinda be our *flavor*-ite!

Makes 2 servings

---

2 boneless, skinless chicken breasts (about 8 ounces each)

1 cup all-purpose flour

½ teaspoon table salt

1 large egg, whisked

2 tablespoons whole milk

2 cups panko bread crumbs

⅓ cup vegetable oil, plus more if needed

2 tablespoons unsalted butter

⅓ cup Frank's RedHot Original sauce

1. First, butterfly each chicken breast by cutting through it horizontally almost to the other side and opening it into one wider, flatter piece. Place a piece of plastic wrap on top of each piece and use the smooth side of a meat tenderizer to pound the chicken to ½ inch thick. This will help it cook more quickly.

2. Next, make a chicken-breading assembly line. In a large zip-top bag, combine the flour and salt and give a shake to mix. In a shallow bowl, whisk the egg and milk. Place the panko in a separate zip-top bag. Place a piece of chicken in the flour and shake-shake-shake until it's completely coated. Remove and dredge in the egg-milk mixture, then place it in the panko bag, where you again shake-shake-shake until it's completely coated. Repeat with the second chicken breast.

Blue cheese crumbles, for serving

Blue Cheesy Mashed Cauliflower (page 107), for serving

Side salad with celery and ranch dressing

3. Set a large nonstick skillet over medium-high heat. Add the vegetable oil, give the pan a swirl to coat the bottom, and lay the chicken down flat in the pan. If you can get both butterflied pieces in the pan, great, but don't overcrowd. Cook until golden brown with a hard crust on the bottom, 4 or 5 minutes. Flip and cook the other side for 4 to 5 minutes, until cooked to 165°F—be sure to check. If you need to add a little oil after flipping, go ahead.

4. Meanwhile, in a shallow microwave-safe bowl, melt the butter, add the Frank's sauce, and stir to combine.

5. To serve, pour the sauce onto dinner plates, then dip the chicken into the sauce to glaze both sides. Toss a few blue cheese crumbles on top.

6. Serve with our delicious Blue Cheesy Mashed Cauliflower, and be sure to zigzag a little leftover Buffalo butter sauce on them. We also make a little side salad with celery and ranch dressing so we have all of the major Buffalo chicken food groups sitting somewhere on that plate!

Mary, queen of Buffalo.

NAPA VALLEY CHICKEN DINNER

WHEN OUR YOUNGEST, SALLY, WENT TO COLLEGE, WE KNEW THAT IN THE EVENT OF A dining hall emergency, she could make her own food. She was extensively trained in toasting an Eggo waffle and spraying a three-inch mound of Reddi-Wip on the top like she was working at Dairy Queen—which at that time would have been her dream job. So she could survive—albeit on a limited diet.

Then, in her senior year, she wanted to impress her boyfriend (and future husband), Ali, so she announced she was going to start cooking. She was going to school in Texas, where she'd eaten chicken enchiladas a million times, so she started with them. She wrapped up cooked chicken in a tortilla, and she was done. When Ali and his roommate, Andrew, arrived, Sally was pulling the entree from the oven. Andrew eyeballed the entree and said, "It's pizza night?" Crestfallen, Sally learned the value of using an actual recipe.

Kathy sent her a cookbook of quick and easy casseroles—for which, as they say in Food Network parlance, they dump and stir. But Sally was using tasty ingredients—and suddenly friends were inviting themselves over at dinnertime, saying, "Ali, your girlfriend is an amazing chef!"

Chef? At that point the only chef Sally knew was Boyardee. So she took the compliment—she loved his Beefaroni.

This past year all three of our kids got married, and they all needed quick and easy things to make using their new kitchen wedding gifts. So Kathy came up with this recipe, which she calls Napa Valley Chicken Dinner, because Kathy's from California and a single glass of her native chardonnay from Napa Valley adds a wonderful flavor to the chicken. As Kathy has explained, wine goes great with almost anything. Just don't try it on Eggos, Sally!

Waffle House.

Makes 4 servings

2 boneless, skinless chicken breasts

Table salt and freshly ground black pepper

2 tablespoons unsalted butter, plus more as needed

1½ tablespoons olive oil, plus more as needed

One 10-ounce package mushrooms, thinly sliced (we use Baby Bellas)

1 cup white wine (we use chardonnay) or chicken stock

One 10.5-ounce can condensed cream of mushroom soup

⅛ teaspoon garlic powder

Smoked Brussels Sprouts with Bacon (page 112), for serving

1. Slice both breasts horizontally in half to make 4 thin similar-size cutlets. Cover with a sheet of plastic wrap and use the smooth side of a meat mallet to gently pound them to even thickness. Season them lightly with salt and pepper.

2. In a large nonstick skillet, melt the butter in the olive oil over medium-high heat. Swirl the pan to combine the butter and oil. Working in batches if necessary, add the chicken and cook, undisturbed, until the chicken has golden highlights around the edges, about 5 minutes. Flip and cook until the second side also has golden brown edges and is cooked through to 165°F, about 5 minutes more. Remove the chicken to a plate. If cooking in batches, add a bit more oil and butter as required.

3. Add the mushrooms to the pan, toss them in the pan oil, and add a grind of pepper. Cook for about 5 minutes, stirring occasionally, as they release much of their liquid. Add the wine and bring to a quick boil, not just on the edges but across the center of the pan. Cook for about 1 minute as the wine flavors the mushrooms.

4. Open the can of cream of mushroom soup and stir the garlic powder and ¼ teaspoon pepper into the can (it's easier to mix them in this way). Pour the soup into the pan, mix with the mushroom/wine sauce, and bring to a boil. Reduce the heat to medium, return the chicken to the pan, flip it over in the sauce, and simmer for 3 to 5 minutes to bring the chicken to serving temperature.

5. Serve the chicken with a healthy heap of creamy mushrooms on top. A great side dish is our Smoked Brussels Sprouts with Bacon.

SHRIMP AND CAULIFLOWER GRITS

ON OUR FIRST VACATION TO THE LOWCOUNTRY OF SOUTH CAROLINA, I FELL IN LOVE
with fried green tomatoes, shrimp and grits, and a cocktail called Firefly that I enjoyed so much over the course of one very long night that I can never have another, or the CDC will come to our home and confiscate my liver.

Naturally we tried to re-create the food when we got home. Fried green tomatoes were challenging, because no nearby New Jersey stores sold green tomatoes. They have plenty of red tomatoes that are still green, but that dog don't hunt. So we turned our attention to shrimp and grits, which I loved so much when we initially stayed at the Sanctuary Hotel on Kiawah Island that I actually ordered it for every meal. Yes, they serve it for breakfast, lunch, and dinner, and I had it every time—that's what vacation is for! Besides, I think they have the best shrimp and grits in the whole wide world . . . sorry, Bubba Gump.

Maybe we should . . . RUN!

Kathy loved it, too, but the kids were a different story. When they hear *grits*, they think it's gritty, which it isn't, of course. It's actually creamy and delicious. But trying to persuade kids to try something can be about as easy as trying to teach your poodle to speak Dutch.

So I decided we'd try making our own version, without grits! We use riced cauliflower, because the whole world is now cauliflower-centric. It's a snap to make, and everybody adores it . . . probably because of the cheese. To quote Albert Einstein, "The Cheddar makes it better."

Okay, he didn't really say that—but it's true!

Makes 3 servings

Half a medium head cauliflower

One 4-ounce package diced pancetta

1 large garlic clove, thinly sliced

½ red bell pepper, cut into medium dice

½ medium red onion, cut into medium dice

1. To make the cauliflower rice, trim the leaves and cut the head into 1-inch chunks. Place in the food processor and pulse until uniformly grainy. Cauliflower rice is smaller than regular rice and a little "gritty," and that's what we're going for.

2. In a large nonstick skillet, sauté the pancetta over medium-high heat until crispy, 4 to 5 minutes. Remove it to a plate. Add the garlic, bell pepper, and onion to the pan with the pancetta oil and sauté until the onion softens and gets some golden highlights on its edges, about 5 minutes. Remove to the plate with the pancetta.

½ pound extra-jumbo shrimp (16/20 count), deveined and tails removed

1 teaspoon Creole seasoning (we use Tony Chachere's Original)

¼ cup white wine or chicken stock

½ cup shredded Cheddar cheese

Thinly sliced green onions, for garnish

3. Add the shrimp to the same pan in a single layer, sprinkle on the Creole seasoning, and cook until the bottoms of the shrimp are pink, about 3 minutes. Flip and cook the other side until the meat is opaque and cooked through, about 3 minutes—slice into a shrimp to make sure. Remove the shrimp to the pancetta and onion plate.

4. Add the wine and cook a couple minutes to deglaze the pan, scraping any crunchy remnants off the bottom, then add the cauliflower rice and sauté for 4 to 5 minutes, rotating the rice from the bottom to the top a couple times to soften it and heat it through. Toss in the Cheddar and the cooked pancetta, vegetables, and shrimp and stir until the cheese is melted, about 3 minutes.

5. We serve in bowls and snip some very thin green onion rings on top—then immediately devour!

The Shrimp and Grits Girls.

ELLEN'S ELEGANT SALMON CAKES AND SALAD

KANSAS HAS THE DISTINCTION OF BEING THE GEOGRAPHICAL CENTER OF THE FORTY-eight contiguous United States of America—in other words, it's a long way to any ocean. When I was growing up there, that was fine when it came to typhoons and hurricanes, but when it came to seafood, so far from the Atlantic and Pacific, we had basically three options: Chicken of the Sea tuna salad, the Filet-O-Fish at Mickey D's (always a good choice, because we got fries), or my mom's crispy crunchy salmon patties, which were a fond memory of Fridays during Lent. It was tough enough for a kid to give up candy *and* pop for forty days—but meat, too?

Mom never wrote down any of her recipes, so my sisters and I have spent the last thirty years reverse-engineering them to come up with the tastes of our childhood. This recipe is in the spirit of my mom's patties, but better than any we've ever had. It was developed by our friend Ellen Storms, who designs all of Kathy's jewelry, and this recipe is an absolute gem!

Ellen spent a year studying at the French Culinary Institute in New York City and cleverly infuses fresh herbs and flavors into freshly chopped salmon—unlike the canned salmon my mom used in the 1960s, which contained bones and skin that Dad said were fine to eat. "Lot of calcium, kids!"

Kathy and I just finished making a batch of these cakes with fresh salmon, and when these were frying on the stove, just that smell took me back forty years or so, to a time when my mom was in the kitchen, my dad was watching Walter Cronkite, and I was a young lad who knew that the privacy of any phone call depended on the length of our rotary phone cord and whether any nosy neighbors were listening in on the party line.

Makes 8 cakes

SALAD

⅓ cup vegetable oil

2 teaspoons soy sauce

3 tablespoons apple cider vinegar

1 tablespoon sugar

1 teaspoon table salt

¼ teaspoon red pepper flakes

1 large English cucumber, peeled, seeded, and cut into medium dice

3 green onions, cut into ⅛-inch rings

1. To make the salad: In a medium bowl, whisk the vegetable oil, soy sauce, vinegar, sugar, salt, and red pepper flakes to combine. Add the cucumber and green onions and give them a stir. Refrigerate until you're ready to serve with the salmon.

2. To make the salmon cakes: Set up a bowl of ice and water. In a medium saucepan, bring a couple inches of lightly salted water to a boil over medium heat. Add the green beans and cook until crisp-tender, 3 to 4 minutes. Drain the beans and drop them into the ice bath to stop the cooking, then drain again.

3. Cut the salmon into ½-inch cubes. In a large bowl, combine the salmon, cooled green beans, jalapeño, garlic, basil, eggs, bread crumbs, 1½ teaspoons salt, and the black pepper and mix well. Divide the mixture into 8 portions. Ellen was taught in culinary school to make her cakes perfectly symmetrical by using a 3-inch ramekin. Mist a ramekin with cooking spray, then give a

SALMON CAKES

Table salt

1½ cups medium-chopped trimmed green beans

1¾ pounds fresh or thawed frozen salmon fillets, skin and any pin bones removed (ask the seafood department to do it)

1 jalapeño pepper, seeded and finely diced

2 garlic cloves, minced

1 cup fresh basil leaves, finely shredded

3 large eggs, whisked

1 cup plain dried bread crumbs, plus more for coating the cakes

½ teaspoon freshly ground black pepper

Cooking oil spray

Vegetable oil

little shake of bread crumbs into the ramekin. Press 1 portion of the salmon mixture into the ramekin and pack it down a bit. Dust the top with a few more bread crumbs, then place your hand on the top of the ramekin and quickly invert it and pop it out into your hand. Place on a plate and proceed to make the rest of the cakes.

4. Preheat a large nonstick skillet for a few minutes over medium-high heat. When very hot, add enough vegetable oil (we use about 3 tablespoons) to coat the bottom of the pan. Working in batches as needed so as not to crowd the pan, place the salmon cakes in the pan and fry undisturbed until the cakes have substantial golden-brown crust on the bottom, 3 or 4 minutes. Carefully flip and cook until the second side has a nice crust as well, 3 to 4 minutes longer. Insert an instant-read thermometer into a cake to make sure the salmon is completely cooked to 145°F.

5. Set the cakes on a paper towel momentarily to absorb any excess oil and invert a plate over them to keep them warm until ready to serve.

6. To serve, give the salad another stir and use a slotted spoon to remove the salad from the bowl to the serving plates while draining off some of the dressing. Set a salmon cake or two next to or on top of the salad—and enjoy!

Wrapped up in a call.

CREAMY DREAMY CHICKEN MARSALA

THE DOOCY FAMILY HAS PROUDLY BEEN IN FOOD SERVICE FOR DECADES. BOTH MY grandmas cooked at cafés in northern Iowa—seventy years ago. My sisters Cathy, Lisa, Ann, and Jenny all worked in, managed, or owned restaurants. Then there's me. The closest I got to food service was working as a DJ at a disco in college. The place was going bankrupt, and they told me they could not afford to pay me anymore. I said they didn't have to—I would work for beer. And I did, until they went out of business. Best part of being paid in beer? No W-2 form for the IRS.

That was my only food service work—until I got hired to be the fry-guy for Guy Fieri.

Guy had just opened another location of his Chicken Guy franchise, and they asked if I'd like to see the chicken frying secrets of the most famous guy on TV. I said yes, and faster than you could say "We're riding the bus to Flavortown!" I was wearing a Chicken Guy T-shirt, with an industrial apron cinched around my middle. As the TV cameras taped us, Guy showed me how to bread tenders and fry them to golden perfection in a state-of-the-art commercial fryer.

His recipe was delicious—but what do you expect—he is the King of Cooking TV. At the end of the Fox News segment I said, "And that concludes this episode of *Diners, Drive-Ins and Doocy*." Guy giggled, and I wondered if I could trademark that. I could probably *try*, but then the next time I'd see Guy it would probably be with his lawyer guy.

The reason I mention that Guy Fieri taught me how to fry chicken is that I read that the recipe Guy's kids ask him to make most often is his chicken Marsala. He told me exactly how his kids like it, and it sounds delicious. This recipe is our family's favorite, and when you make it you'll see why—we finish ours with cream cheese, which makes it creamy and dreamy.

By the way, the last time I made this at home, I put on my official Chicken Guy T-shirt from that TV shoot. Kathy came into the kitchen, sat down, tasted the chicken, looked around the room, and then said, "Shut the front door!" (Guy Fieri's famous line when he's tasting things on *Triple D*.)

Waiting for her to compliment the Marsala, she explained, "Sally left the door ajar when she went for a walk—so could you *shut the front door—please*."

Kathy could be Vice Mayor of Flavortown— if they're hiring. I know they have aprons.

Chicken lovin' guys.

Makes 4 servings

2 boneless, skinless chicken breasts

½ cup all-purpose flour

Table salt and freshly ground black pepper

½ teaspoon garlic powder

3 tablespoons olive oil

1 large garlic clove, minced

1 medium shallot, sliced into medium rings

One 10-ounce package mushrooms, thinly sliced (we use Baby Bellas)

¾ cup Marsala wine

1 cup vegetable stock (we use Better Than Bouillon vegetable base flavor)

4 ounces cream cheese, at room temperature

Cooked angel hair pasta, for serving

1. Slice both chicken breasts horizontally in half to make 4 cutlets of equal size. Cover with plastic wrap and use the smooth side of a meat mallet to pound it down to about a ½-inch thickness.

2. In a large zip-top bag, mix the flour, 1 teaspoon salt, 1 teaspoon pepper, and the garlic powder. Working one at a time, add a chicken breast to the bag and shake until coated.

3. In a large nonstick skillet, heat the olive oil over medium-high heat. Working in batches as needed, add the chicken cutlets to the pan and cook, undisturbed, until they have substantial golden-brown highlights on the bottom, about 5 minutes. Flip and cook until the chicken is cooked to an interior temp of 165°F, another 5 minutes. Remove the chicken to a plate and keep warm.

4. Add the garlic, shallot, and mushrooms to the pan, lightly salt and pepper them, and sauté for 5 minutes as the mushrooms release their liquids. Pour in the Marsala wine; it will boil immediately around the edges of the pan, but keep it boiling until it bubbles in the center of the pan. Stir in the chicken stock and bring to a boil for 2 minutes. Reduce the temperature *slightly* and stir in the cream cheese. Use a spatula to smoosh it down in the pan and help it melt. Keep mixing until smooth; it will take about 5 minutes. Return the chicken to the pan and warm it to serving temperature.

5. Serve the chicken with the mushroom-Marsala sauce on top of angel hair pasta.

BUFFALO CHICKEN ENCHILADAS

WHEN I WAS ABOUT FIVE YEARS OLD, LIVING IN RUSSELL, KANSAS, MY PARENTS SENT MY sister Cathy and me over to the neighbor's house to drop something off. I knocked on the door and waited about thirty seconds . . . nothing. "Nobody home," I said in the direction of my three-year-old sister, who I spied nibbling on a bright red Swedish Fish candy. A little jealous, I wondered where she got it—and then I noticed that she was standing next to what looked like bright red candies, but were actually what we later found out was a whole planter of bright red Thai hot ornamental peppers, which had a Scoville index of about 80,000 units.

Cathy ate the whole pepper.

There was a delayed reaction of about twenty seconds before she felt it. First she had a facial expression one would associate with oral surgery without novocaine. Then she started screaming that her mouth was on fire. We ran home, where our parents alternated between feeding her milk and bread. That might have worked for somebody who'd downed a little jalapeño, but because she ate one complete Thai hot pepper *and its seeds,* her taste buds were toast and Mom and Dad's home remedies were like using squirt guns to douse a towering volcano.

Cathy cried herself to sleep and woke up the next morning vowing she'd never to eat another spicy pepper again. But it's funny how things work out in life—Cathy wound up managing two Mexican restaurants. I loved visiting her because the food was always fantastic and she'd give me free chips. I thought it was a perk because I was her brother, until I noticed she gave them to everybody. Blood wasn't thicker than salsa.

Cathy tutored us on how to properly sauce and build the enchiladas—which are incredible thanks to the cream cheese!

Makes 10 six-inch enchiladas

Cooking oil spray

One 19-ounce can red enchilada sauce

¼ cup Frank's RedHot Wings mild sauce, plus more to taste

Breast meat from 1 rotisserie chicken (save the rest for something else delicious)

1 tablespoon vegetable oil

½ red onion, finely diced

One 8-ounce package cream cheese, cubed, at room temperature

2 cups shredded Mexican blend cheese

1. Preheat the oven to 350°F. Mist the bottom and sides of a 9 × 13-inch baking pan with cooking spray.

2. In a medium bowl, combine the enchilada sauce and the wings sauce. Give a taste; if you'd like it spicier, add 1 more tablespoon of Frank's at a time.

3. Shred the chicken breast meat into a bowl and add ½ cup of the enchilada–hot sauce mixture. Toss to coat the meat.

4. In a large nonstick skillet, heat the oil over medium-high heat. Add the onion and sauté until the edges start to brown, about 5 minutes. Reduce the heat to medium, add the cream cheese, and use a silicone spatula to cut it up and smoosh it to help it melt a bit, for about 30 seconds, then quickly add 1 cup of the shredded Mexican cheese and the chicken mixture and heat, stirring often, until the cream cheese and Mexican cheese are melted and the mixture is evenly creamy.

Ten 6-inch yellow corn tortillas

Blue cheese crumbles, for garnish

Ranch dressing, for serving

4 green onions, dark green parts only, cut into ⅛-inch rings

5. Pour 1 cup of the enchilada–hot sauce mixture into the prepared baking pan. Use a spoon to coat the bottom of the pan with sauce.

6. To assemble the enchiladas, wrap the tortillas in a damp paper towel and microwave them on high for 30 seconds to make them flexible. Spoon ⅓ cup of the chicken-cheese mixture evenly down the middle of a tortilla, then roll it closed and set it seam side down in the baking dish. Repeat to roll and arrange the rest of the enchiladas, then pour the rest of the enchilada/hot sauce over all the enchiladas. If there are any bald spots, use a spoon to scoot some sauce to cover them; otherwise the tortillas will get too dry. Top with the remaining 1 cup shredded Mexican cheese and scatter the blue cheese crumbles on top.

7. Bake until both kinds of cheese have melted, about 25 minutes. Serve the enchiladas with ranch dressing drizzled on top and a sprinkle of green onions.

SWEET CHILI-SAUCED PORK CHOPS

ONE NIGHT WHEN I WAS ALMOST DONE COOKING PORK CHOPS I REALIZED TOO LATE THAT my favorite bottle of Kansas City barbecue sauce was empty! The only way to get to KC and back in five minutes was if Elon Musk flew me on SpaceX, but sadly he won't return my calls.

I immediately thought about my grandma Doocy's recipe boxes, which were crammed full of a lifetime of great foods. Her collection had started in the 1950s and included lots of casserole and cookie recipes. The humbling discovery was her go-to recipes for things that she apparently could not buy at the local grocery store in Bancroft, Iowa; basic staples of today such as pickles, salad dressing, and BBQ sauce. If Grandma was there with me right then she'd just smile, put on an apron, and make me a new bottle of BBQ sauce.

Then I snapped out of my nostalgic cloud. Who was I kidding? If Grandma were still alive, she'd yell at whoever ate the last of the sauce and tell them to go to the store and get more—before she got mad. At that point people would be running out of the building.

Scanning the fridge for a flavorful and suitable substitute, I grabbed a bottle of a sauce we keep on hand for egg rolls but a friend puts on everything, from French fries to sandwiches to eggs: Thai sweet chili sauce. Kathy's idea was to quickly warm it up a little and use a small amount to glaze the meat, not drown it in sauce. This recipe is that simple.

"Stephen, your chops have a delicious sweet and sour and zesty taste!" I can hear Grandma say. "Now enough with the small talk—help me do these dishes so we can make some mayonnaise!"

End of dream sequence.

Makes 2 pork chops

2 tablespoons vegetable oil

Table salt and freshly ground black pepper

2 boneless pork chops (about 6 to 8 ounces each)

¼ cup Thai sweet chili sauce, plus more for serving

Simple Creamy Mashed Cauliflower (page 107), for serving

1. In a medium nonstick skillet, heat the oil over medium-high heat and give the pan a swirl to coat the bottom. Lightly salt and pepper the pork chops and place them in the pan. Cook, undisturbed, until they are seared golden brown on the bottom, about 5 minutes. Flip and cook until that side is also golden brown and the chops are prepared to your level of doneness, another 5 minutes. (145°F is the official safe temperature for pork. Check!)

2. Remove from the heat and transfer the pork chops to a plate. Drain any grease, then take a couple paper towels and carefully clean out and discard any remaining oil in the pan. Pour the sweet chili sauce into the still-warm pan, then quickly drag the chops through the sauce on both sides to give the pork a nice glaze. Leave them in the pan a moment and drizzle a little more sauce onto your serving plates.

3. Serve the chops in the sauce and drizzle a little more on top. Chop-chop, it's pork chop time! These are perfect with our creamy mashed cauliflower.

KIELBASA KEBABS

MY SISTER LISA'S LONGTIME BOYFRIEND, GREG, IS A GREAT GUY WHO'S BEEN A FIXTURE in our family for many years. When he travels from Kansas to New Jersey to visit his mother, he sometimes drops by our house. Born in Tarnobrzeg, Poland, Greg always celebrates his heritage by bringing us delicious foods like pierogies, pastries, and candies. I remember when he brought a batch of paczki pastries, which are jelly-filled doughnuts, and candies called *krówki*, which translates to "little cows" and is a delicious semi-soft Polish fudge. And then there were little roundish chocolates, which the kids gobbled up like they were on death row waiting for a call from the governor. One of our kids downed three in a row and then started sounding like they were speaking Swedish. Greg was giggling as he explained that the roundish chocolates were actually chocolate kegs filled with whiskey! He forgot to tell us that they were not for kids. The remaining pieces immediately went up on a high shelf (and *wow* they were tasty!).

During another visit, Greg and Lisa came to our house for dinner. It was a beautiful night and we were going to grill, but we lost interest in cooking—probably after a couple of the chocolate barrels of whiskey—so we went out to eat and had a lovely evening. The next day we had to do something with the Polish kielbasas and vegetables that we had planned on grilling the previous night. Kathy had been helping Sally with an upcoming tailgate party and suggested we make a colorful kaleidoscope of kielbasa kebabs. They were delicious, and so easy.

This is a perfect recipe for grilling or a tailgate because you can prep the kebabs the night before and refrigerate. And because the meat is already cooked, there's no worry of contamination. It's a whole meal on a single stick . . . kind of like how those chocolate kegs are a whole saloon in a single sweet.

These Kansans love kielbasa.

Makes 5 or 6 servings

One 1½-pound package Steamables small red potatoes

One 14-ounce package cooked kielbasa, cut into 1-inch-thick chunks

1 orange bell pepper, cut into 1½-inch squares

1 yellow bell pepper, cut into 1½-inch squares

1 red bell pepper, cut into 1½-inch squares

2 medium zucchini, cut into ½-inch rounds

10 cherry tomatoes

1 red onion, cut into 1½-inch square chunks

Vegetable oil, for the grill grates

Olive oil cooking spray

Table salt and freshly ground black pepper

Pickle and Pasta Garden Salad (page 98), for serving

1. Preheat the grill to 450°F. Soak about a dozen 12-inch bamboo skewers in water for at least 15 minutes so they don't burn up on the grill.

2. Microwave the potatoes until cooked through according to the package directions (about 8 minutes). Let them cool for about 5 minutes before you assemble the kebabs.

3. There's no right or wrong way to thread the meat and vegetables onto the skewers. Just make sure you leave about 1 inch of skewer stick on each end, so they're easy to place on the grill. We try to alternate the colors as we put things onto the skewers—the vegetables are easy, just make sure that every stick has at least one piece of meat and a potato. We also like to surround each piece of meat with a slightly curved piece of colorful pepper on each side of it, so the pepper appears to be wrapped around the kielbasa. Poll your guests to see which ingredients they like—and custom-build their kebabs.

4. Reduce the temperature at the center of the grill to medium-high, with both sides still at the higher heat. To lubricate the grill grates so the food won't stick, pour a small amount of vegetable oil on a paper towel, then use tongs to rub that oily paper towel on the center grill grates.

5. Lightly mist the outsides of the kebabs with olive oil spray, then lightly salt and pepper them. Place them on the center grill grates and leave them undisturbed to cook for about 5 minutes, or until they have good grill marks. Carefully flip them over and grill the other side, about another 5 minutes, until everything is gorgeously grilled.

6. Place the kebabs on a platter and serve. We love to serve this with my grandma Doocy's creamy pasta salad.

TATER-TOPPED BUFF CHICK MINI LOAVES

"KIDS, IF YOU WANT DESSERT, YOU HAVE TO FINISH YOUR DINNER." I HEARD THIS OFTEN over the first eighteen years of my life, until I went to college, where I learned a tougher lesson: *"If you want dessert, you have to stop drinking beer."*

When my mom was begging us to finish dinner, she could have tricked us with this next-level entree—a little chicken meatloaf muffin with mashed potatoes on top. It looks like a cupcake . . . simply brilliant!

Our daughter Mary did her undergraduate work at Boston College where she developed not a sweet tooth but an iron gut and fell in love with any and everything covered with hot sauce. At the same time, she loved anything cupcake-y. When Mary landed her first job out of law school, Kathy and I created this recipe to celebrate. My grandmother sometimes put mashed potatoes on top of her meatloaf—and that's where this idea came from.

"Mary, congratulations on the new job in our nation's capital," we wrote on a card. "These cupcakes are the perfect example of how things in Washington are not always as they appear. XO, Mom and Dad."

Tater topping time.

Makes 4 large or 7 standard-size muffin meatloaves

---

1 tablespoon unsalted butter

1 celery stalk, finely diced

3 green onions, sliced into ⅛-inch rings, white parts and green tops kept separate

1 large garlic clove, minced

1 large egg, whisked

¼ cup Frank's RedHot Original sauce, plus more for drizzling

1 pound ground chicken breast

½ cup bread crumbs (we use panko)

½ cup blue cheese crumbles

Cooking oil spray

One 4-ounce package instant mashed potatoes (we use Idahoan Buttery Homestyle)

1. Adjust an oven rack to the center position and preheat the oven to 375°F.

2. In a small nonstick skillet, melt the butter over medium heat. Add the celery and sauté until softened, 3 to 4 minutes. Add the white parts of the green onions and the garlic and cook until the onions have golden highlights, about 4 to 6 minutes. Remove the vegetables to a small plate to cool down.

3. In a large bowl, combine the egg and hot sauce and whisk well. Add the chicken, bread crumbs, cooked onions/celery, uncooked green onion tops, and blue cheese crumbles and mix well. Because we have so many latex gloves left over from the pandemic, I've been wearing a pair and using my hands like my mom did when she made old-school meatloaf.

NOTE: Muffin tins come in three sizes: mini, standard, and large (or jumbo). This recipe can be used with either a standard muffin tin, which will yield 7 appetizer-size meatloaves, or a large (or jumbo) tin, which will yield 4 full meal-size meatloaves.

4. Mist the wells of your muffin tin with cooking spray, dividing the meat mixture into 4 or 7 portions, depending on what size loaves you're making. Add the portions to the wells and push down gently to fill the wells, then level the tops.

5. Set a sheet pan under the muffin tin, transfer that setup to the oven, and bake until the tops are deeply golden with a few darker highlights around the edges, 22 to 27 minutes, depending on the size of the loaves. And we always use an instant-read thermometer to verify they're at least 165°F.

6. About 15 minutes before they're done, prepare the instant mashed potatoes according to the package directions (we use the microwave method). Let them cool a bit (but not too much) until the meatloaves are done.

7. To serve, you can use a knife to spread a few tablespoons of the potatoes on the top of each meatloaf—just like frosting a cupcake. Or, for a more fun look, pipe the potatoes on top using this easy method. Carefully scoop the still very warm potatoes into a zip-top bag, work them toward one corner on the bottom, then use scissors to snip off a ½-inch diagonal corner. Squeeze the potatoes out to decorate the tops of the meatloaves.

8. Drizzle hot sauce on top and enjoy the cupcakes—I mean meatloaves . . .

HOMEMADE HIBACHI SHRIMP

WHEN I WAS GROWING UP, MY DAD TAUGHT ME TWO IMPORTANT SKILLS: HOW TO WHIS-tle and how to toss a piece of popcorn in the air and catch it in your mouth. He learned how to whistle on the farm, and he picked up the popcorn trick when he was working at the movie theater in Bancroft, Iowa. I whistle all the time, but the only time my popcorn-catching ability has come in handy is when Kathy and I would take the kids to a hibachi steak house for dinner. It's at the end of the appetizers, when the tableside cook would toss a shrimp tail straight up and catch it in their tall white chef hat, then they'd offer to toss a piece of shrimp into the mouth of a diner. I always volunteered, and I caught it every time—until one time when a shrimp lodged in the back of my throat and blocked my air supply. Kathy saved my life with a modified Heimlich—and I was forever done going to those places.

But the kids loved the hibachi joint, and Kathy would take them whenever I was out of town on assignment. Over time it started to bother her that the cook used only one spatula for the entire meal. Raw eggs, chicken, steak, and lobster—all were all moved around the grill with that single spatula from start to finish. She politely asked the guy to change spatulas, but he just laughed.

Kathy revealed a secret: "I'm from the Board of Health, and unless you change spatulas, I'm closing you down."

He motioned over the boss, who listened and then said, "We only use one . . ."

Wrong answer. Kathy gathered the kids and left, the manager watched her walk out to the parking lot, no doubt wondering if she was in a Board of Health vehicle. She was not. But he could see her drive across the street to the local pizza joint that has used the same pizza peel on every pie made since 1978—*and we don't care*.

We make our own hibachi shrimp now at home—with a twist. We use riced cauliflower—because the whole world has gone crazy for cauliflower—and we have the exact same sauce they serve at the hibachi restaurants. It's sold by different names, such as yum yum sauce, white sauce, Japanese-style steak house sauce, and almost all grocery stores carry it—but Terry Ho's brand is our hands-down *flavor*-ite. It tastes exactly like the sauce at the place where I used to catch shrimp like a trained seal.

Makes 3 or 4 servings

1 pound frozen shrimp (16/20 count), thawed, peeled, deveined, and tails removed

½ cup teriyaki sauce or lower sodium soy sauce

One 20-ounce bag microwavable frozen riced cauliflower (or see page 102 to make your own)

1 tablespoon unsalted butter

⅓ cup yum yum sauce (we use Terry Ho's brand), plus more to taste

2 to 3 green onions, dark green parts only, cut into ⅛-inch rings

1. Place the thawed shrimp in a zip-top bag and add the teriyaki sauce. Seal, shake, and marinate in the fridge for at least 30 minutes or up to 8 hours.

2. Microwave the riced cauliflower according to the package directions.

3. Meanwhile, dump the shrimp and marinade into a large nonstick skillet over medium-high heat and spread out the shrimp so they cook evenly. Bring the marinade to a quick boil for 3 or 4 minutes, then flip the shrimp and fully cook, 3 to 4 minutes. The shrimp is done when it gets bright pink—but because it's frying in a dark sauce, it's hard to tell. Slice a shrimp in half to make sure it's completely opaque and cooked through.

4. When the riced cauliflower is done, open the bag and pour it into a serving bowl. Stir in the butter and let it melt. Top with the cooked shrimp and drizzle on the yum yum sauce. We use ⅓ cup but if you'd like a little extra, add it—after all, it's yum-yummy.

5. Top with some green onion rings and serve immediately. Stir at the table and enjoy—Health Department's orders!

MAMIE'S CREAMY ARTICHOKE CHICKEN

BECAUSE I GREW UP IN ABILENE, KANSAS, THE BOYHOOD HOME OF OUR THIRTY-FOURTH president, Dwight David Eisenhower, when friends see this recipe for Mamie's Creamy Artichoke Chicken, they assume the Mamie refers to Ike's wife and America's former first lady, Mamie Eisenhower. Great guess—but not even close. No actual person named Mamie assisted in this recipe. Let me explain.

One night Kathy pulled a can of artichoke hearts from the cupboard and announced she was going to make her friend Martha Hockman's artichoke dip from our first cookbook. "Hold it!" I said, and explained that I'd already planned on using that can of 'chokes to make Amy Baier's artichoke chicken casserole from our second cookbook. We couldn't agree on which recipe to make, so we opted to make them both—in one recipe.

A couple of tweaks later, we'd made a version of Martha's creamy artichoke dip on top of Amy's artichoke chicken casserole, and it's magnificent!

So, who's Mamie? There is no Mamie! The recipe name is an homage to the dishes' originators: Martha + Amy = Mamie.

A tip of the hat to them both; they certainly know their artichokes. I hope they don't get *choke-d* up over the name . . .

Makes 6 servings

½ cup all-purpose flour

½ teaspoon table salt

½ teaspoon freshly ground black pepper

¼ teaspoon garlic powder

6 boneless, skinless chicken thighs

1 tablespoon unsalted butter, plus more as needed

2 tablespoons olive oil, plus more as needed

1 cup chicken stock

4 ounces cream cheese, cut into cubes

One 14-ounce can quartered artichoke hearts, drained

One 4-ounce can diced green chiles, undrained

Cooked rice, for serving (we like basmati)

Fresh Corn Chip Salad (page 105), for serving

1. In a small bowl, mix the flour, salt, pepper, and garlic powder. Unroll the chicken thighs and lightly dust them on both sides with the mixture.

2. In a large nonstick skillet, melt the butter in the olive oil over medium-high heat, then swirl the pan to combine. Working in batches if necessary, add the chicken thighs and cook undisturbed until they have a nice golden crust on one side, about 10 minutes. Give them a flip and cook the other side until that side also has a nice crust and the interior temperature reads 165°F on an instant-read thermometer, 8 to 10 minutes. Remove the chicken to a plate. If cooking in batches, add more butter and oil if needed.

3. Add the chicken stock to the pan. It will immediately bubble, making it easy to deglaze the pan, so get a silicone spatula and scrape loose any delicious crunchy chicken bits. Add the cubed cream cheese and smoosh it around the pan until it melts evenly into a uniform creamy color. Reduce the heat to medium and add the artichoke hearts and green chiles. Return the chicken pieces to the pan, smooth side up. Don't spoon the sauce on top—you want the golden-brown fried chicken peeking out from the creamy sauce. Let the chicken and artichokes warm up to serving temperature.

4. This dish is great with a side of rice or our Fresh Corn Chip Salad.

EASY HONEY-MUSTARD CHICKEN THIGHS

IF YOUR FAMILY IS LIKE OURS, YOU'RE OFTEN EMPLOYING FAMOUS FUNNY QUOTES WHEN real life mirrors something from the movies or TV. For years when our kids were growing up outside New York City in New Jersey, when we would drive them somewhere, if we came to a stoplight and a very expensive luxury car would pull up next to us, one kid (usually the boy) would affect a high-society accent and say through a rolled-up window, *"Pardon me, would you have any Grey Poupon?"* Then all the kids would convulse in laughter—because somebody said Poupon.

Peter always enunciated that line with great gusto because our windows were closed, and it was a show only for the people in our car. Until the one time he didn't realize my driver-side window was down, and as soon as he delivered the Poupon punch line, the luxury car passenger, who was barely three feet away, swiveled her head and stared directly at him. "Yes!" she answered him. "The Grey Poupon's right here in the glove compartment!" She and the driver exploded in laughter, and he floored it when the light changed.

This mustard and honey chicken recipe is from my mom, who was cooking with thighs long before Julia Child's TV show ran in our town, because we were broke and thighs were cheap. Mom made this recipe a lot when I was a kid in the 1970s, and in the 1980s when that famous commercial had started running. But Mom used her own European brand of mustard . . . French's. In doing research for this cookbook, I discovered that the French's company was never actually headquartered in France, and today their corporation is based in Chester, New Jersey—just down the road from where that Doocy kid disturbed the rich people in the Rolls-Royce. Now he's on their XM radio doing the news live from the White House. *Pardon me, would you have any headlines?*

Makes 6 thighs

Cooking oil spray

4 tablespoons honey

4 tablespoons Dijon mustard (we use Grey Poupon!)

6 boneless, skinless chicken thighs (bone-in work, too; just bake longer)

Sea salt and freshly ground black pepper

Garlic powder

Side salad with ranch dressing, for serving

1. Preheat the oven to 375°F. Line the bottom of a 9 × 13-inch baking pan with foil and mist the foil with cooking spray.

2. Make the honey-mustard glaze. My mom's ratio of honey to mustard was one to one, but because measuring honey is a pain (it's so sticky), she had an easier way. Squeeze 3 tablespoons of the honey into a little bowl, then eyeball the same amount of Dijon mustard and put that in the bowl. Stir well, and if it's a little glossy but also a little runny, it's perfect. If it's a little dry, you need some gloss—so add more honey. If it's too runny, add more mustard.

3. Unroll the thighs and lightly season each one with salt, pepper, and garlic powder. Brush honey-mustard glaze on each side. Place the thighs in the prepared baking dish with the smooth side of the thighs on top. Drizzle any remaining glaze over the thighs for added flavor. (Put the honey-mustard bowl in the dishwasher; you can't use it again, and we'll make more honey-mustard fresh for serving.)

4. Bake the chicken until golden brown and completely cooked through to 165°F on an instant-read thermometer, about 30 minutes. (For bone-in thighs, it will be about 45 minutes.)

5. In a clean new bowl, mix the remaining 1 tablespoon honey with the same amount of mustard. Stir until glossy and drizzle or brush that on the cooked chicken. Let the glaze set for a couple of minutes.

6. Plate or platter the chicken and serve. A lovely side salad with ranch dressing is a perfect pairing. *"Pardon me, would you have any Hidden Valley Ranch?"*

PORK CHOP AND ARTICHOKE PICCATA

YOU EVER WONDER WHY TV REPORTERS CHOOSE CERTAIN LOCATIONS FOR THEIR ON-CAMERA stand-ups? Peter Doocy, the TV correspondent who used to live upstairs at our house, told me that when he's reporting from Iowa, when given the opportunity he will often find a reason to drive to Davenport by the end of the day. He has a great stand-up location near the Mississippi waterfront, but he's not there because it's picturesque (although it is)—he's there for the pork chop.

Pork chop on a stick.

"Dad, it's not just any pork chop, it's the Presidential Pork Chop!"

The Blackhawk Hotel opened in 1915, and over its long and illustrious history it has hosted presidents Hoover and Nixon. President Obama dropped into Davenport in 2011 and had dinner at the Blackhawk's Bix Bistro. Mr. Obama selected a pork chop off the menu, and as soon as POTUS ordered it, they changed the name to the Presidential Pork Chop. When Peter saw it during a presidential campaign, he wanted to dine on the same thing as the commander in chief. And of course Peter was on an expense account.

"Delicious, double cut, bone-in," Peter reports, sounding like somebody whose mom writes cookbooks.

For the curious, the Presidential is, according to the restaurant's menu, an Iowa-raised Berkshire pork chop brined in apple and cinnamon and finished with a mustard demi-glace and served with bacon-braised cabbage and little loaf of corn bread. According to online reports, Mr. Obama liked it so much he had the White House chef call and get the recipe.

Iowa is the number one pork producer in America, and when you travel across the state you see a lot of pigs. We're a family of pork chop lovers; we shared our Doocy family Ritz cracker–breaded chops and mushroom gravy pork chops, both from Iowa, in our first two cookbooks. This year we've been doing a lot with artichokes and piccata recipes, and this is a simple and delicious combo. If the White House chef calls, we're happy to share the recipe. Here it is—Hail to the Chef!

And if you ever find yourself in Iowa at the Blackhawk Hotel restaurant and you spy a tall blond correspondent carving up a pork chop, that's probably the younger Mr. Doocy. Peter says he generally gets there so late that he has to have dinner at the bar. Wait . . . there's a bar?

That changes everything! He's not there for the pork chop, he's there for the Pabst Blue Ribbon!

Makes 4 servings

½ cup all-purpose flour

½ teaspoon table salt

½ teaspoon freshly ground black pepper

¼ teaspoon garlic powder

4 center-cut boneless pork chops, about 8 ounces each

2 tablespoons olive oil

¾ cup white wine or chicken stock

¾ cup low-sodium chicken stock

1 teaspoon cornstarch

One 14-ounce can quartered artichoke hearts, drained

2½ tablespoons capers, undrained (brine included)

1 teaspoon grated lemon zest

Juice of ½ lemon

2 tablespoons unsalted butter

1. In a medium bowl, combine the flour, salt, pepper, and garlic powder. Lightly dredge each chop in the mixture, taking care to flour the sides!

2. In a large nonstick skillet, heat the olive oil over medium-high heat and swirl it across the pan. Add the pork chops and let them sear, undisturbed, until golden brown on the bottom, 4 to 8 minutes (depending on their thickness). Flip the chops and cook the other side until equally golden and to your level of doneness, usually another 4 to 8 minutes. (The USDA's safe temperature for cooked pork is 145°F.) Just know they'll continue to cook a bit more from residual heat as they rest. Remove the chops to a plate and cover to keep warm.

3. To make the piccata sauce, set the skillet over medium-high heat and add the wine. It will immediately start boiling. Let it boil 1 or 2 minutes as it reduces by one-quarter. In a measuring cup, combine the chicken stock and cornstarch and whisk until smooth. Pour that mixture into the reduced wine, then add the artichokes, capers (and caper brine), lemon zest, lemon juice, and butter. Stir well and return the pork chops to the skillet to let everything warm up for a couple of minutes. Flip the chops in the sauce to coat them well.

4. Spoon the caper sauce on top of the chops and serve the artichokes on the side.

I ♥ Iowa.

PERFECT PARISIAN POACHED CHICKEN

HOW OFTEN DO YOU WANT TO MAKE A RECIPE AND NOTICE THAT IT CALLS FOR 2 CUPS OF shredded cooked chicken? Next time instead of using a rotisserie bird—poach!

Our neighbor Leanna used to live in Paris, where she picked up this *très facile* (very easy) technique from a friend. It requires literally 2 minutes of prep, and in less time than it takes to watch an episode of *Diners, Drive-Ins and Dives* you have a couple of moist and delicious chicken breasts.

The bonus is that the chicken not only winds up perfectly poached, it can also be flavored by adding an extra ingredient or two (or three) to the pan to enhance your final recipe. Some of Leanna's favorite additions: garlic cloves, green onion tops, a ginger knob, lemon slices, fresh thyme or parsley sprigs, or a glug of white wine from the bottle you didn't finish last night. Serving the chicken with something that has garlic? Toss a couple garlic cloves into the pot and start flavoring your chicken from minute one. Preparing an Asian dish? Slice some peeled fresh ginger and throw that in. When Kathy makes rosemary potatoes, we throw a couple sprigs of rosemary in with the chicken, and the chicken winds up with a built-in hint of rosemary. And poaching the chicken in chicken stock instead of water gives it an even richer flavor.

Of course, you can also poach it perfectly plain for a neutral addition to a salad, sandwich, or casserole. Leanna makes extra pieces of chicken for meals in the next day or two.

This is one of the best cooking shortcuts we've ever discovered! Try it—as they would say in Paris, it's in-Seine-ly simple!

Makes 2 chicken breasts or about 2½ cups shredded chicken

---

2 boneless, skinless chicken breasts (6 to 8 ounces each)

1. On a cutting board, pound down the chicken breasts to no thicker than 1 inch. Set the breasts in a medium saucepan with water (or chicken stock) to cover the top of the chicken by just ½ inch. If you'd like to boost the taste of the finished product, add any flavoring you'd like to infuse the chicken with (for some ideas, see the headnote).

2. Cover the saucepan and set over high heat. Bring the liquid to a good, solid boil—not just little bubbles around the edges, lots of big bubbles in the middle. Boil for about 2 minutes to make sure the boil is really good, then turn off the heat and leave the pan on the stove—with the lid on tight! The chicken poaches in that hot water over the next 20 minutes (or more time for a really large breast). Check the temp with an instant-read thermometer—it should be 165°F. Leanna says you can leave the chicken in the water with the lid on tight for up to 1 hour.

3. By the way, if you're going to shred the chicken using our stand mixer method on page 152, hot straight out of the pan is a good way to do it!

CREAMY CRUSTED HORSERADISH SALMON

HORSERADISH: THERE'S SOMETHING MAGICAL ABOUT THAT TASTE. OR IS IT MEDICINAL?
Through history horseradish has been used to treat everything from tuberculosis to rheumatism. I've read the Greeks used it as a rub for lower back pain and, oddly, as an aphrodisiac. Wait, what? Who needs Viagra when you can just discreetly buy a jar of *that pungent stuff* over by the mustard. "Can you put that in a brown paper bag, please?"

I've always loved horseradish. When I was a kid, once a week my mom bought horseradish and bacon chip dip. Remember that? This recipe is a flashback to my childhood, when our family couldn't eat that horseradish chip dip fast enough. I can still see the broken shards of wavy chips at the end of our appetizer hour—back at a time when *double dipping* only referred to an accounting scam—not snacks.

Our family ENT, Kenneth Remsen, is fond of its "pungent aroma and spicy flavor." After he'd contracted Covid and lost his sense of smell, you know what he used as a test to see when it returned? Every morning he'd go to the fridge and open the jar of horseradish. For weeks he couldn't get a whiff of anything, then one morning he sniffed it and could again sense its "pungent aroma and spicy flavor." He knew then that he was over Delta. Dr. Ken uses it not only to cook—but to diagnose!

This salmon recipe is a collaboration with Ken and his wife, Erika. One day in early 2022 they made it for their friend Gary, a longtime boxing promoter who said he'd spent a lifetime ordering horseradish salmon in restaurants, and this was "one of the best dishes I've ever had—anywhere!" He then offered to pay the Remsens to make it for him once a week. Dr. Remsen is considering that proposal; he's just trying to figure out what a fair co-pay is on an entree.

The horseradish Remsens.

Makes 4 servings

3 tablespoons unsalted butter, at room temperature

¼ cup bread crumbs (we use panko)

2 tablespoons grated Parmesan cheese

¼ teaspoon freshly ground black pepper, plus more to taste

¼ cup plus 2 tablespoons prepared horseradish (we use Reese brand)

4 skin-on salmon fillets, about 1½ inches wide

½ cup sour cream

Brosotto (page 101), for serving

1. Adjust an oven rack to the center position and preheat the oven to 450°F. Line a sheet pan with foil.

2. In a medium microwave-safe bowl, melt the butter. Stir in the bread crumbs, Parm, pepper, and ¼ cup of the horseradish. Mix well.

3. Place the salmon skin side down on the prepared sheet pan and divide the horseradish mixture among the salmon fillets, making a neat crust on each fillet.

4. Bake until deeply golden brown on the top and the inside temp is 145°F on an instant-read thermometer, about 15 minutes. Turn the oven to broil and finish the salmon under the broiler for a minute or two, until the crust gets a few crispy brown highlights. Just watch carefully so it doesn't burn.

5. While the salmon is in the oven, make the creamy horseradish sauce for serving. In a small nonstick skillet, warm up the sour cream over medium heat, keeping it moving in the pan with a silicone spatula until it's hot and much thinner. Remove from the heat and stir in the remaining 2 tablespoons horseradish and a couple grinds of pepper. Mix well and you're done!

6. Use a thin spatula to remove the cooked salmon from the sheet pan—the skin will come off automatically—and place the salmon on plates. Drizzle the sauce on the salmon and enjoy.

7. The Remsens serve the salmon with a side of our veggie-packed Brosotto.

GRANDMA'S BRAIDED BACON MEATLOAF 2.0

WE ATE MEATLOAF AT LEAST ONCE A WEEK DURING MY WONDER YEARS. I THOUGHT MOM made it because it was simply delicious, but actually she made it because we'd eat it and it was cheap. At six or seven I remember asking Mom who showed her how to make it, and she said "Gunga," which was how I had pronounced *Grandma* when I was three, and that nickname stuck for her entire life.

My grandma Sharp was 100 percent Swedish. Did you know that Sweden is famous not only for Volvos and IKEA but for meatloaves? In Stockholm they call them *köttfärslimpa*, which I would say out loud if I had any idea how to pronounce those special letters with the double-dots above them. Now you see why I called her Gunga.

In the 1960s, Mom was very clever in the kitchen with the limited resources she had. In Russell, Kansas, nobody really had canned tomato products in the house, but we always had ketchup, so if something needed "a little *red* something," Mom would squeeze in a squirt of Heinz. She also had a technique so she'd always know when the meatloaf was done; she'd put a piece of bacon on the top and when it was finally crunchy, the meatloaf was seemingly always perfectly done. That bacon was like the pop-up timer you might see on a roasted turkey.

This recipe has elements that we've collected over our lifetimes: the ketchup, Gunga's ground meats, and a blanket of bacon inspired by our friends at Masterbuilt, the smoker company, who showed us how to make a bacon weave, which they call a fatty—we call it fabulous. The glaze that we added candies the bacon—and that blasts it off the charts! This meatloaf may be made of memories, but it's also the best meatloaf we've ever had—just saying.

Makes 6 to 8 servings

Cooking oil spray

1 tablespoon unsalted butter

1 medium sweet onion, cut into medium dice

2 garlic cloves, thinly sliced

1½ cups ketchup

¼ cup packed light brown sugar

½ teaspoon smoked paprika

2 large eggs

2 tablespoons A.1. sauce

1 tablespoon Worcestershire sauce

1 teaspoon table salt

1 teaspoon freshly ground black pepper

One 4-ounce can diced green chiles, undrained

1 cup bread crumbs (we use panko)

2 pounds ground meatloaf mix (beef, veal, and pork)

1 pound thin-sliced bacon (16 slices in the package)

1. Preheat the oven to 350°F. Lightly mist a 9 × 13-inch baking pan with cooking spray.

2. In a large nonstick skillet, melt the butter over medium-high heat. Add the onion and garlic and sauté until the onion is soft and turning golden brown on the edges, 4 to 6 minutes. Remove from the heat to cool.

3. To make a glaze, in a small bowl, mix ½ cup of the ketchup, the brown sugar, and smoked paprika. Set the ketchup glaze aside.

4. In a large bowl, combine the remaining 1 cup ketchup, the eggs, A.1. sauce, Worcestershire sauce, salt, and pepper and stir well. Add the diced green chiles, bread crumbs, and cooled onion-garlic mixture and mix again. Finally, add the ground meat mixture and combine until all the ingredients are well mixed. I go old-school and use my hands—but I go new-school by wearing a pair of disposable food prep gloves from our PPE stash. Form the meat mixture into a large meatball and leave it parked in the bowl.

5. Now for the creative part! Let's make the bacon weave. If you've never built a bacon weave, it's unbelievably easy; google "How to make a bacon weave" and you'll find 122,000 videos in less than a second. If you'd prefer written instructions, see the opposite page. Just make the bacon weave on a sheet of wax paper or parchment paper.

6. Pour the ketchup glaze in the middle of the bacon weave and quickly spread it almost to the edges. Shape the large meatball in the bowl into a traditional loaf about 11 inches long, then place the top of the loaf squarely in the middle of the bacon weave. Pulling up the wax or parchment paper that's under the bacon weave, cinch the bacon up to both long sides of the loaf. Once you've got a good handle on it, flip the whole setup upside down into the prepared baking pan, with the bacon weave on top. Remove the paper gently, and if any bacon slices got jostled out of place, carefully put them back into position. As needed, reshape the meat mixture underneath the bacon with your hands to make it look like a perfect loaf.

7. Bake the meatloaf, uncovered, until the interior temperature at the thickest part of the loaf reads 160°F on an instant-read thermometer, about 1½ hours. Cooking times will vary depending on how thick your loaf is.

8. Let the meatloaf rest 10 minutes before serving, and don't cut it until you take a picture; it's the coolest looking meatloaf—ever.

HOW TO MAKE A BACON WEAVE

Set out a large, sturdy piece of wax or parchment paper and lay 8 bacon slices on the paper, side by side, horizontally. Working on the left side of the slices, starting at the bottom, fold 1 slice to the right a few inches. Skip the piece above that, then fold the next, folding up *every other piece*. Grab a new slice of bacon from your stash and lay it vertically on the left side, from top to bottom. Now, unfold all the bent pieces. That first piece of the weave is now done.

To add a second vertical slice, once again start at the bottom. This time you're going to fold only the pieces you didn't touch the first time. So skip that bottom piece and fold the one above it all the way *to the left* until it touches that first vertical piece. Skip the next, fold the next, and repeat. Take another unused piece of bacon and place it vertically just to the right of the first piece, then unfold all the bent pieces. See the pattern?

For the third row, fold the same pieces as you did on the first one—but they'll all go to the left this time. Repeat the pattern until you have 8 rows and 8 columns of bacon, beautifully woven into a grid pattern.

If you still can't visualize this weaving, don't worry—watch a video online and it will make perfect sense! I can make one now in about 5 minutes, and the end result is *soooo* worth it. Good luck!

COQ AU NO VIN

JULIA CHILD, WHEREVER YOU ARE, COVER YOUR EARS: NOT EVERYBODY LIKES TO COOK with wine. This recipe is something we started making last year New Year's Day, when I was torturing myself with a combination of the keto diet and Dry January.

We love coq au vin (which means chicken in wine), so we keto-ized Julia Child's legendary recipe of red wine, mushrooms, onions, bacon, and chicken. The keto diet loves bacon and chicken, so it was a natural to adapt.

Instead of wine, we used beef stock and tomato juice; thirty minutes of simmering makes this an absolutely tender, savory treat with a flavor that's first-class. No longer on keto, we've added back the original vegetables to this recipe—but it's still booze free.

We call it coq au *no* vin. I mean, *wine* not?

Makes 6 servings

Cooking oil spray

½ pound bacon (5 to 8 slices), cut into 1-inch pieces

½ cup plus 2 tablespoons all-purpose flour

6 boneless, skinless chicken thighs

Table salt and freshly ground black pepper

1¾ cups beef or chicken stock

One 10-ounce package whole mushrooms, trimmed and halved (we use Baby Bellas)

2 garlic cloves, thinly sliced

4 carrots, peeled and halved crosswise

1 large yellow onion, peeled and quartered

1 teaspoon herbes de Provence

1¾ cups tomato juice

Mashed potatoes, for serving

1. Lightly mist the bottom of a 10-inch soup pot with a lid or a Dutch oven with cooking spray. Set over medium-high heat and fry the bacon for 6 to 8 minutes. Flip and cook to your level of crispy, 4 to 7 minutes longer.

2. Meanwhile, place ½ cup of the flour in a shallow bowl and—without unrolling the thighs—lightly dredge them in the flour. Sprinkle them lightly with salt and pepper.

3. Remove the bacon to a plate, add the chicken thighs (still rolled up, so they all fit in the pot) to the hot grease and cook them, undisturbed, until they get color and a bit of a crust, 5 to 7 minutes. Carefully turn them over and cook another 5 minutes on the second side. Remove the chicken to a plate.

4. Add ¼ cup of the beef stock and the mushrooms to the pot. The stock will immediately boil. Deglaze the pan by scraping a spatula on the bottom, creating a little sauce. Coat the mushrooms in the sauce and cook them for 3 to 4 minutes, as their liquid starts to release. Toss in the garlic, carrots, and onion and season with ½ teaspoon salt, 1 teaspoon pepper, and the herbes de Provence. Mix to combine, then sauté until the onions have significantly softened, 5 to 7 minutes. Add the remaining 2 tablespoons flour and mix to coat.

5. The stuff stuck to the bottom of the pan has the best flavor, so add another ¼ cup of the beef stock and deglaze the pan again to get that flavor. Add the remaining 1¼ cups beef stock and the tomato juice, give a stir to mix them in, then move the vegetables to one side and return the chicken to the pot.

6. Bring the liquid to a quick boil, cover the pot, reduce the heat, and simmer until the chicken is at 165°F (check with a thermometer) and the sauce has thickened beautifully, about 40 minutes.

7. When ready to serve, microwave the cooked bacon a quick 15 seconds to lightly warm it up. Serve the chicken and vegetables on plates or a platter, with some bacon on top of each serving. We always serve this with a small side of mashed potatoes with a splash of the pot's juices as gravy on top.

Kathy can stir the pot.

MONA LISA'S CHICKEN

IN JULY 2001 MY BROTHER-IN-LAW ROB AND HIS WIFE, GWEN, INVITED US ON AN EX-travagant two-week vacation in Europe. My favorite single day was in Paris, where Gwen had booked an all-day guided tour of the Louvre Museum with their top English-speaking guide, a deb-onair *homme* named Girard who either knew every detail of every work of art or was just making it up. He showed and explained to us the Venus de Milo, the Raft of the Medusa, and the most famous work of art in the world, the Mona Lisa, who smiles faintly on a wall behind bazooka-proof glass.

After the morning hours spent gawking at incredibly old famous stuff, Gwen had reserved us a table for lunch at the Louvre's fancy restaurant. The menu was in French. Having had four years of college-level Romance language instruction, with an emphasis on French, I briefly scanned the menu and ordered the *poulet à la moutarde*. I knew *poulet* was chicken, and it was the only chicken dish, so I ordered it. I had no idea what *moutarde* was, but as long as it wasn't gizzards, I was going to eat it.

To my delight they brought me a perfectly portioned piece of crispy chicken in a creamy *moutarde* (mustard) sauce, which I would not have ordered in a million years: I'm just not a big mustard chicken guy, although I grew up on French's yellow mustard, which I discovered is not French—it's made in Missouri.

Back to the mustard chicken—there was an herby hint of something I'd never eaten. I asked the waiter what those green flecks were in the cream sauce, and he re-vealed the secret ingredient in this recipe: "tarragon." When we got home, we found an easy *poulet à la moutarde* in a cookbook—but it didn't include tarragon, so we added it at the end, and it's become a family fa-vorite. Of course we don't call it *poulet à la moutarde*—people might think it includes gizzards—so at our house we simply refer to it as Mona Lisa's Chicken.

Try it—you'll Louvre it!

Makes 6 servings

Lunch at the Louvre.

½ cup all-purpose flour

1 teaspoon table salt

1 teaspoon freshly ground black pepper

½ teaspoon garlic powder

6 boneless, skinless chicken thighs

3 tablespoons unsalted butter, plus more as needed

2 tablespoons olive oil, plus more as needed

1 cup chicken stock (we use Better Than Bouillon chicken base)

1 large or 2 small shallots, sliced into thin rings

2 garlic cloves, thinly sliced

3 tablespoons Dijon mustard (we use Grey Poupon)

1 cup heavy cream

20 to 25 fresh tarragon leaves, minced

Smashed Brown Potatoes (page 99, minus the cheese and other extras), for serving

1. In a shallow bowl, mix the flour, salt, pepper, and garlic powder. Unroll the thighs and lightly dust them with the flour mixture.

2. In a large skillet, melt 1 tablespoon of butter in the olive oil over medium-high heat, then swirl the pan to coat the bottom. Working in batches, place the floured thighs in the pan smooth side down and cook undisturbed until the thighs have a nice golden crust, 7 to 9 minutes. Flip and cook the other side until the thighs read 165°F on an instant-read thermometer, 7 to 9 minutes longer. Remove the chicken to a plate and keep it warm. If working in batches, add more butter and oil as needed.

3. Pour ½ cup of the chicken stock into the skillet, set over medium-high heat, and deglaze the bottom, scraping off the tasty crunchy fried chicken remnants. Add the shallots and garlic and sauté for a couple minutes to soften the shallots and reduce the stock a bit. Reduce the heat to medium and add the remaining ½ cup chicken stock and the mustard. Mix until the sauce is a uniform golden color. Add the remaining 2 tablespoons butter, the heavy cream, and half of the minced tarragon. When the butter is melted, mix everything together, then return the chicken to the pan, smooth side up, and cook for about 5 minutes to warm to serving temperature. As the sauce bubbles around the sides, stir a bit so it doesn't separate.

4. Serve the chicken on plates or a platter, with sauce spooned over each portion. As the pièce de résistance, scatter the remaining tarragon on top. A great side accompaniment is our easy smashed potatoes.

5. Once plated—dig in! It's so delicious it would make the Mona Lisa smile—if she were a smiler.

The kids orbiting Venus—de Milo.

BEER-BATTERED COCONUT SHRIMP

EVERY TIME WE'D GO TO A CERTAIN SEAFOOD PLACE FAMOUS FOR ITS SHRIMP, I'D TRY to impress Kathy as I'd recite the line from the movie *Forrest Gump,* when Bubba Gump was marveling at the many ways people could cook shrimp: "You can barbecue it, boil it, broil it, bake it, sauté it . . ." That was the easy part, but then I'd struggle. Which came next, the Creole or the gumbo? Maybe it was the kebabs? Point was, I stopped. Midspeech, Bubba actually mentioned what is today our favorite shrimp dish—one that we had for the first time during a family vacation in Hawaii.

In 2004, the kids had worn us down begging to go to Hawaii, asking at least nineteen thousand times at dinner. We said yes, which meant we saved and planned for a year. Kathy booked us at a very famous luau one night, with traditional Hawaiian music and of course hula dancing. At that time both of our daughters, Mary and Sally, were taking dance lessons, so they leaped from their seats and started dancing alongside the professional hula dancers. Kathy and I were fine with it, because we were five time zones away from anyone we knew, so I got up and joined them.

Dinner was amazing—at least the parts I could identify. For the first time we all tried chicken long rice, taro, *kālua* pork, and other things that we still can't find using the usually reliable Wikipedia. Of course, when in Rome . . . Kathy and I each ordered a mai tai, not really our favorite adult beverage of choice, but we were at a luau, in Hawaii! Kathy remembers it was sweet and smooth. I remember they were $18 apiece . . . *in 2004*!

The smash hit dish that night was coconut shrimp. My colleague Jay Soroko at Fox News shared this recipe that his parents, Jordan and Judy, have perfected over the years. It's just as wonderful as that version we had in the middle of the Pacific, and when we make it, it takes us back to the night our kids were dancing at the luau. The highlight was when guests at another table walked by on the way out and said, "Hi, Kathy and Steve!" They were from our town, and they'd been watching us all night.

"We got some pictures of you dancing, Steve," they said, at which point I offered them $75 for their disposable camera. They thought I was kidding . . . but anyway, the Doocys no longer dance in public.

Aloha! You'll love this shrimp . . .

Makes 4 servings

DIPPING SAUCE

One 8-ounce jar apricot preserves

⅓ cup sherry

1 teaspoon fresh lemon juice

2 tablespoons salted butter

1. To make the apricot dipping sauce: In a medium saucepan, combine the apricot preserves, sherry, lemon juice, and butter. Mix over medium heat until the preserves and butter are melted and the sauce is smooth, 3 to 4 minutes. Remove from the heat but keep warm.

2. To make the battered shrimp: First, make the batter. Separate the eggs and put the egg whites in the bowl of stand mixer or in a small bowl and the yolks in a medium bowl. Whisk the yolks until smooth, then add the flour, salt, and pepper and stir to combine.

BATTERED SHRIMP

2 large eggs

2 cups all-purpose flour

½ teaspoon table salt

¼ teaspoon freshly ground black pepper

1 cup beer (we use Coors)

2 cups sweetened coconut flakes, plus more if needed

1 pound jumbo shrimp (16/20 count), peeled and deveined, tails left on

Vegetable oil, for frying

Rice Cooker Coconut Rice (page 119), for serving

Sugar snap peas, for serving (optional)

Great chow at the luau.

Pour in the beer and mix. It's going to be gloppy, but keep mixing until you have a very thick slurry. Set that in the fridge for about 10 minutes. Whip the egg whites a few minutes on medium speed, or until they are foamy white and frothy. Set that bowl in the fridge as well to chill for 10 minutes.

3. Remove both bowls and gently fold the egg whites into the yolk mixture. Keep folding until the bubbles disappear and you have a smooth-shiny batter.

4. Set up a dredging station, starting with the batter. Next, place the coconut in a wide, shallow bowl for dredging. Pat the shrimp dry with paper towels. Working with one at a time, dip the shrimp in the batter, shake off any excess, and roll it in coconut flakes. If the coconut bowl gets too much wet batter in it, swap it out for some fresh coconut. Set the shrimp on a plate or wax paper until all are done.

5. Pour about ¾ inch of vegetable oil into a large wide saucepan and heat over medium heat to 350°F. If it's too hot, it will quickly burn the coconut, so we use an instant-read thermometer to make sure it's in the right neighborhood.

6. You'll have to cook the shrimp in batches. When the oil is ready, place the shrimp into the pan without crowding and fry about 1 minute as the edges quickly turn golden. Gently flip the shrimp and cook the other side about 1 minute more until it's also golden and crunchy all over, for a total of 2 minutes of frying time. Remove the shrimp to drain on paper towels while you fry the rest of the shrimp.

7. Serve the coconut shrimp with the warm apricot dipping sauce. These shrimp go great with our Rice Cooker Coconut Rice (also from a Hawaii vacation). Jordan and Judy serve with sugar snap peas. Enjoy!

7

PASTA AND PIZZA

WHEN I WAS GROWING UP, TAILGATING WAS when you got too close to the car you were following. But Kathy and I were tailgating in the modern sense before people called it that. In cold parking lots, out of the back of our Eddie Bauer Ford Explorer, snack mom supreme Mrs. Doocy would help distribute and organize the snacks and drinks at our kids' games, scout trips, Academic Decathlons, and dance competitions. Had I invested in Capri Sun back in 1998, I'd be lighting our charcoal grill with fifties.

Snacks were an excuse for Kathy to go to every game and practice, just in case one of our kids got hurt or needed moral support. For my part, I felt that sports could be an easier way for our children to get into a great college than being great at trigonometry—which triggers people.

We knew from the time he was five that Peter Doocy was destined to attend Harvard on a soccer scholarship, so we signed him up for Kinder Kickers. The season started as the weather turned cold, and Kathy was more worried about him catching a cold than a pass—so we thoroughly insulated him in long johns under a polar fleece sweat suit, topped with a final layer of the team jersey and shorts. He had the flexibility of Pinocchio, without the worry of termites.

Is it snack time yet?

A few seasons in, we knew no Ivy League soccer scholarship was in the offing, so Peter moved to softball. Always a good soldier with a positive attitude, he came ready to play—but his coaches wanted to win and usually played our town's stars. Peter got almost zero playing time. "Hey, Coach, aren't you supposed to play the kids at least half of the game?" I'd ask, and they'd say yes and that Peter would play more next week—but he never did. The only Doocy who got to routinely take the field was snack mom Kathy—at the end of the game.

Toward the end of the season the coach must have thought we were going to turn him in for not playing Peter, who'd warmed the bench all year, and out of the blue the coach asked him to pinch-hit for one of the starters. Kathy and I were terrified. Peter had never pinch-hit for anybody. Nonetheless Peter scooted up to the plate, knocked some clods off his cleats as if he knew what he was doing, and assumed the ready-batter position that he and I had worked on at the batting cages for five years.

Moments before the pitcher was about to throw the first ball, a local luminary—Phil Simms, the two-time Super Bowl quarterback who lived in our town—arrived at the game, along with his son Chris. There was some murmuring and pointing, and before you knew it every head in the stands was staring at the Simmses. Not one person was looking at Peter—including the pitcher.

Remembering why he was on the mound, the pitcher did an impressive wind-up and then threw his first pitch. It was terrible—*waaaaay* too low and outside. But Peter was thinking the coach would never put him in again, so he took a big step across the plate toward the ball and whacked it hard. The crack of the bat surprised both teams back to the game—but they missed the hit and had no idea where the ball was. Peter rounded first, with his coach yelling, "Take three!" This meant he was supposed to stop at third base. But Peter had never gotten this far in his dream and didn't want it to end, so he ran right past third and headed for home. I got a terrible feeling in the pit of my gut.

Twenty feet from home, with the catcher blocking the plate, Kathy was yelling, *"Slide, Peter, slide"* in that *"Run, Forrest, run"* voice. Every person there knew he should have stopped at third, because the best player in our town had just thrown the ball to the all-star catcher, and Peter was about to be tagged out at home and humiliated.

That's when Peter did something I'd never seen in rec ball. He took a giant leap and flew as far as he could toward the plate, then slid on his belly, kicking up a huge cloud of dust just as the catcher caught the ball. One millisecond later, the ump yelled, "He's safe!"

Later Phil Simms said to Peter, "Great play, kid." And he meant it, because the lanky boy who'd ridden the bench all year had hit an inside-the-park homer on his first at-bat.

Over dinner that night, Peter told us that his dream was to make the high school baseball team, but they only took kids who played a lot in rec their last year, and so far he'd only really made one play. We estimated in his final year of rec ball, Peter would have to play every single game, but that meant he needed to be recruited by a coach who understood his real potential. Who was that in our town, we wondered. In the end, the guy who drafted Peter was a rookie who was quite honestly completely unqualified for the job. That's right—I volunteered to be his coach. Before that the only thing I'd ever volunteered for was to be an organ donor.

He never gave up.

My first official coach task was the town draft. I didn't know what to do, but Peter did. He made a list with the names of the town's best players on the back of our gas bill, and through a series of luck and flukes, I recruited all the boys on the list except one. Before the games Peter was essentially the manager, assigning players to positions, making sure everybody played half a game, and devising a strategy. He loved to play ball, and it showed. The season played out like a Hallmark Movie of the Week, and we wound up in our town's world series. Because he played so much that year, he wound up making the high school baseball team.

My mission was accomplished. At our end-of-season celebration at the Dairy Queen,

I announced to the team I was retiring after one season of head coaching. The boys gave me a big cheer—but I think they really just wanted another round of ice cream treats. I said yes—and let their parents deal with them bouncing off the walls on a sugar high.

As I handed Kathy the $100 gift certificate the boys' parents had just given me as a thank-you gift, I noticed the long faces of Mary and Sally, who apparently had thought I was going to be their coach, too. *Change of plans*—I immediately announced I was un-retiring. A cheer went up—and I worked the soccer sidelines for another ten years, even though I still can't explain what offsides means.

Sally's and Mary's teams were much younger than Peter's, and coaching younger players requires a lot of vocal volume in always polite, direct terms.

Mary, Arthur Ashe Kids' Day.

With each practice I lost a little more of my voice, and by the end of the first month I woke up sounding like Lauren Bacall. "You've got a bad case of preacher's notch," the ENT doctor told me. The condition was named after the hellfire-and-brimstone preachers who ministered to their congregation at a high volume for a long time. "You a stock trader, Steve?" my doctor asked, and immediately revealed himself to be a CNN viewer.

The doctor's instructions were for me to rest my voice as much as possible—which is hard when you host a three-hour talk show every day. As a coach, I became the Marcel Marceau of North Jersey and started doing a lot of pointing and pantomiming. My signature play was pulling a dollar bill out of my athleisure pants pocket and waving it over my head. When somebody spotted it, they'd yell, "dollar offense!" The kids thought it was fun, and I imagined the parents in the stands were very impressed that their daughters' coach had names for the plays. In reality, *dollar offense* meant that whoever scored a goal got a dollar. I bring this up only because the statute of

Peter at bat.

limitations has certainly run out. But if the Feds want to pursue legal action, they should come talk to me at my morning job—at CNN.

Late one afternoon the *Fox & Friends* producer called and said, "Tomorrow Cal Ripken is coming on—can one of your kids play catch with him?" Our youngest, Sally, was the only child available, and while Sally loved the idea, she didn't actually know how to catch the ball. However, when given the chance to be on TV playing ball with one of baseball's most beloved players, she said yes! So the night before, we practiced in the backyard until way past dark. On TV the next morning, Cal Ripken tossed Sally a dozen balls, and she caught every one.

I complimented her skill later that day, and she said something gobsmacking: "Dad, I want to pitch!"

Oh no! Kathy has told me many times that the loneliest people on the sidelines are the parents of pitchers and goalies. Brilliant observation—and true!

Her smile says it all.

Best ever—and Cal Ripken Jr.

I wasn't worried about Sally losing the game for the team—I could do that on my own. We lived in New Jersey, and I was worried about the parents, who could be a rough audience. I worried that might impact her self-confidence, so I made her the Cal Ripken deal—"Let's practice," I said. "If it works out, you can pitch this year."

Two months later, with one inning left in the season, I announced that Sally was going to pitch. The girls all joined hands with my daughter and hugged her for good luck. I took the opportunity for a moment of Vince Lombardi-esque inspiration: "Sally, as William Shakespeare used to say before every performance—get out there and kick some butt!"

Her smile was so broad it could be seen from the Google Earth satellite. I could not tell if it was because she was pitching or because I had just said "butt."

Sally the swimmer.

The loneliest people on the sidelines are the parents of pitchers and goalies.

Sally walked the first five batters and hit another—with no outs. I could feel some Type-A parents were giving me the stink eye—Sally's pitching was cutting into their lunch plans—but right then I did not care. I had happily volunteered and spent 150 hours with their children that season, and for a couple more minutes they were going to invest a little time in my kid, whose dream was to pitch.

In her pitching dream, Sally never got past walking up to the mound; the actual pitching was hard stuff. She knew she was supposed to throw strikes and get outs, but it wasn't working that day, and she got frustrated and a little embarrassed, but *she never gave up.*

And after thirty-six minutes of flop sweat for Kathy and me, the ump called, "Strike three!"

Our team ran to the mound and hugged Sally, whom I hoisted to my shoulders and carried off like she'd just won the Super Bowl. Kathy and I both had tears running our mascara . . . Sally was our *Rudy.*

While Kathy was picking up the orange peels, juice boxes, and baseball bats, one of the parents walked by said, "Coach, what place did we finish this year?"

"Fifth, I think." I paused. "Actually it could be sixth."

For a moment I thought to myself, *If he was so concerned about his kid's team standing, why didn't he volunteer to coach?*

In our basement we have trophies from our three kids' entire sports careers. Those trophy ceremonies were exciting and fulfilling and meant something to them—for about five minutes. Now they are simply shiny reminders of those wonderful years I spent playing ball with my kids and their friends.

A couple times a year I'll be running errands and a young adult will wave and say, "Hi, Coach!" I'll wave back and say, "You're all grown

Paddleboarding in Florida.

up!" I'll ask how their parents are, and silently wonder to myself if I ever paid them a dollar for a goal.

As for the Doocy sports stars—Sally eventually retired from softball and went on to lead her high school's varsity swim team as captain, and she swam in the state finals. Peter made the high school baseball team all four years and played in the New Jersey state championships.

And Mary, who was a stand-out soccer, softball, and lacrosse player and never once in her life rowed a boat, was recruited as a walk-on to the Boston College crew team and became the first Doocy in family history to be a Division 1 university athlete.

Of course, Kathy and I know our kids couldn't have done it without their parents—who brought the snacks.

JASPER'S SECRET
MILLION-DOLLAR PASTA SAUCE

SIXTY-EIGHT YEARS AGO IN KANSAS CITY, LEONARDO MIRABILE AND HIS SON JASPER opened their eponymous eatery Jasper's that would one day be one of America's best Italian restaurants. In the beginning they cooked up the family's Old World recipes, but they were always looking for new ideas. Jasper was on a trip to New York City when he told a waiter in a midtown ristorante that he loved their red sauce. "What kind of tomatoes you use?" he asked—but everybody clammed up. They weren't in the business to give away their secrets to some guy from the Midwest. He left the place empty-handed, but just out the door, he passed what he realized was the restaurant's garbage can. Jasper scanned the street, nobody was looking, so he lifted the lid, and got his answer. It was full of empty Hunt's tomato cans. That's just good detective work, Jasper!

Then, while eating at a lovely trattoria on a family trip to Rome, Jasper ordered the *capelli d'angelo* (angel hair) and fell in love with it. Once again he quizzed the staff, but nobody was going to give away their secret recipes to some guy from America. So the next night he came back and ordered the same thing. And the night after that he ordered the same thing. He made notes, and once back in Kansas City he worked with his wife and their chefs to crack the code. It was *perfect*! It was Jasper's gem.

When customers would ask Jasper for the recipe, he would shake his head and say, "Sorry—can't." He knew if he gave away the recipe, they could make it at home and they might never come back to his restaurant. So it remained a secret his entire life.

That recipe was his restaurant's number one best-selling pasta dish for more than fifty years! After he passed away, as a tribute to his incredible life's work, Jasper's family decided to share the recipe for that signature dish to keep his memory alive. His secret sauce is revealed below.

Kathy and I adore this—Jasper was a genius, and the recipe is simple and over-the-top delicious. We whip up this restaurant-quality dish at home in less than half an hour. The best part? You didn't have to rummage through a garbage can to get the recipe.

Makes 4 or 5 servings

Table salt

2 teaspoons unsalted butter

One 4-ounce package diced prosciutto

1 cup thinly sliced button mushrooms

8 ounces long pasta (Jasper used angel hair; the Doocys use bucatini)

½ cup frozen green peas

1. In a large pot, start salted water boiling for the pasta, but don't cook it yet.

2. As the water's heating, in a large skillet, melt the butter over medium-high heat. Add the prosciutto and sliced mushrooms and sauté until the mushrooms release some of their liquid and get some golden highlights, about 5 minutes.

3. While the prosciutto and mushrooms are cooking, add the pasta to the boiling water and cook to al dente according to the package directions. In the last 2 minutes of boiling, toss in the frozen peas.

1½ cups jarred marinara sauce (the Doocys use Rao's brand)

½ cup heavy cream

¼ teaspoon red pepper flakes

1 cup grated Pecorino Romano cheese

Buttery crusty bread, for serving

4. When the meat is crispy and cooked, stir in the marinara, cream, pepper flakes, and Romano and use a silicone spatula to mix until the cheese melts and forms a smooth, delicious sauce.

5. Drain the cooked pasta and peas, toss in with the sauce, and mix well. Serve immediately with some buttery crusty bread.

TURKEY MEATBALL STROGANOFF

DURING MY SUMMERS IN COLLEGE, WHEN MY DAD WORKED IN CONSTRUCTION, HE GOT me the best-paying jobs for a kid my age. I was paid union wages, but I earned them, doing incredibly hard manual labor jobs of roofing and plumbing. Quitting time was 3:30 in the afternoon and Dad would drive us home. Within five minutes I'd be in deep REM sleep, which you'd think was impossible in broad daylight sitting straight up in a Chevy Vega bucket seat with the window open, the AC broken, and one arm dangling out as an aerodynamic wind foil.

Every night my mom would welcome her hard-working men home with an amazing meal of comfort food. She made a magnificent meatball and mushroom stroganoff like this one, and Kathy adapted it to use frozen turkey meatballs to save time and effort.

Dad loved Mom's cooking, but he loved his green Naugahyde La-Z-Boy recliner even more. After dinner he'd retire to that chair with a big bowl of ice cream, and by the time the closing theme of *The Waltons* was playing, he'd be dead asleep. "Jim, time to go to bed," Mom would say, and Dad would reply within seconds, "I'm not sleeping . . . I'm resting my eyes."

She'd prod him again in an hour, when he was full-on snoring, and he'd repeat, "I'm just resting my eyes." That went on every night of my childhood in Kansas. I miss that.

The next day, Dad would come to my room at 4:30 a.m., shake my foot, and say, "Rise and shine, sunshine!" He never complained about the hour or the work or the pay; he always smiled and made the best of everything. We loved working together, and at the end of the summer I'd return to college and he'd go back to driving to and from work alone.

I miss our father-to-son chats. But this recipe is a happy reminder of when we were both working the Dawn Patrol. His legacy is that I'm still working it.

Dawn Patrol Doocys.

Makes 5 servings

Cooking oil spray

One 16-ounce package frozen turkey meatballs

Table salt

One 12-ounce package egg noodles

1. Preheat the oven to 350°F. Mist a sheet pan with cooking spray.

2. Place the frozen meatballs in a single layer on the sheet pan and bake according to the package directions until nice and hot. Remove to a plate and keep warm.

2 tablespoons olive oil

1 large yellow onion, cut into medium dice

One 10-ounce package mushrooms, thinly sliced (Baby Bellas work great)

One 10.5-ounce can condensed cream of chicken soup

One 1-ounce packet Lipton onion soup mix

1½ cups low-sodium chicken stock

2 teaspoons all-purpose flour

½ teaspoon freshly ground black pepper

4 ounces cream cheese, cubed, at room temperature

Side salad, for serving

3. Meanwhile, bring a pot of salted water to a boil for the noodles. Cook the entire bag according to the package directions.

4. Now let's make the fantastic sauce. In a large skillet, heat the olive oil over medium-high heat. Add the onion and mushrooms and sauté until the mushrooms release their liquid and the onion softens and they both cook down substantially, about 10 minutes. Mix in the cream of chicken soup, onion soup mix, chicken stock, flour, and pepper. When the mixture is bubbling around the outside of the pan, add the cream cheese cubes near the bubbles so it melts quickly. Let sit a minute or two, then vigorously mix until the sauce is a uniform creamy color.

5. Into the pan go the meatballs. Warm everything to serving temperature.

6. Serve the meatballs and gravy over the noodles. Round out the plate with a side salad—and it's time to eat!

CREAMY PLT PASTA
PANCETTA, LETTUCE, AND TOMATO

OUR DAUGHTER MARY GETS MOST OF HER RECIPES OFF SOCIAL MEDIA, AND SHE JUST SENT me a crazy idea where somebody deconstructed two Quarter Pounders, wrapped them in puff pastry and made a Big Mac Beef Wellington. Don't know if we'll be trying that, but I love the creativity!

A while back Mary also sent us that viral recipe with a bunch of cherry tomatoes and a block of feta cheese. Kathy has been baking fancy cheeses for a while; just look at our Billionaire Bacon and Cranberry Brie (page 22). For our version of a melted cheese and pasta dish, we use Boursin cheese, because it has all the spices and flavors already installed in the cheese, so all we do is heat, stir, and eat! The dish is flavored with pancetta and served on fresh arugula, so we call it PLT Pasta—for pancetta, lettuce, and tomato.

From pasta to POTUS . . . as I'm typing out this recipe, our son, Peter, is traveling with the president in Wilmington, Delaware. Peter's rental car is parked in the Greenville Shopping Center parking lot by Janssen's Market near Joe Biden's home. Reportedly the president frequents Janssen's, where back in the cold case they have a stack of premade Joe Biden sandwiches built with maple turkey, Havarti cheese, fresh arugula, and champagne mustard.

Now if they had a tomato on there it could be another PLT: *POTUS,* Lettuce, and Tomato.

Makes 4 servings

Olive oil cooking spray

2 pints grape tomatoes

Table salt

One 5.2-ounce package Boursin Garlic and Fine Herbs

One 4-ounce package diced pancetta

½ pound bucatini or spaghetti

3 to 4 cups baby arugula

1. Adjust an oven rack to the center position and preheat the oven to 400°F. Mist an 8 × 8-inch baking dish with olive oil cooking spray.

2. Place the tomatoes in the prepared dish. Give them a light misting of cooking spray and lightly season with salt. Clear an area in the center of the pan and place the Boursin cheese in it, then scatter the pancetta evenly over the tomatoes.

3. Bake until the tomatoes are shriveled and blistered and the round of cheese is a beautiful golden brown, 35 to 40 minutes.

4. Meanwhile, when the tomatoes and cheese are about halfway done baking, start a small pot of salted water boiling for the pasta. Add the pasta to the boiling water and cook according to the package directions. Time when you add the pasta so that it's done just as the tomato and cheese dish is finished cooking.

5. When you remove the dish from the oven, use a spatula to gently press down on the tomatoes to release their tasty juices. Stir up the cheese to coat the tomatoes and meat. Drain the pasta, add to the sauce, and mix until creamy and dreamy.

6. To serve, place ¾ to 1 cup of arugula on each plate and spoon the pasta and sauce on top. Time to eat up!

CAST-IRON SKILLET PIZZA ON THE GRILL

AT BIRTHDAY PARTIES OR ON BABYSITTER NIGHTS WHEN OUR KIDS WERE LITTLE, KATHY would order simple cheese pizzas from a local joint and ask them to cut the pizza into little two-inch squares that she called a "kid cut," so the kids weren't holding a foot-long triangle of molten cheese that dripped on their shoes. With the kid-cut pieces, they didn't need a plate or napkins; they could just grab and go, and if they needed a napkin, they'd use their shirts. That's why God invented Shout Triple-Acting stain remover.

When our kids got older they graduated to more exotic pizza configurations. Here's a recipe for two different pizzas, both college favorites. One, of course, involves Buffalo sauce and the other is a little salad-y. We make both on our outdoor grill, which gets much hotter than our kitchen stove—creating a brick-oven pizzeria-quality crust at home!

And as you stand next to the grill waiting to take the pizza out, you can admire the neighbors' well-maintained yard and notice that they've been blowing their leaves into your backyard . . . which is actually good, because now you don't feel so bad about putting a dozen empty wine bottles into their recycling bin last Tuesday.

Makes one 6-slice pizza

BOTH PIZZAS

One 16-ounce ball store-bought pizza dough

Olive oil, for brushing

Cornmeal, for dusting

BUFFALO CHICKEN FINGER PIZZA

¼ cup ranch dressing, plus more for garnish (we use Ken's brand)

½ cup shredded mozzarella cheese

½ pound breaded chicken tenders, cooked according to the package directions

¼ cup Frank's RedHot Original sauce, plus more for garnish

¼ cup blue cheese crumbles

1 green onion, dark green part only, cut into ¼-inch rings

FIRST STEPS FOR BOTH PIZZAS

1. Preheat the grill to high.

2. Let the dough ball warm to room temperature on a lightly oiled plate and covered with a kitchen towel for 1 hour (or 4 hours if frozen).

3. Make sure you use an ovenproof skillet for this recipe. We use a 12-inch Lodge cast-iron skillet. Brush the bottom and sides of the pan with about ½ tablespoon of olive oil.

4. Lightly dust a work area with about ½ tablespoon cornmeal. The easiest way to roll out the dough is to flatten the ball with your hands and dust the top of the dough with some more cornmeal. Using a rolling pin and starting in the center of the dough, roll it out in every direction until it's round and about ¾ inch thick. Pick up the whole dough by the edge and slowly walk your hands around it so the weight of the dough stretches it thinner.

5. Toss a little cornmeal across the bottom of the skillet to help the dough release later. Place the pizza crust into the pan and use your fingers to press it in place and form a nice raised rim around the edge. We then use a pizza docker and run it over the entire pie and crust (it cost $8 on Amazon) because it pokes holes all over the dough to

BLT PIZZA

One 4-ounce package diced prosciutto or pancetta

½ cup shredded mozzarella cheese

1 large or 2 medium tomatoes, very thinly sliced

Table salt and freshly ground black pepper

¼ cup shredded Parmesan cheese

2 cups baby arugula

Ranch dressing (we use Ken's brand), Chick-fil-A sauce, or Hidden Valley Ranch Secret Sauce, for garnish

Have a slice day.

ensure there are no air bubbles that blow up during the baking; you can also use a fork. Brush the outer edge of the crust with ½ tablespoon olive oil so it turns a gorgeous golden color as it bakes.

6. The steps below are specific to each kind of pizza—but why not throw a party and make both?

FOR THE BUFFALO CHICKEN FINGER PIZZA

1. With the dough in the pan, spread the ¼ cup ranch dressing on the crust as the base sauce, running it up to 1 inch from the edge of the crust. Scatter the mozzarella over the ranch.

2. Chop the cooked chicken tenders into small pieces and toss them in a medium bowl with the hot sauce, coating every piece (add more sauce if you need it). Sprinkle the sauced chicken over the cheese.

3. Place the skillet with the pizza on the grill and close the lid. Bake for 4 minutes, then sprinkle on the blue cheese crumbles. Close the lid and bake until the crust is browned and beautiful, another 4 to 5 minutes. Taking care when working with the super-hot pan, remove the pan from the grill and transfer the pizza to a cutting board.

4. To serve, top the pizza with the green onion rings and drizzle with more ranch dressing and/or more hot sauce, according to your preference. Let the pizza rest a couple minutes, then slice up and enjoy!

FOR THE BLT PIZZA

1. In a small skillet, fry the prosciutto over medium-high heat until crispy, about 5 minutes, and set aside on paper towels to absorb the oil.

2. With the dough in the pan, scatter the mozzarella over the crust, leaving the outer edge bare. Top the cheese with a single layer of sliced tomatoes, then lightly salt and pepper the tomatoes. Sprinkle the tomatoes with the Parmesan.

3. Place the pan with the pizza on the grill and close the lid. Bake until the crust is golden brown and the tomatoes appear cooked, 7 to 9 minutes. Taking care when working with the super-hot pan, remove the pan from the grill and transfer the pizza to a cutting board. Let it rest for 2 to 4 minutes; the tomatoes are hot!

4. To serve, toss the arugula on top of the pizza, then the crisped prosciutto. Drizzle with ranch dressing—although sometimes we'll swap out the ranch dressing for Chick-fil-A sauce or Hidden Valley Ranch Secret Sauce, for a zesty tang. Slice and serve!

CACIO E PEPE AND PANCETTA

CACIO E PEPE IS ITALIAN FOR CHEESE AND PEPPER. BUT THERE'S ONE OTHER INGREDIENT, hot water. It wouldn't surprise me if the person who invented this dish was busy making a cheesy cream sauce and realized they didn't have any cream and resorted to using the pasta-boiling water, so they took a ladle of that, mixed it with the cheese and some grinds of pepper, and a star was born.

My friend Jasper Mirabile Jr. is second-generation Italian and loves to go to Italy. During one family trip to Rome at a lovely restaurant, his daughter, who speaks perfect Italian, introduced the family as the Mirabiles of Kansas City. The Italians left the table and googled them and discovered they owned one of the Midwest's best Italian restaurants, and brought out the owner and chef, who canceled Jasper's wife Lisa's ravioli order. "Absolutely not, that's what we serve tourists," he said. "You're having the house specialty." He brought out cacio e pepe for the whole table. *Cheese and pepper*. And it was amazing.

Jasper loved it, so he asked the natural question of his Italian hosts: "How do you make it? Everybody from the restaurant suddenly clammed up. With cacio e pepe, the grated cheese-to-hot water ratio is like the secret recipe to Coca-Cola, so they sent the family on their way with a lovely tiramisu dessert—but no recipe.

Back in his Kansas City restaurant kitchen, Jasper spent days perfecting his version, which is one of the most popular items on his menu today. This recipe is what Jasper and I came up with after he suggested we add meat. We did, and it's delicious.

But I'm biased—my sisters Ann and Jenny worked at the Mirabile family's restaurants thirty years ago, and my daughter Sally went to college at SMU with Jasper's daughter Alex and was in her wedding, so we've got a real family connection. And today we use Jasper's recipe—which is lots easier than flying to Rome, trying to bribe a waiter with a twenty-euro bill, and asking, "So how much of the Romano?"

Makes 4 servings

Table salt

8 ounces bucatini or other strand pasta, such as spaghetti or linguine

4 ounces diced pancetta

1 cup grated Pecorino Romano cheese

½ cup grated Parmesan cheese

1 teaspoon freshly ground black pepper, plus more to taste

1. Bring a large pot of salted water to a boil. Add the pasta and cook to al dente according to the package directions.

2. Meanwhile, in a large nonstick skillet, cook the pancetta in a single layer over medium-high heat, stirring occasionally, until it has a few golden dark highlights, 5 to 7 minutes. Remove the pancetta to paper towels but leave the grease in the skillet for flavor.

3. Start the sauce just as the noodles are finishing cooking. Using a ladle, carefully remove about ½ cup of the hot pasta water and pour it into the skillet over medium heat. Stir in both cheeses and whisk into a smooth, Alfredo-like consistency; it will be a little gritty until all the cheese melts. If it's too thick, ladle a little more water in and mix.

4. Ladle another ½ cup of the hot pasta water into a Pyrex measuring cup and set it aside. Drain the noodles and place them in the skillet with the cheese sauce. Add the pepper and mix thoroughly. If you think the cheese sauce is too thick or clumpy, add a little of the reserved hot water until it's the texture you want. But don't overdo the water—you don't want it too runny. Finding the happy medium is what makes it perfect. (By the way, I've noticed that bucatini needs more water than spaghetti.)

5. Add the pancetta and mix until combined, then remove from the heat. Serve immediately, with more pepper to taste. And marvel at what you just did with a little cheese and hot water!

SIMPLY LAZY LASAGNA

KATHY MADE LASAGNA ON OUR FIRST DATE. AT THE END OF THE NIGHT I TOLD HER WE would one day be married. She immediately asked me to leave. It must have been the carbs talking. We were married about six months later and that was thirty-six years ago. We now call that recipe Engagement Lasagna.

When our younger daughter, Sally, was at SMU in Dallas, she went out on a date with a very handsome young man who sent her heart aflutter. A little nervous, and remembering our first date history, Sally ordered the lasagna, and so did he. But he never mentioned they'd be married some-day. After six years of dating, Kathy took Sally aside and said flat out she'd invested a lot of time in this guy. "Sally, if you're serious about Ali, long term, it's time you learned how to make *the lasagna*." Understanding the significance of Kathy's recipe, Sally finally got the lasagna lesson.

Two weeks later, Ali popped the question. Apparently Kathy's Engagement red sauce is the *magic* part. And the first thing Sally cooked for Ali in their New York City apartment? Lasagna.

At one of our book events, a woman said she'd heard and loved our Engagement Lasagna story; the actual recipe is in our first *Happy Cookbook*. "I don't have time to make that," she said, and instructed us to come up with a speedier recipe. She said her friend makes "Lazy Lasagna" out of frozen ravioli and a jar of sauce. She said it takes fifteen minutes to prep, and once it's baked, it's on the table and terrific! We loved that idea, but we've also incorporated a couple of the critical elements of Kathy's legendary Engagement Lasagna recipe into that brilliant lazy lasagna concept. From the taste you'd never guess how easy it is to make . . . and the magical part of the recipe? It's made with love . . . and a little wine. Which makes it luscious and lazy!

Makes 9 servings

Cooking oil spray

1 tablespoon olive oil

1 yellow onion, cut into medium dice

1 pound sweet Italian sausage (casings removed if links)

½ teaspoon freshly ground black pepper

½ cup red wine (cabernet works great)

One 28-ounce jar marinara (Rao's is our hands-down favorite)

Two 12-ounce bags large round frozen cheese ravioli, not thawed

1¼ cups whole-milk ricotta cheese

1½ cups shredded mozzarella cheese

Colorful garden salad, for serving

1. Adjust an oven rack to the center position and preheat the oven to 350°F. Mist an 8 × 8-inch baking dish with cooking spray.

2. In a nonstick skillet, heat the olive oil over medium-high heat. Add the onion and sauté about 1 minute. Crumble the sausage into very small pieces, toss into the pan with the onion, and add the pepper. Mix well and cook until the sausage is fully cooked and the onion has softened and has golden highlights, 10 to 12 minutes. Pour in the wine, it will come to a quick boil. Boil for 30 seconds, give it a stir, then cook another 30 seconds to reduce by half—make sure you don't boil it all away!

3. Remove from the heat. Add the marinara and mix well. The hot pan will warm up the sauce a bit.

4. To assemble the lazy lasagna, spoon about ½ cup of the meat mixture into the prepared baking dish, then lay 9 ravioli in a single layer in the dish, with the rounded side facing up. It works perfectly as 3 rows with 3 ravioli each. Spoon half of the remaining meat sauce over the ravioli. Dollop out the ricotta in tablespoons (it's thick) over the sauce, then smooth it out a little with a rubber spatula. It doesn't have to be perfect!

5. Add another layer of 9 ravioli, then the rest of the meat sauce, then the mozzarella.

6. Place foil over the dish and bake for 1 hour. Remove the foil and turn the oven to broil. Set the dish under the broiler for a few minutes to get some golden highlights on the cheese, watching carefully so it doesn't burn. Remove from the oven and let rest for 10 minutes.

7. Spoon out one "stack" of ravioli for one serving. We serve this with a colorful garden salad. Lazy never tasted this great!

The lasagna lesson.

RACHEL'S ROMAN HOLIDAY ZUCCHINI PIZZA

RACHEL CAMPOS-DUFFY AND HER HUSBAND, SEAN, did something they'd never done before—they took a vacation without their kids. This is a major undertaking because they have nine children. It was the trip of a lifetime—they went to Italy and did all the typical American tourist things. They visited the Vatican, hoping the pope would pop out of a window and wave, but he did not, and they posed with a toga-clad Russell Crowe look-alike at the Coliseum.

The Duffys' European Vacation.

One day for a quick lunch they stepped into a grab-and-go pizza joint. The Duffys don't speak Italian, so they pointed at something they'd never seen—pizza di zucchini. They ordered one, thinking, *When in Rome . . .* Two bites into it and Sean and Rachel agreed—"Why didn't anybody ever tell us about zucchini pizza?"

When they got home Rachel raved about the pizza, but the kids were skeptical. Why eat zucchini when pepperoni is already perfect? To prove her point, Rachel baked three pizzas, two zucchini versions as she remembered them and one meat pie. The verdict from the pint-size panel of judges was unanimous: "Mom—can you make this for my birthday, *puh-lease*?" Now at every special event at the Duffy house they feature Rachel's version of that pizza from their Roman holiday.

Rachel was making her pizza from memory—but we wanted to get it exactly right for this recipe, so we enlisted the help of Sonny Esposito and Gennaro Romeo at Pazza Restaurant in Franklin Lakes, New Jersey, where they make classic Roman-style pizzas with slightly thicker rectangular crusts every day. They knew exactly how the Italians make what we're calling Rachel's Roman Holiday Zucchini Pizza.

Today Rachel dreams of one day having a full-size pizza oven in her kitchen like the place in Rome. Then again she might simply be dreaming of being 4,752 miles away from their nine adorable and amazing children, who often wait until bedtime to announce they forgot to tell her they need five pieces of navy blue poster board from Staples—five minutes after Staples closed for the night.

If you've never had a zucchini pizza, either, *puh-lease* try it!

Makes one 13 × 18-inch pizza

Olive oil for the pan and plate

One 16-ounce ball store-bought pizza dough

3 medium zucchini (2 to 2½ pounds total)

Table salt

½ teaspoon garlic powder

2 cups shredded low-moisture mozzarella cheese

3 garlic cloves, minced

4 tablespoons extra-virgin olive oil

Cornmeal, for dusting

¼ cup plain dried bread crumbs

¼ cup grated Pecorino Romano cheese

Freshly ground black pepper

Red pepper flakes, for serving

1. Adjust an oven rack to the center position and preheat the oven to 475°F. Oil a 13 × 18-inch sheet pan.

2. Place the dough on a lightly oiled plate and let it warm to room temperature for about 1 hour (if refrigerated) or 4 hours (if frozen).

3. Meanwhile, grate the zucchini on the large holes of a box grater, the grating attachment on a mandoline, or the shredding disc on a food processor. Zucchini is full of liquid and needs draining so that your pizza isn't a swampy mess. You have two options: One is to place the zucchini in a colander or sieve, lightly salt it, mix to combine, and let it drain for 1 hour, then firmly squeeze between your palms to get rid of any extra liquid. Or, do what we do: Working in batches, firmly press the liquid out of the zucchini using a potato ricer. This method is faster.

4. When you have removed the excess liquid from the zucchini, place it in a large bowl and sprinkle with the garlic powder. Add the mozzarella, mix very well, and set aside.

5. In a small bowl, combine the garlic and 3 tablespoons of the olive oil. Set aside to infuse.

6. Dust a work surface lightly with cornmeal and roll out the dough to fit the prepared sheet pan. Use a pizza docker (or a fork) to poke holes all over the crust to keep it from bubbling up while baking.

7. Lightly brush the garlic-infused olive oil all over the crust. Spread the zucchini/mozzarella mixture evenly over the crust, leaving about a 1-inch border.

8. In the bowl that held the zucchini, combine the bread crumbs, Romano, a couple grinds of black pepper, and the remaining 1 tablespoon olive oil. Mix until the bread crumbs are well oiled, then spread the mixture over the zucchini.

9. Bake until the zucchini and cheese are bubbling in some spots in the center and the bread crumbs and pizza edges are beautifully browned, 20 to 25 minutes.

10. Let rest a couple minutes, then cut into 4-inch squares and serve. We like it with a shake of red pepper flakes on top.

A TO ZITI LOAF

WHEN OUR KIDS WERE IN GRADE SCHOOL, THE PARENT/TEACHER ORGANIZATION HAD A program to help people in need called the Friendship Basket. After Kathy got knocked over by our dog and broke her kneecap, she had five knee surgeries, culminating in a total knee replacement. After each surgery somebody would bring over a friendship basket with dinner for that night. This meant that while Kathy was in the hospital, I could spend my days reading the laundry labels on the girls' Lilly Pulitzer clothing, trying to figure out if that triangle meant I could put it in the dryer. (I always decided it did.) After a week of me shrinking the laundry, the only person who could possibly wear some of those outfits was Malibu Barbie.

Whenever it was our turn to make dinner in the Friendship Basket rotation, Kathy would prep a crowd-pleasing batch of goulash (courtesy of Paula Deen's son Bobby), along with a loaf of crusty bread, a salad, and a kid-friendly dessert. I was her delivery guy and saw with my own two eyes how appreciative the recipient family would be. It was very thoughtful program, but there was one major problem: Kathy always made a casserole, and nobody *ever* returned the 9 × 13-inch casserole dish—nobody! I had some labels printed with Kathy's name and stuck them on the bottom of the pans so they would eventually see it when they put it in the dishwasher . . . but not one of those pans ever came home. It wasn't just a *making dinner* program, it was a *making dinner* and *giving away our entire Martha Stewart Bakeware Collection* program.

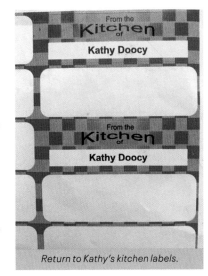

That's when I came up with this recipe idea, based on the bread bowls at Panera. We'd put the meal into a package that didn't need returning—and they could eat it! It has *everything*—the meat, the cheese, the sauce—in one neat package. We call it the A to Ziti Loaf because it includes ziti, obviously, but what makes it possible is the A part of the name—the aluminum foil bag they use to package the store-made garlic bread with the butter and garlic. We bake it in that aluminum—but if we're transporting it as a gift, that store wrapper also serves as a super-convenient way to transport it to somebody else's house. So after you knock on the door and they look at you, wondering, *Where's dinner?* you can accurately say, "It's in the bag . . ."

Return to Kathy's kitchen labels.

And as for our 9 × 13-inch pans, we haven't lost one in more than ten years!

Makes 5 or 6 servings

1 cup ricotta cheese

1 cup shredded mozzarella cheese

Table salt

8 ounces ziti

½ pound sweet Italian sausage (casings removed if in links)

½ cup roughly chopped sweet onion

2 garlic cloves, thinly sliced

2 cups marinara (we use Rao's)

One 16-ounce loaf store-made garlic bread (see Note)

Grated Parmesan cheese, for garnish

NOTE: The key to this recipe is buying a big and wide loaf of garlic bread that's sold in the foil bag in the bakery section of your grocery store, with the butter and garlic already inside. Make sure the loaf is at least 5 to 6 inches wide. This recipe makes more pasta than you need to make the loaf, but if you're making it to give away, you still need something to eat! The couple extra servings of pasta are the reward for your generous gesture.

1. Adjust an oven rack to the center position and preheat the oven to 350°F with a rack set in the middle (or, if you're giving the A to Ziti Loaf away, see A Timeout—If It's Takeout, opposite). In a medium bowl, combine the ricotta and mozzarella and use a fork to mash it together until smooth. Set aside.

2. Bring a big pot of salted water to a boil and cook the ziti according to the package directions.

3. Meanwhile, in a large nonstick skillet, crumble the sausage as small as possible and sauté over medium-high heat until browned and completely cooked, 10 to 12 minutes. Remove to a plate. Add the onion and garlic to the sausage grease in the pan and cook until the onions have softened and have golden highlights, 12 to 15 minutes.

4. Drain the cooked ziti and add to the skillet. Return the sausage to the pan. Add the marinara, mix, and heat to serving temperature.

5. Meanwhile, remove the garlic bread from the package (but keep the foil bag). Separate the top piece of bread from the bottom and set it on a cutting board. Use a serrated knife to cut a large oval out of the top piece: Slice straight down about ¾ inch from the outer edge of the bread, then cut out a large oval all around the loaf. Pull out that middle section of bread and set aside (you can use it later to make delicious croutons for a salad). To maximize space for pasta, scrape out some of the butter and garlic that the store installed and press the bottom and sides of the loaf to compress them a bit. Return the top crust to the bottom crust and set the loaf aside.

6. Time to assemble! Spoon enough of the meat-sauced noodles into the bread cavity to form an even layer that fills the bottom of the loaf about halfway. Drop half of the ricotta-mozzarella mixture on top, as you would when making a lasagna, then smooth it out to form a single layer. Top with another layer of pasta and meat that goes all the way to the top of the loaf. Dollop more cheese on top of the pasta and smooth it out, creating a top crust of cheese that's mounded higher than the top edge of the loaf. Scatter the grated Parmesan on top of the ricotta-mozzarella layer. Carefully slide the loaf back into its foil bag from the store.

A TIMEOUT—IF IT'S TAKEOUT

If you are taking this loaf to somebody, stop here and give the following instructions to finish cooking it.

1. Adjust an oven rack to the center position and preheat the oven to 350°F (if you haven't already).

2. Place the foil-bagged loaf in the oven and bake for 20 minutes. Remove the bread bag from the oven, adjust a rack to about 6 inches from the top of the oven, and turn on the broiler.

3. Taking care to not mess up the hot cheese on top, rip the bag open just along the top and slide the bag onto a sheet pan. Place the loaf on the oven rack and broil for about 1 minute, to give the cheese some golden highlights. It'll burn fast, so keep an eye on it and remove from the oven promptly.

4. Let the A to Ziti Loaf rest for a minute and then remove it from the foil and set it on a platter. We slice it up into 2-inch pieces. And don't forget to destroy the evidence—by eating the bread bowl!

PANCETTA AND PEAS PASTA

WHEN KATHY TALKED ME INTO A WEEKLONG FAMILY TRIP ALONG THE MEDITERRANEAN Sea, she sold me with visions of amazing meals—morning, noon, and night! What she never mentioned was that when we weren't eating, there would be a lot of walking around ancient cities looking for a place to plug in our phone chargers.

We also did a lot of shopping—in Genoa Mary bought an Italian schoolbook bag, and because the World Cup was happening that week, Peter took home a soccer jersey for a player we'd never heard of. For years it was the only jersey in his closet that didn't say JETER. During Kathy and the kids' retail therapy, I would remain outside on the sidewalk, ostensibly to absorb the local flavor of the area, but really to avoid the shopping that was occurring inside, because I do that only the day before Christmas.

When the Doocy family minus one emerged from their morning shop-a-thon, I suggested we have lunch at a cute place I'd been eyeballing across the street. We went in and it smelled incredible. But then the trouble started—the menu was completely in Italian, and the guy behind the counter appeared to not speak one word of English. So we turned to our in-house translator, Peter Doocy, who'd gotten a B– in college Italian. He was reluctant, but I reminded him that we weren't asking him to do air traffic control at Rome International—he just had to order our noodles.

We all watched as Peter said words that sounded Italian—but the giveaway was that everything he said ended with a question mark. Occasionally the cashier would shake his head and ask Peter a follow-up, which Peter didn't understand because he would repeat the exact same words—but louder.

Eventually the order was complete, an Amex card was swiped, and fifteen minutes later our order arrived. Everybody got exactly what they'd ordered—except me. Instead of puttanesca, they brought me what I think was pancetta pomodoro—and it was great! This recipe is our version of that happy accident. Peter may have gotten a B– in Italian, but this pasta is A+.

Serendipity is an unplanned fortunate discovery, which in Italian is *colpo di fortuna*. Peter didn't tell me that, I googled it, and I didn't even have to buy Google a $47 soccer jersey for the translation . . .

Mangia!

Makes 4 servings

Souvenir shopping in Genoa.

½ teaspoon table salt, plus more for the pasta water

One 12-ounce package frozen mini cheese ravioli or tortellini

1 cup frozen peas

One 4-ounce package diced pancetta

2 pints grape or cherry tomatoes

1 large shallot, sliced into thin rings

2 garlic cloves, thinly sliced

¼ teaspoon red pepper flakes

1 cup grated Parmesan cheese

Side salad and crusty bread, for serving

1. Bring a pot of lightly salted water to a boil and cook the frozen pasta according to the package directions. In the last minute of cooking, toss in the frozen peas. When done, drain and set aside.

2. Meanwhile—just after the water starts boiling—make this amazing sauce. In a large skillet, fry the pancetta over medium-high heat until just crispy and done, about 5 minutes. Use a slotted spoon to remove it to a plate, leaving the grease in the pan. Add the tomatoes and ½ teaspoon salt to the pan and sauté for 5 minutes; they'll start to change color. Add the shallot and garlic and sauté until the shallot is softened, 2 to 3 minutes. When the tomatoes have some slightly brownish highlights, use a spoon or spatula to press down on them a little, so they burst and squirt their sauce into the pan. Add the cooked pancetta, pepper flakes, and drained pasta and give everything a stir.

3. Add the Parmesan, let it melt a minute, then stir to combine. Serve with a side salad and some crusty bread to sop up the sauce!

Jersey kid gets Italian jersey.

CHILI FLATBREAD PIZZA

PICKY EATING IS A COMMON THING. HARRY S. TRUMAN HATED ONIONS. BARACK OBAMA avoids beets. George Herbert Walker Bush went ballistic over broccoli.

So everybody's picky about something—but usually there are many whole categories and varieties of foods that people will eat, unlike a New York friend of mine who won't sit down for a meal—any meal—unless the main component is hamburger meat. And that's his wife's beef with him.

She has tried to be very creative within the universe of ground chuck. She'll make him burgers, meatballs, and meatloaf, and sometimes she'll take it right up to the line and make pasta with meat sauce. But he'll inspect it like Matlock to make sure there's not one molecule of sausage in there . . .

"Can't be too careful!"

Stuck in the ground beef rut, his wife wanted to branch out and make him a pizza—because their kids love pizza. This would have to be a meat lover's pizza, but with just one meat to love. So the wife concocted a thick meat-and-bean pie that's a snap to make, and *he loved it*!

Today the family eats this once a week. It has a ton of flavor, thanks to the caramelized onions—which Harry S. Truman would never touch. President Truman once said, "If you can't stand the heat, get out of the kitchen." Which makes sense when you know his picky food history—it's where the onions live!

Makes 8 servings

---

1 pound lean ground beef

1 medium red or yellow onion, roughly chopped

4 garlic cloves, thinly sliced

One 1.25-ounce packet chili seasoning mix

One 6-ounce can tomato paste

One 15-ounce can red kidney beans, drained

2 tablespoons apple cider vinegar

1 package prebaked flatbread crusts (a 14.1-ounce package with 2 crusts or a 16.2-ounce package of 4 crusts both work)

Optional toppings: taco sauce, spicy mayo, or Herdez Avocado Hot Sauce (my favorite)

1. Preheat the oven to 400°F.

2. In a large nonstick skillet, crumble the meat and cook over medium-high heat until browned and cooked through, 8 to 10 minutes. With a spatula, move the beef *waaaay* over to one side of the skillet. Add the onion and garlic and sauté until the onion is softened and the garlic is golden, 4 or 5 minutes. Mix the onion into the hamburger. Tilt the pan to the side and spoon out any excess grease.

3. Stir in the chili seasoning, tomato paste, kidney beans, and vinegar and mix well. It needs to be very thick so it will stick to the top of the flatbread. Cook for a few minutes to thoroughly warm the beans and blend the flavors.

4. Lay out the flatbread crusts and divide the meat mixture among them, spreading the mixture to about 1 inch from the edges of the crusts. Place in the oven directly on the rack and bake according to the flatbread package directions for a crispy crust. You're looking for some dark golden highlights on the outer edges, which usually takes 8 to 12 minutes.

5. Remove the pizzas from the oven with a wide spatula or a rimless cookie sheet and let them cool a few minutes, then cut them into wedges using a pizza cutter. If you want, top with a zigzag of your sauce of choice.

TORTELLINI ALI-FREDO WITH PROSCIUTTO AND PEAS

FOR OUR TWENTIETH ANNIVERSARY, KATHY AND I CELEBRATED BY TAKING THE KIDS ON a family cruise from Barcelona to Rome. This recipe was how I remember the chef made Alfredo pasta at our tableside every day that I'd order for lunch. Midtrip the captain heard it was our anniversary and sent a *very* fancy bottle of champagne to the Doocy room . . . the Peter Doocy room. He was still a minor, so I immediately impounded it as a public service and shared food-tester duties with Mrs. Doocy.

A highlight was a stop in the ritziest place in Europe, Monte Carlo. We knew lunch would cost a fortune, so we stopped by a café and ordered Cokes. They were *$7 each*! Later Peter and I went to the famous Monte Carlo Casino you've seen a million times in movies and immediately lost twenty euros—three Cokes—on a dumb game. Aside from that beverage order, we ate all our meals on the ship, where I watched a chef, who was set up at a buffet table, make the most delicious pasta sauces on the spot. We tried all of them, but my favorite recipe (which I memorized) was the world's simplest Alfredo sauce. But I'd never made it for our family before the pandemic.

In March 2020 I announced to Kathy that I was going to make comfort food every day—until the pandemic was over. Our dinner meal would give us something to look forward to during days when there wasn't much else to look forward to. Today we still look forward to having this simple recipe, because it reminds us of the time when we were all together every day and became even closer as a family. My now son-in-law Ali *loves* this dish, and because he was always asking for it, I've dubbed it Ali-fredo. He was isolated with me for 261 meals, and he says I made this at least fifty times while we prayed that the cloud would lift and we could go out to eat someplace—*anyplace*—even if Cokes cost seven bucks.

Makes 6 servings

Table salt

One 4-ounce package diced prosciutto

One 19-ounce package frozen cheese tortellini

½ cup frozen peas

4 tablespoons (½ stick) unsalted butter

⅔ cup heavy cream

½ cup grated Parmesan cheese

⅛ teaspoon garlic powder

1 tablespoon shredded fresh basil leaves (optional)

1. Bring a pot of salted water to a boil over high heat.

2. Meanwhile, in a large nonstick skillet, sauté the prosciutto over medium-high heat until browned and crispy on the edges, 5 to 7 minutes. Remove the prosciutto to paper towels and set aside.

3. As soon as the water hits a rapid boil, add the tortellini and cook according to the package directions. Add the peas 2 minutes before the pasta is ready.

4. As soon as you add the tortellini to the boiling water, make the sauce. Wipe out the skillet with a paper towel and return it to medium heat. Add the butter, cream, and Parmesan and cook, stirring, until it's completely melted and smooth. Mix in the garlic powder. When the sauce starts to bubble around the outside of the pan, turn the heat to low until the pasta is done.

5. Drain the pasta and add it to the skillet, along with the cooked prosciutto. Stir well to coat and warm the prosciutto and serve immediately. If you'd like, garnish with shredded basil leaves.

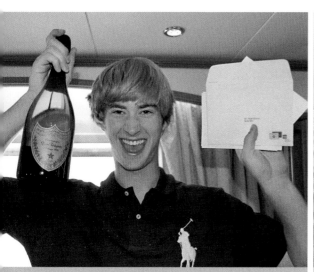

That's my champagne, Peter!

No jokes— $7 Cokes.

SWEETS

*W*HEN MARY WAS IN HIGH SCHOOL I asked her what she thought my life was like growing up in Kansas in an actual little house on the prairie, and she deadpanned, "I bet you sat around and popped a bunch of corn pills."

First of all, I don't know if corn pills were actually ever a thing—but back in the 1960s and 1970s, nobody would have strayed from the straight and narrow to use corn pills because of the fear that getting caught with contraband would wind up on your *permanent record*—every school's nuclear option to keep you in line. Make a prank call to shop class—*there goes Yale*. And back then any single black mark on my *permanent record* could derail my parents' plan for me to be America's first pope—a job opportunity I dismissed when I realized priests have to work weekends *and* Christmas.

Recently Kathy was asked by our neighbor Leanna to write a story for our local newsletter entitled "A Day in the Life of Steve Doocy." Kathy's been listening to me for thirty-six years, so she's my official biographer, and she wrote a great article—but this single quote was something that stood out because I'd not thought about it in decades. She wrote:

Big hair, big tie, big dreams.

During his career Steve has covered every major event of the last forty years. Growing up in Abilene, Kansas, the boyhood home of President Eisenhower, Steve was in sixth grade when school was adjourned so everyone could attend Ike's funeral.

Reading that line, something dawned on me that I'd never consciously realized about my early days—so I added one more thing:

It was at the Eisenhower funeral that Steve saw Presidents Nixon and Johnson, and every major American military figure and became interested in the news business.

All true.

Where I grew up just north of Abilene, the boyhood home of our thirty-fourth president, President Eisenhower was a very big deal. For years my parents ran the Best Western President's Inn on the north side of town. A couple times after he left the White House, the former president stayed there, reportedly in the motel's biggest room, which they referred to as the Presidential Suite. My mom would put Kathy and the kids and me up in the Presidential Suite when we'd visit because it had very good water pressure and a love seat for napping and was a thirty-second walk to the Sirloin Stockade, where we took all our meals. Kathy was clearly from California—she'd never seen gravy on a salad bar.

When Eisenhower died at age seventy-eight, the commemorations on television were substantial, because he'd led the D-Day invasion of Western Europe at Normandy and helped save the world. His coffin was transported via an old-style funeral train for the trip back home to Kansas. On April 2, 1969, the

Sixth-grade Steve.

train arrived in Abilene, and estimates said that our town of five thousand had grown to one hundred thousand people, with so many there to pay their respects.

I was in sixth grade and attended an honest-to-goodness one-room schoolhouse in Industry, Kansas. Only fifteen miles north of Abilene, our whole school attended—all eleven of us. Our teacher, Mrs. Hazel Lloyd, led us through the commotion and haphazardly stopped at the only empty spot on a North 2nd Street sidewalk.

We stood there and waited about fifteen minutes, until the funeral train pulled into town, and as luck would have it we were only fifty feet from all of the action. One of my younger classmates asked me who that old guy in the dark coat was, and I told him that was the president of the United States, Richard Nixon.

"He looked familiar," the kid said.

As luck would have it, where we were standing the networks' live television cameras were situated to the left and the right of us, and those famous correspondent faces from the evening news were close enough that I could hear them solemnly describing the honor guard that was carrying the casket to the hearse. I listened to the newsmen describing what they were seeing to their television audience, which was the same thing I was watching live, and that's when it dawned on me—*I could do that!*

Once the president's family was secure in their limos, the motorcade commenced and the hearse turned down Buckeye toward the Eisenhower Presidential Library. Realizing there was no more to see, the crowd dispersed. The kids from the one-room schoolhouse got to go out to eat. I'd seen two US presidents *and* had a chicken-fried steak—to me that was a win-win.

When I got home, my mom was watching Walter Cronkite's coverage, and I walked over to the TV and touched the screen to show exactly where I was standing, and I recounted in granular detail all that I'd seen that day. She listened to my every word, because I had tidbits she'd not heard on our Magnavox. I was reporting to my audience of one—my mom—and realized that I wanted to do that every day for the rest of my life.

Ten years later I was out of journalism school and working as the statehouse reporter at the NBC affiliate in Topeka, assigned to return to Abilene and cover the funeral of Eisenhower's wife, Mamie. This time I was in the actual press section, with credentials and Secret Service clearance—and getting paid four bucks an hour.

Remember, the day of the presidential funeral my teacher arbitrarily picked our vantage point. If she'd randomly parked us just one block over in any direction, I would have missed the cameras and correspondents and commentary. And it almost never happened, it was a complete fluke.

As I turned sixty-five this last year, I've thought a lot about beginnings and that was mine.

An ancient proverb says, "When eating fruit—remember the one who planted the tree."

Our son, Peter, is a famous correspondent today, and people think he followed in my footsteps on purpose. That could not be further from the truth. His plan was to either get an MBA or go to law school, period. Zero chance of a TV career. But when you look back at Peter's young life, there was a series of random events that changed him and his circumstances, and it started at a grocery store.

The Market Basket in Franklin Lakes, New Jersey, has lots of very high-end foodstuffs. We joked that because things were so pricey there, he wasn't a stock boy, he was a stock analyst. *Who knew Rolex made a salsa?*

Peter had been a pretty quiet kid before that job; he'd worn braces for five years, and it actually hurt him to talk. But this job required him to talk to total strangers as they'd interrupt him while stocking the shelves. "Hey, kid, where's the bucatini?"

Peter didn't know what bucatini was, but it sounded Italian so he assumed it was in the

Our favorite stock analyst.

sauce and noodle aisle. So he'd lead them on a treasure hunt. One afternoon a flustered man flagged Peter down and pointed at an item on his shopping list. Peter had no idea what that listed ingredient was and had no idea where to start, so he called to the store manager, "Hey Fil"—then read directly off the paper—"Where's our *anus*?"

Fil had the young Doocy show him the list, then he pointed toward the produce department. "Let's go, I'll show you where it is. And Peter—it's pronounced *anise*."

Having nonstop conversations with total strangers all day turned Peter into a very verbal and in many respects fearless young man. At the same time, Peter was on the high school varsity baseball team, where he played third base and developed a skill that would distract the opposing team—he had a booming voice on par with the high school public address system.

At the team dinner at the end of his high school years, one of the speakers mentioned Peter and said something to the effect of Peter had a lot of hustle, great spirit, and was without a doubt the loudest kid on any team in New

Peter the prince of produce.

Jersey. As his father, I knew that was true, as does President Joe Biden, who has discovered that Peter's baritone voice can actually be heard over Marine One.

During his college tour we visited Penn State in State College, Pennsylvania. A long way from home, we would overnight at the Nittany Lion Inn. Almost to the building, the big front door popped open and a guy on his way out held open the door for the Doocys. It was coach Joe Paterno, Mister Penn State, the winningest coach in NCAA history.

"This must be a swanky joint," I said. "Look who's the doorman!" Paterno laughed with the rest of us and left. At breakfast the next morning Peter announced his college search was over, and during an info session, we paid Peter's first-year fees and room and board, so the admissions department couldn't change their minds. In the parking lot we made it official by putting a Penn State bumper sticker on our car. His search was over. Period.

Until it wasn't. A few weeks later, Villanova—where Peter had been waitlisted—called. The dean of admissions, Michael Gaynor, said they had one spot left in the freshman class, and Peter had twenty-four hours to decide. Penn State had a big, beautiful campus like my alma mater, Kansas University, and I told him I really wanted him to go. Kathy, however, wanted him to go to Villanova, a Catholic university. "You can go to church *every day*!" Kathy reminded him.

Joe Paterno or church every day? Seemed like a slam-dunk easy choice to me.

He went to Villanova.

To this day we're not sure if he actually ever went inside the church during his four years at Villanova, other than when we were with him for the opening and closing ceremonies.

He was a political science major, and when he was a junior, just starting the application process for business school, one of his professors told the class they could get extra credit if they went to a town hall that night, so Peter went. The town hall was to be televised on MSNBC, and the featured guest was Senator John McCain, who at the time was the GOP nominee for president. Before the show went live, a producer asked the crowd for a show of hands if anybody had a question. A couple did, none apparently that good. Then Peter, the very loud boy from third base, held up his hand. The producer listened to the question and said, "That's pretty good, but can you make it more interesting?" Peter thought about it, waved the producer back over, and posed his question. "That's better," the producer said with a big smile. "You'll go second."

Half an hour into the show, Kathy and I were watching at home when Peter popped up on MSNBC.

Live from Villanova!

"Hi, Senator McCain, my name is Peter Doocy, and I'm a junior here. I'm sure you saw one of your democratic opponents Hillary Clinton recently drinking whiskey shots with some potential voters. Now, I was wondering if you think she's finally resorted to hitting the sauce because of some unfavorable polling. And I was also wondering if you would care to join me for a shot after this . . ."

The question brought down the house; there was a full minute of laughter from the crowd. McCain was a great sport, who told me later he *loved* the question. That night eventually he answered Peter, "Whatever makes Senator Clinton happy," just before the host called young Mr. Doocy a "wiseass."

And with that one single funny question, the path of Peter's entire life changed. The kid who was absolutely going to go to business or law school, should have been at Penn State that night if he'd listened to me. Suddenly out of the blue Peter was being lobbied by Fox producers to join the team as a college-aged correspondent. Kathy and I said *absolutely not*. The producers kept asking, and finally at graduation,

Congrats, Peter! Now find a job.

Peter made a deal with us. "If it doesn't work out, I can always go back to grad school." We relented and said okay, because it was a reasonable backup plan.

So far, it has all worked out for the loud boy from the grocery store.

Woody Allen has a line that applies to all of us who try to figure out the future: "If you ever really want to make God laugh, tell him your plans."

When I was a kid, my master plan was to live in Kansas close to my parents and sisters. But there are few great TV jobs there, and if I'd have stayed there, I never would have met Kathy and had these wonderful kids or had this amazing career or written these cookbooks. As a kid from a rural one-room schoolhouse whose family could not afford to send him to college (but who went to journalism school anyway and won scholarships and got jobs and worked hard), I'm living proof that all your dreams can come true.

Oprah had a great quote that perfectly summarizes how people of very modest means feel after they've had some degree of success. "It hasn't changed who I am," Oprah said. "My feet are still on the ground. I'm just wearing better shoes."

Every morning, about half an hour after I get up, my Apple watch reminds me that it's time to reflect for one minute. Usually I think about Kathy and the kids, or I say a prayer of thanks to God. But one morning as I was reflecting, I went rogue with a crazy idea to close a loop.

"Hi, who do I talk to about a copy of my permanent record?" I asked the person who answered the phone later that day at my high school in Clay Center, Kansas. I was ready for a fight—someone told me once that a person had to be dead fifty years before their records could be released.

Peter jostles with Joe Biden during the campaign.

"I can probably help you. What's your name?" The woman inquired. When I answered "Steve Doocy," she said, "Steve? This is Sue Bebermeyer!"

Wait, what? Sue had graduated one year ahead of me and married into the Bebermeyer family, who lived just down the road from me growing up during the 1970s. I was positive the Bebermeyers would remember all the crazy stuff the Doocys were famous for—some details doubtlessly noted in excruciating detail in the forever files of United School District 379.

Sue could not have been more helpful. "Give me your address, Steve, and I'll send it as quick as we can."

Five days later, there I was at the mailbox, looking at a return address and realizing what was in the envelope. I paused a moment, then ripped down the side of the envelope and was face-to-face with the indisputable details of my public school education, efficiently memorialized on two pages.

I got good grades, took nine sick days, and was tardy—once, in four years! Plus—I got a twenty-four on the ACT, which (according to a website I just looked at) could get me into Penn State today!

And that was it.

Where was the stuff I'd wondered and worried about for fifty years? The details of my bachelor living class, which was evacuated after a possum was baked as a class project? Or the big-mouth teacher who announced in a scary loud voice they'd seen 3.2 beer cans near my car, and "*THAT IS GOING ON YOUR PERMANENT RECORD, MR. DOOCY!*"

Not even a corn pill mention.

I spoke to my daughter Mary, who recently confessed that she'd invented the term "corn pills" on the spot. She'd thought it sounded funny, like a drug someone from Kansas might do. Today Mary is in federal law enforcement and an expert on permanent records—of criminals. She told me the legend of the permanent record was an invention to keep chaotic schoolkids "from going to Crazy Town. It's a myth from the cartoons, Dad."

After I rescanned my transcript I called up my high school again and asked Sue Bebermeyer point-blank, "What about high school high jinks? Don't they keep a file of any of the crazy stuff after graduation?"

"Nope—just the grades."

I thanked her and hung up—a little disappointed, but ultimately rather relieved. Because if that's my *official* permanent record—maybe I can still be pope.

PRETZEL CRUST CHOCOLATE PEANUT BUTTER PIE

IMITATION IS THE SINCEREST FORM OF FLATTERY, AND THAT'S WHY I'M FLATTERED THAT through the years different folks have stopped by *Fox & Friends* and gifted me—me!—handcrafted things like a Steve Doocy bag of potato chips.

In my office I have twenty-five-plus years of *Fox & Friends* souvenirs, many made by fans who'd spent hours creating images of me. Somebody was using their noodle when they made my likeness in linguine, although my angel-hair hair was the *mane* attraction. I loved my portrait in a pizza, where I had a very healthy pink Canadian bacon glow. Another artist made a perfectly posed Steve Doocy pretzel—but unlike most pretzels, I was not twisted.

Pretzels go way back in the Doocy family's world of snacks. My dad loved them in a bowl next to his beer. In our first cookbook I told the story of how my mom would bake a chocolate sheet cake for every 4-H meeting, and we would press pretzels into the center of each piece in order to make twenty-four perfectly pretzeled portions. She'd also make chocolate-covered pretzels or pretzel party mix.

This recipe is a happy memory of those days when my mom needed some cooking ingredient crushed. I was good at breaking things into small pieces, like most kids, so she'd call on me to pulverize pretzels, pecans, saltines, or Ritz crackers. It's a delicious flashback to those poignant days in the kitchen with my mom, who'd top a cream pie with chocolate ganache. Of course I didn't know what a ganache was until I was forty; she'd mix melted chocolate chips with whipping cream, and I was always at her side in the kitchen because when she was done frosting, she'd hand me the chocolate-coated spoon and I'd stick it right in my mouth. What a payday!

This goes great with a cup of Joe—like the time a talented barista sketched my image in a hot cup of coffee—thanks a *latte*!

Makes one 9½-inch pie

One 9-ounce bag salted pretzel twists (we use Bachman Thin'n Right)

⅓ cup packed light brown sugar

½ cup (1 stick) unsalted butter, melted

4 ounces cream cheese, at room temperature

½ cup chunky peanut butter

1 cup powdered sugar

½ cup whole milk

1. Adjust an oven rack to the center position and preheat the oven to 350°F.

2. Place the pretzels in a large zip-top bag (or leave them inside the package) and whack them with a rolling pin or crush them with your fingers into small (¼- to ½-inch) pieces. If you smash them into dust they won't work as well, so don't overdo it. Add the brown sugar to the bag and give that a good shake, making sure there are no big sugar clumps. Pour the brown sugar–pretzel mixture into a 9½-inch glass pie plate. Pour the melted butter on top and mix until the sugar and pretzels are well buttered. Remove a big tablespoon or two of the pretzel mixture and place it on a piece of foil, keeping the pieces clumped as close together

One 8-ounce container Cool Whip, thawed for 4 hours in the fridge

½ cup heavy cream

1 cup semisweet chocolate chips

My pizza portrait.

as possible (this will be a garnish later). Back in the pie plate—use a spoon to manipulate the pretzel pieces up the sides and across the bottom to form a crust.

3. Place the pie plate and the foil with pieces in the oven and bake until the crust has a dull finish and the pretzels are tightly fused together, about 10 minutes. Set aside to cool.

4. Meanwhile, in a stand mixer (or a large bowl with a hand mixer), combine the cream cheese, peanut butter, and powdered sugar and mix on medium speed until smooth. With the mixer on low speed, slowly pour in the milk until you have a nice, runny peanut butter mixture. Fold in the entire container of Cool Whip by hand—don't use the mixer. Pour this mixture into the pretzel crust and level it out.

5. Freeze for at least 4 hours.

6. To make the ganache topping, pour the heavy cream into a medium microwave-safe bowl with a lid that fits tightly. Let it sit uncovered at room temperature for 10 minutes to take the chill off, then cover the bowl and microwave the cream for 1 minute. Add the chocolate chips, cover the bowl quickly, and let it rest, undisturbed, for about 3 minutes for the heat of the cream to melt the chocolate. At the 3-minute mark, with the lid on, I vigorously shake the bowl from side to side because the agitation helps melt the chips. Let rest for another 3 minutes, then remove the lid and give the ganache a stir. If there are any tiny lumps, use a rubber spatula to smoosh them down so the mixture is nice and smooth.

7. Pour the ganache over the pie, smoothing it with a spatula right up to the pretzel crust. Break up the foil-baked pretzels and artistically scatter the pieces over the ganache.

8. Pop the pie back into the freezer for at least 1 hour to firm up the top.

9. To serve, bring the pie out of the freezer and let sit for 5 minutes to soften. When you cut the pie and remove slices, there will be pretzel crust pieces left in the pan; scrape them off the bottom and put on the top of the pie as additional garnish. Wow, that's good!

10. Leftovers go back in the freezer—we'll cut up the pie and place the pieces in separate zip-top bags so we can enjoy them on different days.

HAYDEN'S SWEET AND SALTY HAYSTACKS

WHEN AINSLEY EARHARDT BROUGHT A BATCH OF THESE TREATS TO THE STUDIO AND WAS passing them out to the *Fox & Friends* crew, one of the camera guys said, "My mom made these when I was a kid!" Ainsley said her mom, Dale, made them when she was a little girl—"And my mom's a foodie!

"[My daughter] Hayden's school encourages parents to cook with their kids, because it teaches them how to do things in the kitchen, like mixing and measuring." Ainsley added, "And it's a good way to make a memory."

She's right about that. I have memories of my mom making haystack cookies—in her version, with oatmeal and coconut. I remember her stirring the chocolate chips in a double boiler on the stove for what seemed like forever, because the smell was driving us crazy and all we wanted was to grab a batch and take them out to our treehouse, so we could have snacks and tell ghost stories. Today these are a snap to make in the microwave. If it takes you more than fifteen minutes to make two dozen of these gems, you're doing something wrong.

Since everybody's family seems to have an heirloom haystack recipe, here are a couple of new ones to try. Ainsley and Hayden have two versions that are a lot of fun—in fact, one is made with Funfetti-flavored morsels! The other is blended with Nutella—or as we call them, Hayden's Sweet and Salty Haystacks. Ainsley likes the contrast of salt with the sugary morsels, made possible by using crushed cocktail peanuts and pretzels—it's a terrific combination.

By the way, Hayden is the youngest person who's ever contributed to one of our cookbooks, but she's the perfect person to help with this recipe, because Ainsley's nickname for Hayden is *Haystack!*

Can't make it up . . .

Hayden's handiwork.

Makes 2 dozen cookies

HAYDEN'S HAZELNUT HAYSTACKS

½ cup cocktail peanuts

3 handfuls mini-pretzel sticks or twists

Half a 12-ounce bag semisweet chocolate chips (we use Nestlé)

⅓ cup chocolate-hazelnut spread (we use Nutella)

Rainbow sprinkles, for garnish

CONFETTI CAKE HAYSTACKS

½ cup cocktail peanuts

3 handfuls mini-pretzel sticks or twists

One 9-ounce bag Nestlé Funfetti Vanilla Cake-flavored morsels

Rainbow sprinkles, for garnish

INSTRUCTIONS FOR BOTH VERSIONS

1. To crush the cocktail peanuts, place them in a zip-top bag and gently whack them with a rolling pin or the bottom of a pan. You want them substantially crushed but not too small.

2. To break the pretzels, place them in a large zip-top bag and use your fingers to break them up, until all the pieces are smaller than 1 inch. Measure out the broken pretzels; you need 2 cups.

3. In a large microwave-safe bowl, cover and microwave the chips (either chocolate or Funfetti morsels) on high for 45 seconds. Stir, then microwave another 30 seconds. Stir, then microwave in 15-second increments, stirring after each, until silky smooth.

4. If you're making the hazelnut haystacks, stir the hazelnut spread into the melted chocolate until the mixture is smooth.

5. For either version, stir the peanuts and pretzels into the melted chips. Combine with a rubber spatula until they're completely glazed in chocolate. If you're thinking the mixture is very sticky and gloppy—you're right!

6. Lay out a large piece of parchment or wax paper. Using a spoon, dollop the mixture in 1½-inch-wide piles onto the paper. Use your fingers to make the stacks as compact as you can; if there are any stray pieces of pretzel or peanut, tidy them neatly into the little mound. Garnish with rainbow sprinkles on all the haystacks.

7. Let the haystacks rest on the counter for 30 minutes to firm up, then refrigerate. The hazelnut haystacks will be a little tacky to touch until you put them in the fridge; that's normal.

8. After the haystacks have hardened in the fridge, store them in a zip-top bag for up to a couple of days. But don't worry—they won't last that long, especially if the kids in the treehouse need snacks!

COCONUT CARROT CAKE BARS

WHEN OUR DAUGHTER SALLY AND HER FIANCÉ, ALI, WERE PLANNING THEIR FAIRY-TALE wedding, they met with a coordinator, who asked them hundreds of questions about the venue, vendors, food, drinks, lighting, music—you name it, they had to pick it. When asked about the flavor they wanted for the wedding cake, though, they drew a blank. They'd thought of what the outside of the cake would look like, but not the actual flavor inside. After a tasting, they decided on a chocolate cake with ganache frosting. When I asked why, Sally said, "I don't know."

They never got their chocolate cake—that wedding didn't happen, because of the pandemic— but they still wanted to go through with tying the knot, so they found a new venue and a new menu and had to make a new cake choice. But this time it was easier; Theresa at Café Boulud in Palm Beach said, "Get the carrot cake . . . it's the best." So they did, and it was! It was a night to remember, with both carats and carrots to help celebrate.

After Sally started learning the ropes in the kitchen, she wanted to make something carrot-cakey. Kathy remembered a box-cake bar recipe a neighbor had given her about twenty-five years earlier, so we reimagined the recipe and came up with this version. All I can say is that everybody who tries these *loves* the topping. It's positively magical!

Now every time Sally bakes up a batch of these it takes her and Ali back to that happy wedding night, when they followed tradition and fed each other carrot cake. While the photographer snapped away, Kathy and I prayed she wouldn't spill anything on her white wedding dress.

Imagine the stain the chocolate ganache would have left . . .

I do! Love these cake bars!

Makes 16 large or 32 small bars

Baking spray with flour

4 large eggs

½ cup (1 stick) unsalted butter, cubed, at room temperature

One 15.25-ounce carrot cake mix (we use Betty Crocker Super Moist Carrot Cake)

1 cup pecans, roughly chopped

One 8-ounce package cream cheese, cubed, at room temperature

3 cups powdered sugar

½ cup sweetened coconut flakes

1. Adjust an oven rack to the center position and preheat the oven to 350°F. Mist a 9 × 13-inch baking pan with baking spray.

2. In a stand mixer fitted with the paddle attachment (or a large bowl with a hand mixer), beat 2 of the eggs and the butter on medium-high speed until the butter is creamed. Reduce the mixer to medium speed and pour in ¼ cup water. Working a bit at a time, with the mixer running, add the carrot cake mix, scraping the sides of the bowl so that all the mix is incorporated. Add the pecans and mix until evenly distributed.

3. Because this batter is very sticky, lightly mist a clean rubber spatula with baking spray and use the spatula to transfer the batter from the mixer bowl to the prepared pan. Spread the batter evenly in the pan, pressing down on the batter to fill any voids. This will keep the bars from baking unevenly.

NOTE: You really need to use a mixer for this recipe, because the batter gets super thick and hard to beat, so unless your name is Dwayne "The Rock" Johnson—dig out the mixer.

4. Now to make the topping! Clean the mixer bowl and paddle (or beaters). Add the remaining 2 eggs and the cream cheese and mix on medium speed until well blended. Working a bit at a time, add the powdered sugar. When all the powdered sugar is in, increase the speed to high and beat for about 90 seconds to get rid of the sugar lumps. Turn off the mixer and fold in the coconut by hand.

5. Pour and spread the topping evenly over the carrot cake batter and smooth it out. Rock the pan back and forth to make sure it's at an even depth.

6. Bake until it's browned around the edges and has broad golden highlights across the center of the crust, 45 to 50 minutes.

7. Set aside to cool for at least 30 minutes, then cut into 16 large or 32 small bars, cleaning the knife after each cut to keep the topping intact. Just out of the oven it can be a little crumbly, so serve on a plate and enjoy. Once cooled, refrigerate them because that firms them up. *Mmmm* that's good!

That's a carrot cake!

STRAWBERRY-RHUBARB PIE

IN GRANDMA SHARP'S BACKYARD, TOWARD THE END OF MINNESOTA STREET IN ALGONA, Iowa, there grew a crazy-looking plant that had great big green elephant ear leaves sitting on bright red celery-like stalks. Yes, it was rhubarb—and I loved it. Grandma was a short-order cook, and she made us rhubarb pie twice a week during its short late spring/early summer season. Sadly she never wrote down the recipe, and I never found anything close to it again—until Kathy and I went out to lunch one day on vacation.

We were at the fantastic Gallery Grille in Tequesta, Florida, and we were talking to the owner and our new friend Bruce Nierman, who told us we had to save room for his wife, Jeanne's, strawberry-rhubarb pie. When I heard *rhubarb*, I was instantly on board. Over the last twenty years, Jeanne has probably made this recipe a thousand times for their restaurant and her best friends. She's from a family of accomplished cooks, and the strawberry-rhubarb filling is so delightful and delicious that when her kids were young and she was cooking up a batch in the kitchen, they'd constantly taste-test it, sticking their spoons into the pan of tasty goodness, and before she knew it, she wouldn't have enough left to make a single pie. That's when she started making the pies when the kids were in school.

Back to the restaurant—when they brought us that first piece of Jeanne's pie, I instantly noticed a sweet, familiar smell of so many summers long gone. That first magical bite of rhubarb was like entering a time machine; it completely took me back to Grandma's house more than sixty years ago, when Grandma and I would snack on rhubarb pie in the middle of the day while Mom was at work. We'd watch *The Secret Storm,* which was always on before my cartoons started at 3 p.m. Life was so much easier when there were only three channels, am I right?

Enjoy this pie—it's amazing.

Makes one 9½-inch pie

2½ cups all-purpose flour, plus more for rolling out the dough

1 cup plus 4 tablespoons sugar

¾ cup (1½ sticks) cold salted butter

6 tablespoons Crisco shortening

½ cup ice water, plus more if needed

1 pound fresh or thawed frozen rhubarb, cut into 1½- to 2-inch chunks

1 cinnamon stick

⅓ cup cornstarch

1. In a stand mixer fitted with the paddle attachment (or in a large bowl with a hand mixer), combine the flour, 3 tablespoons of the sugar, ½ cup/1 stick of the butter, and the Crisco. Mix on low speed until the mixture is broken down into pea-size pieces of dough; it will take a few minutes. Slowly pour in up to ½ cup ice water, mixing until the dough forms into a thoroughly blended ball. Remove the ball, cut it in half, and refrigerate both halves for 20 to 30 minutes as you prepare the filling.

2. Adjust an oven rack to the bottom third and preheat the oven to 350°F.

3. In a large saucepan, combine the remaining ¼ cup/½ stick of butter, the rhubarb, cinnamon stick, cornstarch, and 1 cup of the sugar and mix well. Set the pan over medium heat and cook,

2 pounds strawberries, hulled and halved or quartered (if large)

Egg wash: 1 large egg whisked with 1 tablespoon water

Whipped cream or vanilla ice cream, for serving

running a silicone spatula through the mixture as the butter melts and the mixture reduces and becomes translucent, 6 to 8 minutes. Add the strawberries, give them a stir to coat, and cook for 3 to 5 minutes to thicken up the sauce a bit. Remove the pan from the heat and set aside.

4. Lightly flour a work surface. Roll one piece of the refrigerated dough into a ball, then flatten it into a pancake and use a rolling pin to roll it into an 11½-inch round (large enough for a 9½-inch pie plate). Place the crust in the pie plate and manipulate it to fit the bottom and sides, just up and over the edge. Remove the cinnamon stick from the strawberry-rhubarb sauce and pour the filling into the waiting pie crust.

5. Roll out the second piece of dough into a 10-inch round and lay it over the pie. Pinch the crusts together where they meet, trimming any extra crust and fluting the edges. Paint the top of the pie with the egg wash, then evenly sprinkle the remaining 1 tablespoon of sugar over the pie crust. With a sharp knife, poke a couple of symmetrical slits in the top.

6. Place the pie on a sheet pan and bake until the crust is golden brown and strawberry filling may be bubbling out of the top slits, 50 to 60 minutes.

7. Let the pie cool before cutting. Serve with freshly whipped cream or vanilla ice cream. Grandma would love this pie!

NONNA'S CANNOLI

SEPTEMBER WAS DECLARED NATIONAL CANNOLI MONTH BY JASPER MIRABILE JR., THE co-owner of Jasper's Restaurant in Kansas City, where he is KC's current Cannoli King—I declared him that, just now. It's not that he has business cards labeled with that title . . . yet. Jasper's famous for cannoli, and he's the first to admit he goes a little crazy over these deep-fried tubes stuffed with sweetened ricotta cheese. In September he makes thirty different flavors in thirty days, including Cap'n Crunch, red velvet, limoncello, apple pie, and German chocolate cake. He has cannoli blends of coffee and ice cream, and makes cannoli shooters, a special creamy drink that's a boozy combo of cinnamon and chocolate. He's also commissioned a full-size Cannolimobile that he personally drives around to hand out free cannoli to the community and local fire and police departments. One September Michael Crane, who's a former commercial photographer (he took Kathy and my wedding photographs) and now runs Crane Brewing, helped Jasper develop and brew an honest-to-goodness cannoli beer, which sounds amazing!

The Doocys have another connection to these cannoli. My sisters Jenny and Ann worked in Jasper's family trattoria and deli back in the nineties, and every time somebody would order a cannolo, my sisters stuffed the pastry tube on the spot with fresh sweet ricotta. My sisters always thought it was Jasper's recipe, but it's a family recipe from his grandma, or *nonna*, as the Italians say. Nonna Josephine probably made a million of them during her lifetime, but if somebody ever suggested that she get behind the wheel of a Cannolimobile to deliver them, she'd think somebody had been sipping the cannoli beer.

These are divine, and so simple!

Makes 6 cannoli

---

2 cups whole-milk ricotta cheese

¾ cup powdered sugar, plus more (optional) for dusting

1 teaspoon pure vanilla extract

¼ cup finely chopped Hershey bar with almonds

¼ cup candied oranges and cherries, finely diced

6 cannoli shells, plain or chocolate (we buy ours from the baker at our grocery store)

½ cup mini chocolate chips or ½ cup finely chopped pistachios

1. In a medium bowl, combine the ricotta and powdered sugar and use a rubber spatula to mix until smooth. Add the vanilla, chopped chocolate bar, and candied fruit and mix well. Cover the bowl with plastic wrap and refrigerate for a couple hours to firm up.

2. When ready to serve, scoop the filling out of the bowl into a zip-top bag (or use a pastry bag, if you have one). Squeeze the filling into one corner of the bag and use scissors to snip off a ¾-inch corner at the bottom of the bag where the cheese is parked.

3. Squeeze the filling into the cannoli shells, filling only as many as you'll eat in this session so the shells don't get soggy. If you need to, make the hole in the bag bigger! The filling should squeeze a bit out of both ends of the shell. Dip the ends into either mini chocolate chips or chopped pistachios. Dust with powdered sugar if you'd like and serve. Great with a cup of coffee . . . unless cannoli beer is available! Refrigerate any leftovers.

WHITE HOUSE COOKIES

GRANDMA DOOCY WAS A PROLIFIC BAKER, AND IF SHE HAD TIME SHE'D ROLL OUT AND bake 5 dozen cookies, but she never had to worry about them getting stale because she'd immediately freeze them in her legendary Cookie Bucket.

I say legendary because while it was *five decades ago*, some of her grandkids still talk about it today. We joke about a hierarchy of who was allowed freezer access to the cookies in that five-quart ice cream pail. "She had a list, Steve," my sister explained, "and I wasn't on it!" That was news to me, because as the first grandchild, I had unlimited access. But my sister Cathy remembers Grandma saying she could never stick her palm in the pail.

My cousin Angi today confesses that she never asked. She'd just grab a cookie out of the bucket when Grandma wasn't looking. I was shocked to hear a Doocy family member confess to grand theft cookie . . . make that *Grandma* theft cookie.

For me this will always be a taste of Grandma's home, where the cookies were frozen and apparently there was an index of who had cookie clearance. Sorry, Cathy—but you weren't on Grandma's *bucket list*!

Don't delete these cookies.

Makes 70 to 80 cookies

3½ cups all-purpose flour

1 teaspoon baking soda

1 teaspoon cream of tartar

1 cup (2 sticks) unsalted butter, at room temperature

1 cup granulated sugar

1 cup packed light brown sugar

1 cup vegetable oil

1 large egg

1 teaspoon pure vanilla extract

1 cup Rice Krispies

1 cup rolled oats

1 cup sweetened coconut flakes

1. Adjust an oven rack to the center position and preheat the oven to 350°F.

2. In a medium bowl, combine the flour, baking soda, and cream of tartar. Mix well with a fork and set that aside.

3. In a stand mixer fitted with the paddle attachment (or large bowl with a hand mixer), combine the butter and both sugars and beat on medium speed until smooth. Next in go the vegetable oil, egg, and vanilla. Mix on medium speed into a smooth, wet batter, about a minute. Reduce the speed and add the flour mixture ½ cup at a time until it's completely combined. Turn off the mixer and fold in the Rice Krispies, oats, and coconut flakes by hand until evenly distributed. This takes some elbow grease!

4. Scoop out about 1-inch balls of dough and drop them onto an ungreased sheet pan about 1 inch apart. Press them down until a little flat. If the dough is a bit crumbly by the end of the batch just roll it around in your hand to make a ball, then put on the sheet pan and squash it down a bit like the others.

5. Bake in batches until there are light brown highlights around the bottom edges, 9 to 11 minutes. Use a spatula to carefully remove the cookies to parchment or wax paper until they have cooled and firmed up, about 10 minutes. These also freeze well, but you knew that . . .

GRANDMA'S GANACHE BROWNIES

GRANDMA DOOCY MADE THESE BROWNIES FOR YEARS. THEY WERE ALWAYS OUT AT HOLI-days and were usually the first thing gone. If you were late, you'd get the chance to have some from the next batch—next Christmas.

On brownie-making day, one lucky grandchild would be chosen by Grandma to receive a special bonus. This recipe took a whole can of Hershey's chocolate syrup (back when it was sold that way), and she'd use a can opener to take off the entire top. Then after she'd pour the syrup into her mixing bowl, she'd give one lucky kid a wink and pour a cup of milk from the fridge into the can, which still had a ton of syrup inside. Then she'd stir it up, making it way more chocolatey than a regular glass of Grandma's chocolate milk. My cousin Angi remembers she once cut her lip on the sharp can edge, but only made that mistake once. After that, she'd pour the super-chocolate milk from the can into her mouth without touching the can. There was another problem and that was Grandma had about a million grandkids all anxious for their moment with the can, but I was lucky, because I was the oldest and the first, so I had my share of chocolate milk mustaches. Thanks, Grandma.

When our kids were growing up, once a summer Kathy and I would take the kids to the place where all that chocolate goodness came from—Hershey, Pennsylvania—and our kids' favorite amusement park, Hershey Park. We'd spend all day riding scary roller coasters and then adjourn to the Hershey restaurants, which highlighted all things chocolate. One lunch I ordered everybody chocolate milks. When the waiter brought them to the table I jokingly asked if it was possible to drink directly out of the next empty Hershey can. Taking me quite

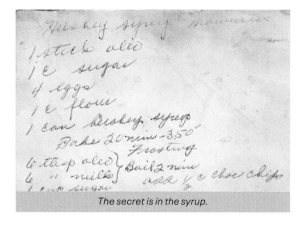
The secret is in the syrup.

seriously, he politely replied, "No, sorry," and explained it was a very big industrial-size container. Then he probably returned to his post and pushed the silent alarm under the counter to notify park security there was a delusional father in Booth 19.

I wasn't delusional; I was nostalgic—although in retrospect it was a nutty thing to ask. It would be like going to Taco Bell and asking to sip out of the nacho cheese vat . . . *which would be amazing!*

After Grandma showed me how to make these brownies as a teenager, I won a blue ribbon for them at Kansas's Clay County Fair. Since then, Kathy and I have updated them with a chocolate ganache that Grandma would love. They don't bake as quickly as boxed brownies, but they're homemade and so chocolatey you'll think you're drinking directly out of the Hershey can.

Makes 28 brownies

½ cup (1 stick) unsalted butter, at room temperature

4 large eggs

1 cup sugar

1½ cups Hershey's chocolate syrup

1 cup all-purpose flour

½ cup chopped walnuts

⅔ cup heavy cream, left at room temperature for 10 minutes

1⅓ cups chocolate chips (we use Hershey's semisweet milk chocolate)

1. Adjust an oven rack to the center position and preheat the oven to 350°F. Grease a 9 × 13-inch baking dish with 1 tablespoon of the butter.

2. In a stand mixer fitted with the paddle attachment (or in a large bowl with a hand mixer), combine the remaining 7 tablespoons butter, the eggs, sugar, and chocolate syrup. Mix on medium speed until the mixture is silky smooth, then incrementally add the flour until it's perfectly blended. Pour the batter evenly into the prepared baking dish.

3. Bake until no longer jiggly in the middle, 55 to 60 minutes. If a butter knife jabbed in the center doesn't come out clean, add another 5 minutes or so until it does. Let the brownies cool in the pan. Leave the oven on.

4. Place the walnuts on a small sheet pan and toast for about 5 minutes, until nicely toasted. (You can also do this toward the end of the brownie-baking time if you're an attentive multitasker.) Remove the walnuts to a plate so they stop toasting.

5. Make the ganache when the brownies have completely cooled. Place the cream in a medium microwave-safe bowl, cover with a tight-sealing lid, and microwave on high for 90 seconds. Quickly add the chocolate chips to the bowl and jostle them so that they are submerged in the cream. Close the lid and let the bowl sit for 2 minutes, undisturbed. Agitate the bowl briskly from side to side so that the chocolate blends into the cream. Keep shaking until the mixture is a consistent deep brown color. Let sit another 3 minutes and give the bowl another shake. All the chips should be melted; if not, microwave another 15 seconds or so and let it sit a little longer.

6. Immediately pour the ganache over the brownies and use a rubber spatula to smooth it evenly over the top. Scatter the toasted walnuts on top.

7. Let the brownies sit for 15 to 20 minutes to firm up. Cut them into 1½-inch squares (4 rows by 7 rows) and enjoy! Grandma never had leftovers, but if you do, cover with plastic wrap and refrigerate.

STATE FAIR CHEESE PIE

WHEN *FOX & FRIENDS* HAD A NATIONWIDE CONTEST LOOKING FOR THE MOST LOVED recipes in America, Pamela Lang of Iowa nominated her mother's cheese pie. She told us that when she was growing up in Omaha, they weren't a big dessert family, but there was one magical night each year when her mom, Peg Ziegler, hosted the Sewing Club in their dining room. Of course if she was going to have all those important ladies over, she was going to have to show off a little, and she knew exactly how to do that: by making this pie.

In 2018 Pam entered the pie in the Iowa State Fair and won five blue ribbons; it won first place in every contest in which it was entered. What an accomplishment! And I can say that, as a fellow blue-ribbon winner myself. Of course my ribbon was for chocolate chip cookies, and my recipe came from the side of the yellow chocolate chip cookie bag. It's fifty years later and the statute of limitations has no doubt expired, but if the Clay County Fair authorities want to confiscate my ribbon, it's in my top sock drawer.

Unlike my cookies, this cheese pie is a real family recipe, already made by three generations, and it's an honest-to-goodness part of the Ziegler family legacy. Yes, it received five blue ribbons at the state fair, and it also won our *Fox & Friends* contest, but for Pam, the most poignant part of this recipe's legacy is that it's a part of her mom, and always will be. Now any time Pam wants to remember those sweet, simple days of her childhood, all she has to do is turn on the oven and beat some cream cheese, and later that day she has the exact pie that wowed the Sewing Club.

It will wow your family, too. Try it—you'll love it!

Makes one 10-inch pie

---

2 cups graham cracker crumbs

½ cup plus ⅔ cup plus 2 tablespoons sugar

½ cup (1 stick) unsalted butter, melted

Two 8-ounce packages cream cheese, at room temperature

2 large eggs

2 teaspoons pure vanilla extract

1 cup sour cream

Ground cinnamon, for dusting

1. Adjust an oven rack to the center position and preheat the oven to 375°F.

2. In an ungreased 10-inch pie plate, combine the graham cracker crumbs and ½ cup of the sugar. Pour the melted butter over the crumbs and stir with a fork until the crumbs are all wet and the mixture is uniform. Press the crumbs onto the bottom and all the way up the sides of the pie plate, just to the rim. We use the bottom of a measuring cup to make it nice and flat and firm.

3. In a stand mixer fitted with the paddle attachment (or a large bowl with a hand mixer), combine the cream cheese and ⅔ cup of the sugar and beat on medium speed until smooth. Add the eggs and 1 teaspoon of the vanilla and beat until completely blended. Pour the mixture into the pie crust.

4. Bake for 20 minutes. Set aside to cool for 15 minutes. Leave the oven on and increase the oven temperature to 425°F.

5. During that 15-minute cool-down, make the topping. In a medium bowl, mix the sour cream and the remaining 2 tablespoons sugar and 1 teaspoon vanilla.

6. When the pie has cooled 15 minutes, gently spread this topping over the pie. The top is very soft, so be gentle! Return the pie to the oven for a final 10 minutes of baking, until the top has leveled itself out and is a bit glossy.

7. Let the pie cool completely on a wire rack. Lightly dust the top with cinnamon and refrigerate for at least 4 hours, until thoroughly chilled.

8. Now it's ready for serving. Slice as you would any blue ribbon-winning pie. Refrigerate any leftovers.

Curt and Pam Lang on Fox & Friends.

GERMAN CHOCOLATE ICE CREAM PIE

IN EVERY PHOTOGRAPH I HAVE OF ME CELEBRATING A BIRTHDAY, I'M BLOWING OUT THE candles on a German chocolate cake.

My mom would spend a couple hours making German chocolate cake for me from scratch right through to my college days. A few years later she invited me home for my birthday. "I'll make your favorite cake," she said, shamelessly bribing me, and I went, and it was delicious—although when I was cleaning up I discovered an empty German chocolate cake mix box in the trash. She was cheating and this actually made me feel so much better! She'd worked so hard her whole life, and I wanted her to have plenty of free time to watch *Merv Griffin* and *The Price Is Right*.

Mom may have used a cake mix for the cake, but she always made the coconut-pecan frosting from scratch, and this is her recipe.

When our kids got to a certain age, they stopped asking for cake-cakes and wanted ice cream cakes on their birthdays. This recipe is a cross between my beloved birthday cake and the kids' ice cream desserts, and it has the same great German chocolate flavors I still adore.

Makes one 9-inch pie

3 cups Dutch Chocolate ice cream (we use Turkey Hill)

One 9-inch premade pecan pie crust (we use Diamond of California)

½ cup evaporated milk

1 large egg yolk

½ teaspoon pure vanilla extract

⅓ cup sugar

1 tablespoon unsalted butter

¾ cup sweetened coconut flakes

½ cup pecans, finely chopped

Whipped cream, for serving (optional)

1. First let's soften the ice cream so it's easy to work with. Let the carton of ice cream sit at room temperature with the lid on for about 15 minutes, then use a rubber spatula to scoop out 3 cups of ice cream. Place the ice cream in the pie crust. Level out the ice cream smoothly; it has to be flat or the frosting will run off the top later. Place in the freezer for at least 2 hours to firm up.

2. Here's the way my mom would make the frosting: In a Pyrex measuring cup, measure the evaporated milk. Add the egg yolk, vanilla, and sugar. Whisk it super-smooth and set aside.

3. In a small saucepan, melt the butter over medium-high heat, then quickly pour in the milk and egg mixture. Stir to combine with the butter and bring to a boil, stirring with a silicone spatula the whole time. After a few minutes the mixture will be getting thicker—that's what you want. Boil until you see a steady stream of bubbles in the center of the pan, then remove from the heat and stir in the coconut and pecans. This mixture is way too hot to put on the ice cream, so scrape it out of the hot pan onto a plate. Spread it out to let cool for 2 minutes.

4. Remove the ice cream pie from the freezer and frost it evenly with this creamy and delicious topping. Return to the freezer for 2 hours to firm up. When it's time to serve, if you want to be really decadent, top it with whipped cream, which is how my mom served it on my birthday. *Wow, thanks for the recipe, Mom— now back to* The Price Is Right, *and the showcase is next!*

BROOKIES

PLATO FAMOUSLY SAID, "NECESSITY IS THE MOTHER OF INVENTION." TURNS OUT HE WAS referring to what happens when you run out of eggs.

Lee Lewittes is the mother of young boys, Benjamin and Jonathan, and early one winter day she rushed home because a blizzard canceled their school. They would spend the rest of the day at home, watching TV and knowing that whatever they were going to eat, they'd have to make themselves, because the Uber Eats guy didn't want to get stuck in a ditch.

Lee asked the boys what they should make as a family activity—brownies or cookies? Benjamin wanted brownies and Jonathan wanted cookies, and at that point, there was no compromising until Mom said, "Okay . . . we'll make both!"

Her boys were delighted. What mother in her right mind would ever suggest her kids have *two* desserts in the middle of the day? Then reality set in—she opened the egg carton and there was only one egg left. With a snowstorm raging, there was *zero* chance she was going out for more. It was time for the mother of the brothers to be the mother of invention. "I've got an idea—let's make *both* in one pan." They made it—and it was delicious!

"Boys, what should we call the recipe?" The boys finally had the chance to immortalize something with a name. "What about Sammy?" That's what Jonathan wanted to name a dog . . . a not-so-subtle reminder of the kids' most fervent wish. So like a trial attorney leading a witness, she said, "A brownie . . . cookie . . . is a . . ." with long pauses in between. They were kids, not ad copy writers, and had no idea where Mom was going with this. Then, like a Vegas hypnotist, she tried to make them think they came up with the title: "Brownie—cookie—*brookies*—Great idea, boys!"

Lee's a veteran TV producer, and "brookies" had popped into her head when she'd opened the brownie box an hour earlier. Clever stuff, thanks to Lee and her boys, who would like a dog someday. But in the meantime I refer to them as the Brookies Brothers.

Makes 24 brookies

Baking spray with flour

1 box brownie mix suitable for a 9 × 13-inch pan (we use Duncan Hines Chewy Fudge Brownie Mix)

Eggs, water, and/or oil, as called for on the brownie mix box (see Note)

½ cup vegetable or canola oil

½ cup packed light brown sugar

¼ cup granulated sugar

½ teaspoon pure vanilla extract

1. Adjust an oven rack to the center position and preheat the oven to 350°F. Mist a 9 × 13-inch baking pan with baking spray.

2. In a large bowl, combine the brownie mix with eggs, water, and/or oil according to the package directions and mix thoroughly. Spread the mixture in the prepared pan and set aside.

3. Now to make the cookie layer! In a large bowl, combine the oil and both sugars until well blended. Add the vanilla, egg, and flour and mix until all the flour has been incorporated and the dough is smooth. Mix in the chocolate chips. (Keep in mind that this is not going to feel like a traditional cookie dough—it doesn't all stick together. Think of it as more of a topping.) Spoon the dough evenly over the brownies; it's okay if you see some of the brownie mix below.

1 large egg

1 cup all-purpose flour

One 12-ounce package semisweet chocolate chips

Vanilla ice cream, for serving (optional)

4. Bake until the cookie layer on top is a deep golden brown and looks a little dry and crumbly, 50 to 60 minutes.

5. Cool before cutting and serving. These are amazing as is, but add a scoop of vanilla ice cream on top and I'm in heaven!

NOTE: If the brownie box gives you the choice of making the brownies fudgy or cake-like, make them fudgy.

GRANDMA'S SCOTCHEROOS

A CIVIL WAR WAS STARTED ABOUT FIFTY YEARS AGO IN OUR FAMILY, AND IT CONTINUES to this day. It's about a breakfast food.

In the 1960s Grandma Doocy cut out of a magazine a recipe for a dessert called Scotcheroos. The Kellogg's test kitchens had come up with the recipe, and not surprisingly you use a lot of their Kellogg's Rice Krispies to make a batch. Grandma Doocy thought that recipe was too much like Rice Krispies treats, and she didn't want to make something like everybody else. So she called an audible and started using Special K—the breakfast food she ate every day. People went crazy for them, and they became a fixture at every town-wide event in Bancroft, Iowa. They were legendary. My memory is that they were like a Rice Krispies treat—on steroids!

Over time Grandma's children grew up, and some started their own families, and they continued to make Scotcheroos, but there was a revolt. My aunts Sherri and Patty began making them the way Kellogg's intended—with Rice Krispies. Meanwhile, my aunt Mary continued to make Grandma's original version. During the holidays on our dedicated Facebook page for the cousins (all of Grandma's grandkids, including me), the number one topic is Scotcheroos, whose version they're making—and which is better. This argument has been going on for *fifty years*—not always on Facebook, of course!

Forget paper or plastic, red state or blue state—the Doocy purity test for my generation is, are you in Patty and Sherri's camp, or are you with Mary and Grandma?

So, whose recipe am I sharing? I've got to go with Grandma's! She's been gone for a while, but every time a Doocy family member makes a batch, she's right there at our side, telling us to stir the peanut butter faster. And we would, because when we were done, she'd let us lick the spoon. That's a lovely lasting legacy.

Makes about 40 bars

---

2 tablespoons unsalted butter, at room temperature, for the pan

9 cups original Special K cereal

1½ cups light corn syrup

1½ cups sugar

1½ cups creamy peanut butter

One 11-ounce bag Nestlé Toll House Milk Chocolate & Peanut Butter Flavored chips

1. Butter a 9 × 13-inch baking dish.

2. Pour the Special K into a large bowl.

3. In a medium saucepan, combine the corn syrup and sugar and bring to a boil over medium-high heat, keeping a silicone spatula moving through the mixture so it doesn't scorch. You'll notice it's hard to stir in the beginning, but as it heats up it gets easier. You'll first spot a ring of little bubbles around the outside rim; wait until you have bigger bubbles in the middle and throughout and then quickly give a quick stir and remove from the heat. The longer it boils the harder it gets, and we don't want that.

4. Quickly fold in the peanut butter and stir briskly until it's melted in. Immediately pour the mixture into the bowl with the cereal and mix quickly so every flake gets peanut butter-ized.

5. Dump the mixture into the prepared baking dish and use a spatula to spread it out evenly, gently patting it into place so it's nice and level. Set aside.

6. In a small uncovered microwave-safe bowl, microwave the chocolate-peanut butter chips on high for 45 seconds, then stir. Microwave again in 15-second increments, stirring after each, until the mixture is perfectly smooth and melted. Note a word of caution from Aunt Mary: "Don't leave in too long or you'll have a helluva mess." She speaks from experience.

7. Quickly frost the bars with a smooth layer of the melted chips across the top. Set aside for 1 hour, then cut into however many bars you would like. To get 40, cut them in a 5 × 8 grid for pieces roughly 2 × 1½ inches. Don't wait too long to cut them or they will get too firm. And that's it—when you make them Grandma's Special K way!

KRUMKAGER COOKIES

IN OUR *HAPPY IN A HURRY COOKBOOK*, MY BOSS, SUZANNE SCOTT, THE CEO OF FOX NEWS Media, shared her Norwegian aunt Astrid's classic rice pudding recipe. It was a hit—so naturally when we started writing this cookbook I asked if she had any other family favorite recipes to include—and she did. And it's another Norwegian specialty, also by Aunt Astrid, called the *krumkager* (or *krumkake*). This translates to "curved cake," but it's not a cake; it's a wafer-thin Scandinavian cone cookie. And while they're Norwegian, they kind of look like unfilled cannoli.

The Gunderson family would spend every Christmas Eve at Astrid's place in Red Bank, New Jersey. Suzanne's brother, Steve, tells me Astrid was a good cook and baker who, once the food was ready on the table, would announce, *"Vær så god!"* which means "Here you go." And they would rush to the table for a hearty dinner of turkey and all the trimmings. The main attraction for the kids was dessert time, which would include her aforementioned classic rice pudding; Aunt Astri (as she was nicknamed) would hide a single nut in one of the pudding portions. Whoever was lucky enough to get that bowl was entitled to claim a gift—for finding the almond and not breaking a tooth.

Astrid proudly served trays of these *krumkager* and many other Scandinavian sweets once a year. And the family, loaded up on treats, would hold hands and sing Christmas carols while walking around the tree. Later, when they got older, they'd put a hand on the shoulder of the person in front of them and sing. Then, when the songbooks were closed, they'd exchange a few Christmas gifts, and Astri would give everyone a festive tin of treats to take home and savor through the holiday season. This lovely parting gift has become part of her legacy.

Today a big cookie factory machine could stamp out these gems in two seconds . . . but this is about family, this is about tradition, this is about Christmas!

Steve and his family have made hundreds of *krumkager* around the holidays using Astri's recipe, which she typed up and then scribbled additional notes on through the years as she perfected this crispy cookie. (And you do need some special tools to make this recipe—check out A Note on Equipment on page 307.) I love these, but the Nordic thing is in my genes; according to my DNA test, I'm 72 percent Nordic . . . which explains why I've been driving a Volvo since 1984, and I love IKEA's furniture sales, because I love a *Swede* deal.

When Steve Gunderson, his daughter, Greta, and wife, Maryann, make these every year deep in December, they play Christmas music in the background to get them in the proper mood. Steve tells me, "The music helps us feel like we're Santa's little elves."

Actually, I consider them *Aunt Astri's* elves—keeping this wonderful Gunderson family tradition very much alive. *"Vær så god!"*

Steve and Astrid.

Makes about 3 dozen cookies

3 large eggs

1 cup sugar

2 cups all-purpose flour

1 cup (2 sticks) salted butter, melted and cooled a bit

1 teaspoon pure vanilla extract

1. In a stand mixer fitted with the paddle attchment (or a large bowl with a hand mixer), beat the eggs and sugar together until smooth. Add the flour, melted butter, and vanilla and mix until you have a perfectly smooth dough. The Gundersons cover with plastic wrap and refrigerate for several hours or overnight to firm up the dough. I've found better luck working with it while at room temperature, so I skip the fridge and move to the next step.

2. Preheat the *krumkake* iron (see A Note on Equipment, opposite) over medium heat for at least 5 minutes so that the entire iron is evenly hot. Place a small ball of dough on the iron to make a test cookie, setting it not in the center but about 1 inch from the iron's hinge. Gently and slowly close the iron when you get to the dough, because the hot iron melts the butter and the weight of the iron helps close the lid. After 5 seconds of it closing on its own, slowly squeeze the handles until the iron is completely closed (this guarantees that the cookie won't be too thick). If dough comes out the side of the iron, you're using too much; adjust until you have the right amount.

3. Once the iron is closed, the cooking time really depends on how hot your iron is. I get best results cooking one side for 25 seconds and then flipping the iron to the other side and cooking another 25 seconds. The cookies come out a lovely light golden brown. Steve Gunderson cooks his for 40 seconds on each side and gets great results and a deeper color. Do a little experimenting to figure out the timing for your iron and your stove and taste the cookies to see if you like them lighter or darker in color.

4. Use a thin metal spatula to remove the cookie from the iron, then drape it over a wooden rolling cone or dowel. Using thermal-gloved hands, gently wrap the cookie around the wood into a tube shape. Place the cookie seam side down on a piece of parchment paper and let it cool for a minute with the dowel inside it. Pull the dowel out when the cookie is firmed up and cooler. Repeat to make the rest of the cookies.

5. The Gundersons love the cookies just like that—wafer thin and crispy. Kathy has been known to fill one up with a little freshly whipped cream. Aunt Astrid would gift them in cookie tins, and it's in one of those sturdy boxes that Steve's family stores any rare leftovers. The key to keeping these cookies crispy is to have them in a container with a tight—but not airtight—lid, or they can get soggy. And we don't want that after all that work. Enjoy—and appreciate Aunt Astrid!

A NOTE ON EQUIPMENT

To make these cookies, you need a *krumkake* iron or pizzelle press that hinges open and you can flip halfway through the process. (It's kind of like a Belgian waffle-maker in that way.) My Nordic Ware press included a wooden rolling cone to shape the cookies into tubes. The Gundersons use a Jøtul brand iron from Norway, and just like Astri, they wrap their cookies around a wooden dowel made from an 18-inch length of wooden closet pole. Thanks, Home Depot!

The cookie result you get depends on two variables: the temperature of the iron and the amount of dough you place on it. If you want your cookies very lightly colored, take them out quickly. Darker? Longer. Just figure out what a good temperature is, leave it set there, and start your timer!

Because there are different sizes and brands of irons, I can't tell you exactly how much dough to use. Astri used 1 teaspoon, Steve Gunderson's family uses "1 heaping soup spoon," and my iron calls for between 1 and 2 teaspoons. You'll have to make a couple test-run cookies until you find the right amount of dough, perhaps starting with 1 teaspoon of dough and increasing from there until you have the cookie that's perfect for you.

You'll also need some thermal gloves to avoid getting burned when you wrap the cookies around the dowel!

ACKNOWLEDGMENTS

When I graduated from journalism school (long before the Morgan Freeman movie *The Bucket List* came out), if I had a lifetime achievement checklist, I'd imagine my long-term dream would have been to someday write a book that somebody would actually read. Here you are at the end of our third cookbook, which is so far beyond anything I could have ever dreamed. Thank you sincerely. That's pretty heady stuff to a kid who grew up in a town of forty-three souls on the wide-open flatlands of Kansas.

This has been another challenging year for all of us, but collaborating with all the people whose names you are about to see was easy, because while so much kept us apart, the one thing that pulled us together was food. So allow us to give credit where credit is due to all the wonderful sharing friends and family members whose fingerprints are on these stories and recipes.

When it comes to *actual* fingerprints, the FBI Crime Lab would certainly find my grandma Doocy's prints on the dozens of 3 × 5 index cards from her heirloom recipe boxes that Kathy and I used for historical reference. We never would have gotten our hands on them if not for my first cousin, Angi Nemmers, in South Dakota. I was chatting with her about how we were writing this *Simply Happy* cookbook—and then she secretly sent us Grandma's recipe card boxes. It was a jackpot of ideas and family history. Angi also helped with a couple recipes, as did her mom, Mary Nemmers, and my aunts, Sherry Nitz, Helen Doocy, and Linda Keenan.

My sisters, Cathy, Lisa, Jenny, and Ann, also were on speed dial, answering my questions regarding what they remembered about the ingredients our mom used fifty years ago in her Kansas kitchen. Their answers were often Miracle Whip, cream of mushroom soup, Fleischmann's margarine, Crisco for frying, and Dream Whip—on top of everything. Those were the days . . .

With their submissions, some of our famous friends can now add cookbook contributor to their Wikipedia pages: Ainsley and Hayden Earhardt, Rachel Campos Duffy, Dana Perino, Greg Gutfeld, Jesse Waters, and John Rich.

At Fox, not only do my colleagues have a nose for news, they have an eye for amazing ingredients and recipes. Hat tip to Lee Lewittes, Stephanie Freeman, and Don Presutti for their clever creations. And thanks to the extended Fox families who shared their family classics: Steve Gunderson, brother to Fox News Media CEO Suzanne Scott. Dan Bongino's wife, Paula Bongino. Judy and Jordan Soroko, parents of Jay Soroko. And special credit to Megan Albano, for nudging the ensemble cast of *The Five* to briefly stop working on their program and start collaborating on a charcuterie board.

Many of these recipes and suggestions originated with friends like Melanie and Marcus Luttrell, Erika and Ken Remsen, Leanna Landsmann, Jeanne Nierman, Jasper Mirabile Jr., Ira Fenton, Pamela Lang, Susan Richie, Mary Wiatr, Madeleine Van Duren, Martha Hockman, and Ellen Storms.

Another round of thanks to America's best food photographer, Andrew Purcell, and his team of food stylists—bravo! Every food portrait is not only beautiful, it looks delicious! As for the cover photo of Kathy and me—that is the handiwork of Danny Coya and his crew at South Florida's Starfish Studios. This past year, not only did he snap that iconic shot, but he also took photos at a couple of the Doocy kids' weddings somewhere in a beach town. And a big shout out to Katie McCaskill for helping with hair and makeup on this cover and at our girl's weddings.

Meanwhile, on the Dawn Patrol at *Fox & Friends*—where I'm so lucky to work with some of television's best producers, bookers, and writers—thank you for the seriously hard work you do every day, dutifully informing America about the day's news. Gavin, Tami, AJ, Kristin, Sara, Julie, and Rachel—you are all wonderful leaders on America's Breakfast TV A-Team.

And to America's number one cable morning show team: Brian, Ainsley, Janice, Carley, Pete, Will, Rachel, Rick, Lawrence, and Adam, thank you for being great friends and honest food testers for this and all our cookbooks— along with all the men and women who we proudly work with in Studio M.

Others who helped us this year in countless ways include the Frank family, the Rhode family, Sileshi Petro, Jim Matthews, Steve Huskisson, Linda Garage, Dr. Patrick Clancy, Dr. Carol Shields, Dr. Jerry Shields, Wills Eye Hospital, and finally the professionals at the Bascom Palmer Eye Institute and Center for Retinal & Macular Degeneration Research. Special thanks to Terry Keeney and Vickie Sonnenberg for sharing their story of hope.

After we wrote out each recipe, we made each one multiple times to make sure they were perfect, and that's why my local ShopRite checkers, Lorrie and Darlene, saw me two or three times on some days. Thanks for letting me cut the line, ladies!

We have the best literary lawyer in America, Robert Barnett. Bob—we are eternally grateful that you assigned your colleague Daniel Martin to do all the actual important legal stuff, because we know most of the past year you were gabbing on Zoom calls with James Patterson, dishing the secret stuff Bob Woodward left out of his latest book. Thanks, Mr. Barnett.

Kathy and I spent a year writing down what we had for dinner the night before, and then in January of this year we boxed up our stories and recipes and transported them to Cassie Jones and her team at William Morrow, who spent months then magically turning all of that into this gem of a book that you're holding. It's our best yet, and certainly worth leaving on your coffee table, so Kathy and I can stare up at your living room ceiling until you pick up the book and cook something tasty. Shout out to the team at Morrow—Jill Zimmerman, Rachel Meyers, Anwesha Basu, Jeanne Reina, Kayleigh George, and Benjamin Steinberg—you are all great publishing partners.

And to all our friends, families, brothers, and sisters—what can we say? William Shakespeare probably said it best in one of the rare quotes where he wasn't talking about cheese: "I can no other answer make but thanks—and thanks and ever-thanks."

Finally, to the many people who have supported us with our cookbook project, thank you, for trusting us with your dinner. Now it's your turn—invite us over sometime. We're always looking for new ideas and free entrees—and we'll bring dessert!

Sincerely,
Kathy and Steve Doocy

UNIVERSAL CONVERSION CHART

OVEN TEMPERATURE EQUIVALENTS

250°F = 120°C

275°F = 135°C

300°F = 150°C

325°F = 160°C

350°F = 180°C

375°F = 190°C

400°F = 200°C

425°F = 220°C

450°F = 230°C

475°F = 240°C

500°F = 260°C

MEASUREMENT EQUIVALENTS

Measurements should always be level unless directed otherwise.

⅛ teaspoon = 0.5 mL

¼ teaspoon = 1 mL

½ teaspoon = 2 mL

1 teaspoon = 5 mL

1 tablespoon = 3 teaspoons = ½ fluid ounce = 15 mL

2 tablespoons = ⅛ cup = 1 fluid ounce = 30 mL

4 tablespoons = ¼ cup = 2 fluid ounces = 60 mL

5⅓ tablespoons = ⅓ cup = 3 fluid ounces = 80 mL

8 tablespoons = ½ cup = 4 fluid ounces = 120 mL

10⅔ tablespoons = ⅔ cup = 5 fluid ounces = 160 mL

12 tablespoons = ¾ cup = 6 fluid ounces = 180 mL

16 tablespoons = 1 cup = 8 fluid ounces = 240 mL

INDEX